Essential
KNIT
SWEATERS

Essential
KNIT SWEATERS

Patterns for Every Sweater You Ever Wanted to Wear Every Day

FRAUKE LUDWIG

STACKPOLE BOOKS

Essex, Connecticut
Blue Ridge Summit, Pennsylvania

STACKPOLE BOOKS

An imprint of Globe Pequot, the trade division of
The Rowman & Littlefield Publishing Group, Inc.
4501 Forbes Blvd., Ste. 200
Lanham, MD 20706
www.rowman.com

Distributed by NATIONAL BOOK NETWORK
800-462-6420

Copyright © 2021 Edition Michael Fischer GmbH, www.emf-verlag.de
This edition of *Pullover stricken—Das Grundlagenwerk* first published in Germany by Edition
Michael Fischer-GmbH in 2021 is published by arrangement with Silke Bruenink Agency,
Munich, Germany.

Cover design, book layout and typesetting: Zoe Mitterhuber
Project management: Isabella Krüger
Editing: Regina Sidabras, Berlin, Germany
Photographs: Corinna Teresa Brix, Munich, Germany
Illustrations: Background: Globe Textures/shutterstock
Translation: Katharina Sokiran

We have made every effort to ensure the accuracy and completeness of these instructions.
We cannot, however, be responsible for human error, typographical mistakes, or variations in
individual work.

British Library Cataloguing in Publication Information available

Library of Congress Cataloging-in-Publication Data

Names: Ludwig, Frauke, author.
Title: Essential knit sweaters : patterns for every sweater you ever wanted
   to wear every day / Frauke Ludwig.
Description: Essex, Connecticut : Stackpole Books, [2024]
Identifiers: LCCN 2023023579 (print) | LCCN 2023023580 (ebook) | ISBN
   9780811772761 (paperback) | ISBN 9780811772778 (ebook)
Subjects: LCSH: Knitting—Patterns. | Sweaters.
Classification: LCC TT825 .L794 2024 (print) | LCC TT825 (ebook) | DDC
   746.43/2—dc23/eng/20230724
LC record available at https://lccn.loc.gov/2023023579
LC ebook record available at https://lccn.loc.gov/2023023580

CONTENTS

PREFACE

This book provides an abundance of pullovers and cardigans featuring various construction types. Here, besides traditional seamed designs, raglan constructions, and circular yokes, you will also find contemporary construction methods that allow for a variety of fit options and, above all, get by without having to seam individual parts. For the projects in this book, a limited color palette was used: white, black, and shades of gray. This way, all designs can be used as a canvas and "painted" with your own color preferences. All garments have been graded for sizes XS–XXL to represent a variety of body shapes. After all, this book is for you wonderful women out there!

To enable every one of you to learn new construction methods step-by-step and expand your overall knowledge of knitting, every chapter contains patterns rated for difficulty levels easy, intermediate, and advanced. This way, knitters of all skill sets can find projects to suit them most. Additionally, this book features a variety of different sleeve options, body shapes, neckline solutions, and cuff variations, which are to some extent also interchangeable with each other, allowing you to choose your own combinations. These different options are described in the section "Possible Combinations" on page 42.

I hope you have as much fun knitting all the different designs in this book as I had when designing them and writing this book—in this respect: Have fun knitting!

Yours truly,

KNITTING
BASICS

LET'S GET STARTED

CASTING ON STITCHES

LONG-TAIL CAST-ON

To start a knitted piece, the required number of stitches must be cast on. In this book, for this purpose, the long-tail cast-on technique is used throughout. This cast-on is easy to work and looks pretty. Care should be taken to work it neither too tightly nor too loosely. Those who tend to cast on very tightly should work this part with needles one or two sizes larger than called for in the pattern. On the other hand, those who cast on rather loosely should use one or two needle sizes smaller for the cast-on than called for in the pattern.

1

First, a beginning slipknot is formed. The yarn tail should be at least three times longer than the planned width of the cast-on row. If uncertain, it is preferable to keep the beginning tail a little longer. It has no doubt happened to every knitter at some time or another that the cast-on row had to be unraveled and redone because the tail had turned out to be too short.

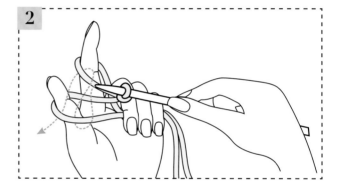

2

To cast on further stitches, lead the end of the yarn connected to the skein from the palm around the outside of the index finger, forming a loop. For better control of the yarn, loop it around the index finger a second time to secure. Now, wrap the long yarn tail around the thumb from back to front, creating another loop. Use the middle finger and the other fingers to help secure the yarn and to control the formed loops. Now, insert the needle from bottom to top into the thumb loop, and pull the front strand of the index finger loop toward you through the thumb loop.

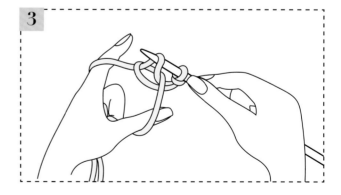

3

Remove the thumb from the loop, and use it to pull the stitches tight on the needle.

Repeat Steps 2 and 3 until the required number of stitches listed in the instructions has been cast on.

BACKWARDS-LOOP CAST-ON

Casting on stitches using the backwards-loop cast-on method is the easiest of all cast-on techniques. However, it does not produce a neat and flexible edge but looks rather shapeless. For this reason, this technique is only applied when stitches can't be cast on any other way; for instance, to cast on new underarm stitches to create positive ease for additional mobility around the arms. For this purpose, the technique is ideally suited since only a small measure of fabric must be bridged. Additional stitches are then worked into the cast-on stitches in the following round.

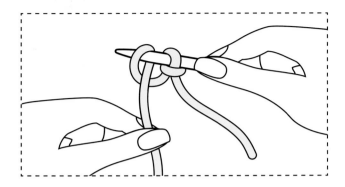

First, just as with the long-tail cast-on, a beginning slipknot is formed. After this, the needle bearing the slipknot is transferred to the right hand.

Again, as for the previous method, the working yarn, emerging from the palm, is led around the outside of the index finger, forming a loop. Then the loop is lifted with the needle, creating a stitch. This step is repeated until the required number of stitches has been cast on.

TIP

Besides the two methods for casting on stitches described in this book, there are a number of other options. The provisional cast-on, for instance, will create a nearly invisible transition when stitches are to be picked up later from the cast-on edge. The Italian tubular cast-on works especially well for ribbing patterns. I recommend watching a few YouTube videos explaining different cast-on methods, a wide variety of which are available.

BASIC STITCHES

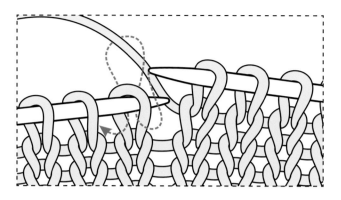

KNIT STITCH

To work a knit stitch, begin with the working yarn behind the knitted piece. Insert the right needle from front to back into the next stitch on the left needle and, using the tip of the right needle, pull the working yarn through to the front. Let the stitch into which you have just inserted the needle slip off the left needle. The newly formed stitch is now sitting on the right needle. The right leg of the stitch sits in front of the needle, and the left leg sits sits behind the needle.

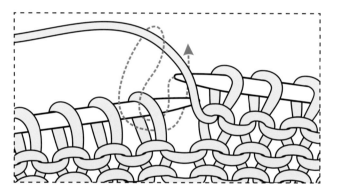

PURL STITCH

To work a purl stitch, begin with the working yarn in front of the knitted piece. Insert the right needle from right to left behind the right leg of the next stitch on the left needle (the right leg is in front of the needle). Now, lead the working yarn from the top around the right needle and, using the right needle, pull this loop back through the stitch. Let the stitch into which you have just inserted the needle slip off the left needle. The right leg of the stitch sits in front of the needle, and the left leg sits behind the needle.

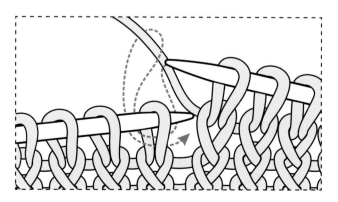

KNITTING THROUGH THE BACK LOOP

To knit a stitch through the back loop, begin with the working yarn behind the knitted piece. Insert the right needle into the back of the next stitch on the left needle and, using the tip of the right needle, pull the working yarn through to the front. Let the stitch into which you have just inserted the needle slip off the left needle. The newly formed stitch is twisted at its base and is now sitting on the right needle. The right leg of the stitch sits behind the needle, and the left leg sits in front of the needle.

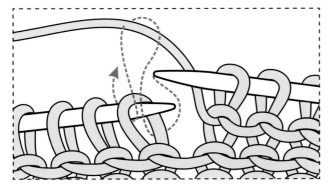

PURLING THROUGH THE BACK LOOP

To purl a stitch through the back loop, begin with the working yarn in front of the knitted piece. Insert the right needle from back to front into the next stitch on the left needle and, using the tip of the right needle, pull the working yarn through to the front. Let the stitch into which you have just inserted the needle slip off the left needle. The newly formed stitch is twisted at its base and is now sitting on the right needle. The right leg of the stitch sits behind the needle, and the left leg sits in front of the needle.

SLIPPED STITCHES

Slipped stiches can be worked with the working yarn either in front of or behind the knitted piece, according to the instructions. Insert the right needle from right to left behind the right leg of the next stitch on the left needle (the right leg is in front of the needle) as if to purl. Now, let the stitch slip off the left needle so that it is now sitting on the right needle. Depending on the pattern, the working yarn is now either placed behind or in front of the work, or a yarn over is formed; which one applies will be stated in the instructions. The stitch is now mounted on the right needle the same way it had been sitting on the left needle.

YARN OVER

Yarn overs are worked for different reasons, but each yarn over creates a new stitch and results in a small hole in the knitting. The holes can be used for decorative purposes. Reasons to work a yarn over can be to increase the overall stitch count, to create buttonholes, or to work lace patterns. In the latter two cases, for each stitch increased by working a yarn over, a corresponding stitch must be decreased.

To make a yarn over, the working yarn is simply wrapped from front to back over the right needle. After this, the stitch pattern is continued according to the instructions, working either in knit (figure 1) or purl stitches (figure 2).

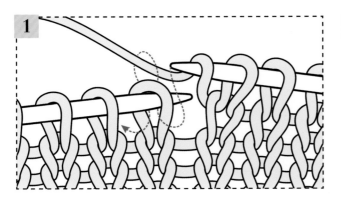

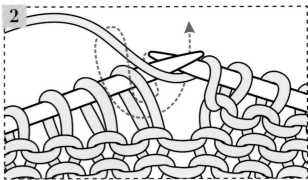

KNITTING IN TURNED ROWS

When knitting in back-and-forth rows with the turning technique, work off all stitches to the end of the left needle, then turn work so that the needle previously held in the right hand is passed to the left hand, and the needle previously held in the left hand is passed to the right hand. The first and last stitches of the row, the selvedge stitches, form the edges of the knitted piece. Depending on the pattern, these first and last stitches can be worked differently to produce different looking edges. An edge composed of only knit stitches in right-side as well as in wrong-side rows will sport little knots. Such a knotted selvedge is especially useful when stitches are to be picked up from this edge later.

When working short rows, work is turned too. Short rows can also be inserted when the knitted piece is worked in the round. Short rows serve to shape particular areas and require special turning stitches.

TURNING STITCHES (GERMAN SHORT ROWS)

Turning stitches are worked in short row sections, which serve to shape particular areas by working more or fewer rows or rounds in these sections than in other parts of the whole piece. This allows one, for instance, to shape the neckline, work sleeve tapering, and to shape the sleeve cap and other areas. Short rows can also be worked to adjust for the properties of different stitch patterns worked together in the same piece.

In this book, for all patterns using short-row shaping, the German short row method with double stitches as turning stitches is used as it produces nearly invisible transitions in almost all stitch patterns and does not create unwanted holes.

Place the working yarn behind the knitted fabric, turn work, and slip 1 stitch as if to purl.

Move the working yarn from front to back over the right needle—this creates the turning stitch, which looks doubled up with two legs sitting on the needle. Both legs together will be worked and counted as one stitch later. If instructions state to *continue in knit*, knit stitches can be worked right away. For purl stitches, the working yarn must first be moved to the front of the work between the needles.

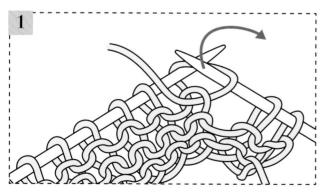

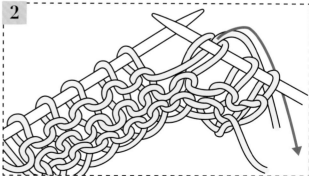

KNITTING IN THE ROUND

Knitting in the round makes it possible to seamlessly work the body and sleeves of sweaters and cardigans in one piece, as well as add collars. To be able to spot the beginning of the round, a stitch marker is placed between the last stitch of the old round and the first stitch of the new one. This marker is often called the "beginning-of-the-round marker" (abbreviated BOR).

Depending on how many stitches need to be worked, the appropriate cable length of the circular needles needs to be chosen. If the cable length is too short, there is not enough space to accommodate all the stitches, and the stitches will be crowded. If the cable length is too long, it is not possible to readily join the stitches into the round. However, the cable length can be shortened by using the Magic Loop method. This simply means that part of the cable will be pulled out between the stitches in any spot in the round, creating a loop on which no stitches sit (hence the term Magic Loop). This makes it possible to use circular needles with a cable length that is longer than needed. However, this is only recommended at the beginning of a knitted piece, such as at the neckline, where more stitches will soon be increased, because in the long run it is tedious and time-consuming to pull out the cord again and again between the stitches.

For sleeves, it works best to use a set of double-pointed needles, distributing the stitches evenly between four needles and using a fifth needle to work off the stitches on the other needles one after another. If, however—for instance when working with thicker yarn weights—a DPN set in the appropriate size is not available, the earlier described Magic Loop method can be employed. Nowadays, special circular needles with extra short tips and cords for knitting sleeves are also available. The best way to find out which method suits you best is to try out different techniques for yourself.

When joining into the round, it is important to make sure that the stitches are not twisted. Otherwise, a Möbius band would be created, which cannot be turned into a pullover. For beginners, it is therefore recommended to first work two rows in pattern before joining into the round, especially with large stitch counts. This way, it is much easier to spot whether the row has been accidentally twisted or not. The small remaining gap can be closed later using the beginning tail.

TIP

When a stranded colorwork pattern is to be worked (such as in Roncita), a couple tricks will improve the product. First, it is important to keep the working yarn at an even tension. It should neither be too tight, drawing in the knitted fabric so it distorts the fit and the pattern in a bad way, nor too loose, again affecting the fit and the pattern and making the fabric curl. Before attempting a larger knitted project in this technique, it is useful to practice it with smaller projects, such as a hat.

Additionally, it is recommended to always cross the strands in the same direction when changing colors. This way, the same color will always be located on top and the other one always beneath it. This makes the pattern much more consistent.

DECREASES

RIGHT-LEANING KNIT DECREASE (K2TOG)

This is the easiest one of all decreases. It looks as if it is leaning to the right, which is why it is used on the left edges of knitted pieces. It is worked by simply knitting two stitches together.

The working yarn is located behind the work. Insert the right needle from front to back first into the first and second stitches on the left needle.

Now, use the right needle to pull the working yarn to the front of work through both stitches at the same time.

Let the two stitches into which you just inserted the needle slip off the left needle.

LEFT-LEANING KNIT DECREASE (SSK)

This decrease looks as if it is leaning to the left and is therefore worked on the right edges of knitted pieces. It is abbreviated as "ssk" for "*slip, slip, knit.*"

Two stitches are slipped knitwise and then knit together as follows: Insert the right needle into the next stitch as if to knit and slip this stitch to the right needle, then slip the following stitch to the right needle the same way. Return the two stitches to the left needle one after the other, so that they are mounted on the needle with the other leg in front, as shown in the illustration. Now, knit both stitches together through the back loop.

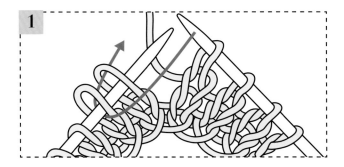

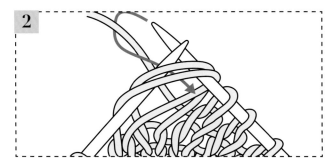

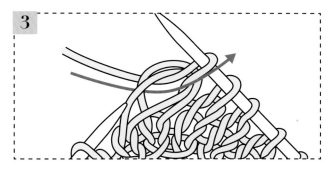

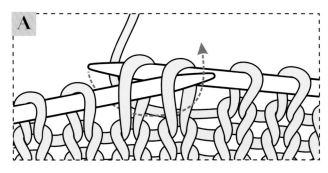

RIGHT-LEANING PURL DECREASE (P2TOG)

Insert the right needle from right to left behind the right leg of the next stitch on the left needle (the right leg is in front of the needle) and into the stitch after that one. Now, wind the working yarn, which is in front of the work, from top to bottom around the right needle. Using the right needle, lead this loop back again through both stitches at the same time. Let the two stitches into which you just inserted the needle slip off the left needle. In this type of decrease, two stitches are purled together. The decrease appears to be leaning to the right and is used to shape the left edge of a knitted piece.

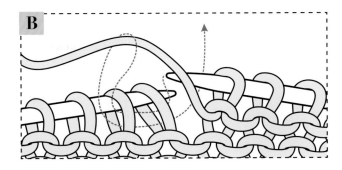

LEFT-LEANING PURL DECREASE (SSP)

This decrease looks as if it is leaning to the left and is therefore worked on the right edges of knitted pieces. It is abbreviated as "ssp" for "*slip, slip, purl.*"

Insert the right needle into the next stitch as if to knit and slip this stitch to the right needle, then slip the following stitch to the right needle the same way. Return the two stitches to the left needle one after the other, so that they are mounted on the needle with the other leg in front, as shown in the illustration. Now, purl both stitches together through the back loop.

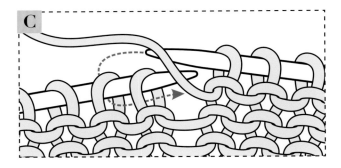

KNITTING 3 STITCHES TOGETHER RIGHT-LEANING (K3TOG)

In this type of decrease, two stitches are decreased at the same time. It corresponds to the right-leaning knit decrease, except for being worked over three instead of two stitches, decreasing two stitches instead of one.

The working yarn is held behind the work. Insert the right needle from front to back first into the third stitch on the left needle, then into the second stitch on the left needle, and finally into the first stitch on the left needle. Now, use the right needle to pull the working yarn to the front of the work through all three stitches at the same time. Let the three stitches into which you just inserted the needle slip off the left needle.

KNITTING 3 STITCHES TOGETHER LEFT-LEANING (SSSK)

In this type of decrease, two stitches are decreased at the same time. It corresponds to the left-leaning knit decrease, except for being worked over three instead of two stitches, decreasing two stitches instead of one.

Insert the right needle into the next stitch as if to knit and slip the stitch to the right needle, then slip the stitch after that one, and then slip the third stitch on the left needle the same way. Return the three stitches to the left needle one after the other, so that they are mounted on the needle with the other leg in front. Now, knit all three stitches together through the back loop.

TIP

Using the same techniques as described here, a larger number of stitches can be knitted or purled together, too. The more stitches that are worked together, the thicker the resulting little lump.

CENTERED DOUBLE DECREASE (CDD) KNITWISE

This decrease leans neither to the left nor to the right. It is worked over three stitches, decreasing two stitches, which disappear behind the center stitch.

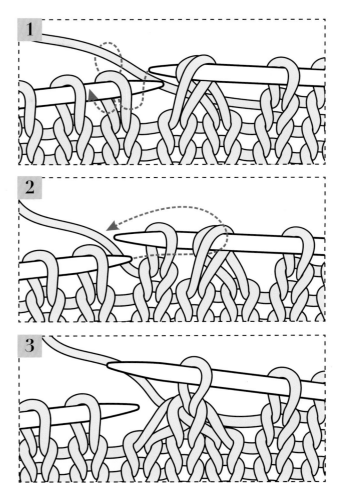

The working yarn is held behind the work. Insert the right needle knitwise into the first two stitches on the left, as if knitting two stitches together, and slip them to the right needle.

Knit the following stitch. Now, pass the slipped stitches over the knitted stitch and off the needle. It is important to pass both stitches together over the knitted stitch, not one after the other.

The illustration shows that in a correctly worked decrease, the center stitch is in front, while the stitches to the right and left of it disappear behind the center stitch.

INCREASES

There are four basic types of increases. The most straight-forward and least noticeable one is the increase from the bar between stitches. This increase is especially suitable for raglan lines or neckline shaping.

INCREASING 1 STITCH KNITWISE RIGHT-LEANING FROM THE BAR BETWEEN STITCHES (M1R)

In this method, one stitch is increased, which leans to the right, away from the stitch worked after it.

Using the right needle, lift the bar between stitches onto the left needle so that the right leg of the stitch created by this maneuver is in the back. The left leg of the stitch sits in front accordingly.

Knit the new stitch just placed on the left needle as usual.

Let the stitch just knitted slip off the left needle. One stitch has been increased.

INCREASING 1 STITCH PURLWISE RIGHT-LEANING FROM THE BAR BETWEEN STITCHES (M1R-P)

In this method, one stitch is increased, which leans to the right, away from the stitch worked after it. This increase works similarly to a knitwise increase from the bar between stitches.

Using the right needle, lift the bar between stitches onto the left needle so that the right leg of the stitch created by this maneuver is in the back. The left leg of the stitch sits in front accordingly. Purl the new stitch just added to the left needle, and let it slip off the left needle. One stitch has been increased.

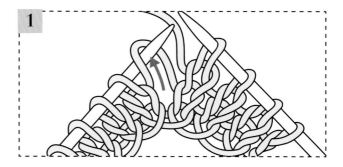

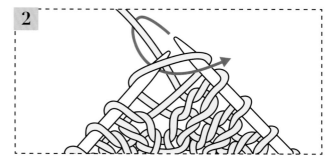

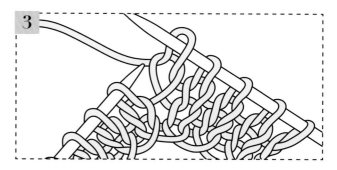

INCREASING 1 STITCH KNITWISE LEFT-LEANING FROM THE BAR BETWEEN STITCHES (M1L)

Here, one stitch is increased, which leans to the left, away from the stitch worked before it.

Using the right needle, lift the bar between stitches onto the left needle so that the right leg of the stitch created by this maneuver is in the front. The left leg of the stitch sits in back accordingly.

Knit the new stitch just placed on the left needle through the back loop.

Let the new stitch just knitted slip off the left needle. One stitch has been increased.

INCREASING 1 STITCH PURLWISE LEFT-LEANING FROM THE BAR BETWEEN STITCHES (M1L-P)

In this method, one stitch is increased, which leans to the left, away from the stitch worked before it. This increase works similarly to a knitwise increase from the bar between stitches.

Using the right needle, lift the bar between stitches onto the left needle so that the right leg of the stitch created by this maneuver is in the front. The left leg of the stitch sits in back accordingly. Purl the new stitch just added to the left needle through the back loop, and let it slip off the left needle. One stitch has been increased.

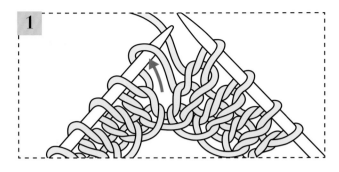

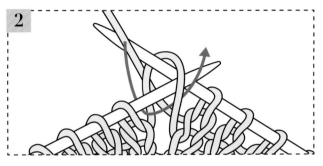

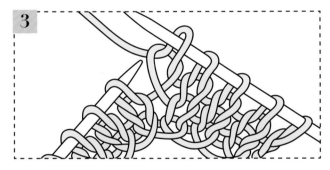

MAKING 2 KNIT STITCHES FROM 1

1

Insert the right needle into the next stitch as if to knit.

2

Pull the working yarn through as for a knit stitch.

3

Do not let the old stitch slide from the left needle yet; instead, slip the old stitch to the right needle as if to purl. One stitch has been turned into two stitches.

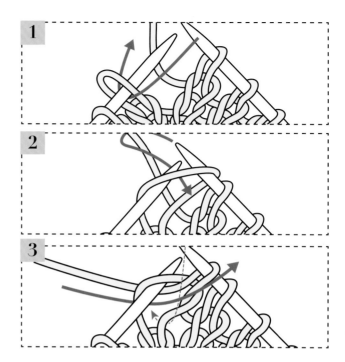

MAKING 2 PURL STITCHES FROM 1

1

Purl the next stitch, but don't let it slide from the left needle yet.

2

Purl the back leg of the same stitch through the back loop.

3

Let the original stitch slip off the left needle; it has been doubled.

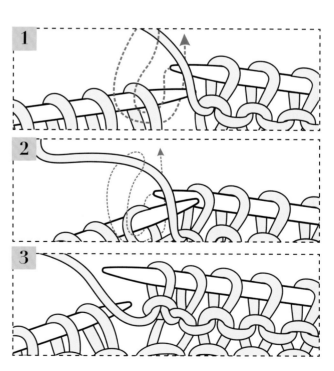

PICKING UP STITCHES

This book features many construction types that don't require sewing knitted pieces together. Individual parts are shaped through increases, decreases, and short rows with turning stitches. Additionally, stitches are picked up later in various spots. For instance, almost all neckbands and collars are knitted on afterwards, which requires picking up stitches from horizontal as well as from curved edges. There are also a few knit-on sleeves and cuffs for cardigans, for which stitches need to be picked up from side edges. For Dorita's ties, stitches must be picked up from within the knitted fabric. All these techniques are briefly described here.

PICKING UP STITCHES FROM A SIDE EDGE

When stitches are to be picked up from a side edge, this is easiest if the piece has been worked with a knotted selvedge. Stitches will be picked up at a rate of two stitches from every little knot. Generally, stitches in knitted fabric are most often wider than they are tall. This makes it necessary to always skip a few stitches to create a flat transition. It is best to pick up the stitches using a needle one size smaller, and then to switch to the correct needle size before working them. This creates a particularly harmonious transition. Depending on the stitch pattern, the number of stitches to be picked up may vary. In stockinette stitch fabric, stitches will be picked up at a rate of three out of four stitches. In garter stitch fabric, the rule of thumb is to pick up one stitch from every garter stitch bump. This means only every other stitch is being picked up. In the patterns in this book, it is always explicitly stated how many stitches are to be picked up to correspond to the pattern's gauge swatch. If too many stitches are picked up, the knitted fabric will bunch; if too few stitches are picked up, the knitted fabric will pucker. If this should happen on account of your own gauge swatch not matching the gauge listed in the pattern, you will need to start over and pick up fewer or more stitches.

PICKING UP STITCHES FROM WITHIN KNITTED FABRIC

Picking up stitches from within knitted fabric must be done from the right side of the fabric. It is important to make sure that stitches are always picked up from the same row only. For this, always insert the right needle through the right leg of every stitch to be picked up and pull the working yarn through. This is a bit fiddly, therefore it is helpful to pull the working yarn through the fabric with the help of a crochet hook and place it onto the right needle. The beginning tail should be pulled through to the wrong side of the fabric with a tapestry needle and woven in there.

PICKING UP STITCHES FROM A HORIZONTAL EDGE

Horizontal edges can be found in the cast-on or bind-off row. From these, stitches can be picked up relatively easily. In this book, from each stitch of a horizontal edge, one stitch will always be picked up. To do this, work your way along the edge from right to left by simply inserting the needle into the stitch under the edge and pulling the working yarn through to the front of work. When working in rows, this will always be followed by working a wrong-side row.

PICKING UP STITCHES FROM A CURVED EDGE

Curved edges are mostly found on necklines or armholes. Here, you will in most cases encounter horizontal as well as slanted edges. From the horizontal part, as usual, one stitch will be picked up from every stitch; from slanted or vertical edges fewer stitches than present in the edge will need to be picked up. Exact numbers are always listed in the pattern instructions. However, here, too, the advice applies—if it seems too loose or too tight, better start over picking up stitches early on, rather than getting frustrated later!

BUTTONHOLES

Generally, there are several options for working button-holes. Which buttonhole is best suited depends on the yarn used and on the type and material of the button. To avoid making buttonholes altogether, use snap fasteners. You can attach them after the completion of the knitted piece, and you never have to worry about buttonholes wearing out. Sew-on snap fasteners can be sewn to the button band at the desired intervals, and a pretty button can be sewn to the outside of the button band where the snap fastener is located on the inside.

In general, when working buttonholes, it is very important to not make them too wide, otherwise the knitted fabric becomes distorted and the button does not close cor-rectly. The easiest method to create a buttonhole is to knit two stitches together and make a yarn over. This results in a small hole, which in most cases will be large enough to accommodate a button. If particularly large buttons are to be used or the stitches are rather tiny, there is another method for working buttonholes.

For this in a right-side row two or three stitches are bound off and, in the same spot in the following wrong-side row, the just-bound-off number of stitches is cast on again using the backwards-loop cast-on method so that the total stitch count is the same as before. This allows for shaping somewhat larger buttonholes.

For delicate yarns, it is recommended to reinforce the buttonholes afterwards using a decorative embroidery stitch. Since this makes the buttonholes slightly smaller again, it should be considered in advance, and the size of the finished reinforced buttonhole be planned to fit the button.

TIP

If possible, the planned buttonhole should be tried out on a small swatch to make sure that the button fits well, that the buttonhole is neither too loose nor too tight.

SPECIAL TECHNIQUES AND STITCHES

WORKING CABLES

Cables are created by crossing one or more stitches. In all cables a certain number of stitches is temporarily moved to an auxiliary needle, called a cable needle. This cable needle is then, according to the pattern instructions, held either in front of or behind the work. Next the stitches from the left needle are worked in the listed stitch pattern, then the stitches from the cable needle are worked. How many stitches need to be placed on the cable needle, whether held in front of or behind the work, and how many stitches are to be worked in the stitch pattern will always be stated in the instructions. To demonstrate the concept, these illustrations show how to work a cable with knit and purl stitches over a width of eight stitches, held in front of the work. In the pattern instructions, this would be noted as: "hold 3 stitches on a cable needle in front of work, knit (the next) 3 stitches, p2 stitches, then knit the 3 stitches from the cable needle."

Place the next three stitches onto a cable needle and hold it in front of the work.

Knit the following three stitches on the left needle, while the cable needle bearing the cable stitches stays in front of work.

Purl the next two stitches on the left needle.

Knit the next three stitches from the cable needle. For especially wide cables, it will be easier to first return the stitches to the left needle before working them.

The cable has been crossed, and you will now continue to work the pattern as listed in the instructions.

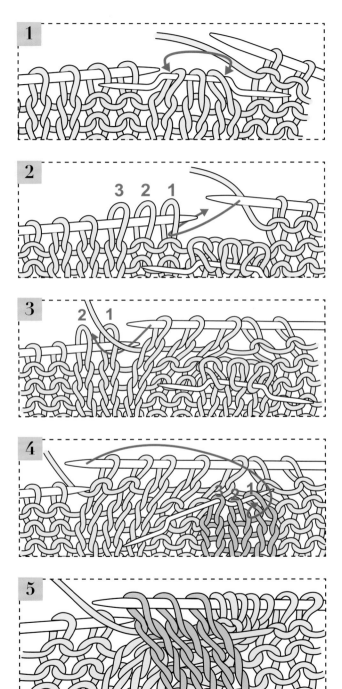

CROSSING STITCHES TO THE RIGHT

Crossing two stitches to the right is nothing more than a tiny cable, worked over two stitches. However, no cable needle is needed to do this. To work this, the right needle is inserted knitwise into the stitch after the next stitch on the left needle, and the working yarn is pulled through. Now, the right needle is inserted knitwise into the stitch before this one (i.e., the first stitch on the left needle), and the working yarn is pulled through to the front of work. Then, both stitches are slipped off the left needle.

BOBBLES

Bobbles are a three-dimensional stitch pattern for which one stitch is turned into several stitches, which are then worked even over a few rows before the stitch count is reduced again to the original number. This works as follows: Insert the right needle knitwise into the next stitch on the left needle, pull the working yarn through to the front of work, place a yarn over onto the right needle, insert the right needle once more into the same stitch as before as if to knit, and pull the working yarn through. Make another yarn over and insert the right needle a final time into the same stitch as if to knit, then pull the working yarn through. You have created a total of five stitches from one. Now, turn your work and purl these five stitches, then turn the work and knit these five stitches. Two times more, "turn work and work the stitches as they appear" (i.e., knit the knits and purl the purls). Finally, one after the other, pass four stitches from the right needle over the first stitch on the right needle, so that only one stitch remains of the original five stitches. Continue in pattern.

I-CORD

To create an I-cord, you can either very conveniently use an I-cord tool or knit it manually with knitting needles. For the latter, two double-pointed needles or a circular needle with short cord can be used. As stated in the instructions, cast on the stated number of stitches, usually three or four. Do not turn the work, but instead slide all stitches to the other end of the needle, then knit all stitches. Again, do not turn your work, but slide all stitches to the other end of the needle, then knit all stitches. Repeat these steps continuously to create a cord. To finish the cord, break the working yarn, use a tapestry needle to thread the end through all stitches on the needle, and pull taut.

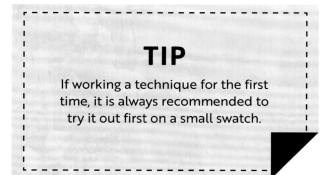

TIP

If working a technique for the first time, it is always recommended to try it out first on a small swatch.

BINDING OFF (FINAL ROW OF A KNITTED PIECE)

BINDING OFF

To finish a knitted piece, all stitches must be removed from the needles in such a way that they are secured. This is accomplished by binding them off. Generally, attention should be paid to not binding off the stitches too tightly, which would cause the knitted fabric to constrict, becoming too tight and crimpy.

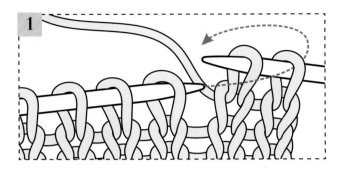

BINDING OFF BY PASSING OVER

This is the easiest method for binding off; it can be used with all stitch types and results in a neat edge. In this example, binding off in knit stitches is shown.

Knit the first two stitches, then insert the left needle from left to right into the stitch worked first.

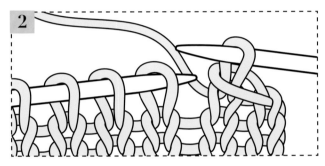

Pass the stitch over the stitch worked after it, and let it slip off the needle so it is placed around the stitch worked after it; it has now been safely bound off. Knit the next stitch on the left needle, and pass the stitch worked before it over the stitch just worked in the same manner as before.

Repeat this procedure until only one single stitch remains on the needle. Now, break the working yarn, leaving an end of 4 inches (10 cm)—long enough to be woven in—and pull it through the last live stitch to secure. With this, all stitches have been bound off.

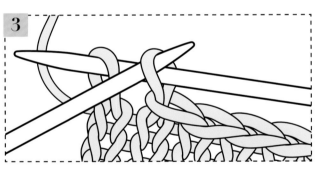

ELASTIC BIND-OFF

The elastic bind-off is similar to the regular bind-off—just with a little trick to prevent the bound-off edge from turning out too tight, in case that poses a problem for you when using the regular bind-off method. All pattern instructions in this book state at the end to "bind off loosely." This can be achieved with a regular bind-off, but using an elastic bind-off method makes it much easier.

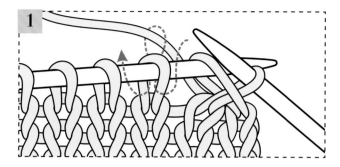

Work the first step as for a regular bind-off, but leave the passed-over stitch on the left needle.

Bypassing this stitch, knit the next stitch on the left needle.

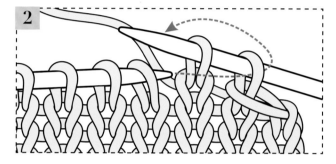

Let the passed-over stitch and the just-worked stitch slip off the left needle together.

Repeat this procedure to the end. This creates a looser bound-off edge—the knitted piece looks much neater and does not pucker.

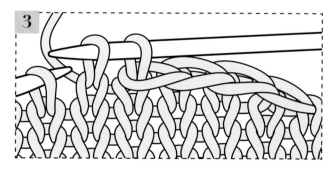

BINDING OFF WITH APPLIED I-CORD

Another way to bind off is an applied I-cord edge, which creates a cord running along the edge of the knitted piece. Its width depends on how many stitches are worked for the cord. This edging is generally very elastic, smooth, and pleasing to the eye. The exact stitch count to be cast on during the first step will always be noted in the instructions. In this example, the I-cord is worked over three stitches.

Cast on two stitches.

Turn work, and knit the two just cast-on stitches.

Knit the next two stitches together left-leaning, using skp. There are now three stitches on the right needle.

Place all of them back onto the left needle one after the other.

Again, knit the first and the second stitch on the left needle and knit the next two stitches together left-leaning, using skp. Place the three stitches back onto the left needle.

Repeat the steps continuously, until you have reached the end of the row or round. When working in rows, place the stitches back onto the left needle a last time. Then, knit the first stitch, knit the next two stitches together left-leaning, using skp, and pass the previously worked stitch over. Break the working yarn and pull it through the last live stitch to secure. When working in rounds, graft the last three stitches together with the three stitches at the beginning of the round in Kitchener stitch.

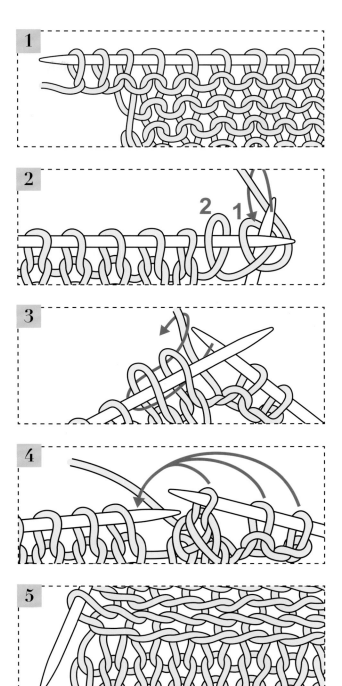

THREE-NEEDLE BIND-OFF
(BINDING OFF TWO EDGES TOGETHER)

As the name suggests, the three-needle bind-off method makes it possible to bind off and connect two edges with live stitches using a third needle. This method is used in this book for joining shoulder seams.

Place the two edges with live stitches together with right sides facing each other, wrong sides facing out. Insert a third needle knitwise into the first stitch on the needle in front, then, also knitwise, into the first stitch on the needle in back.

Wrap the yarn around the third needle as if to knit and pull the working yarn through both stitches to the front of the work and let the two stitches slip from the two needles.

As done before, wrap and pull the working yarn through the next pair of stitches to the front of the work, and pass the previously worked stitch on the right needle over the newly created stitch. Repeat this step continuously to the end of the row.

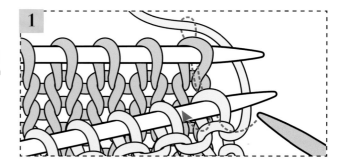

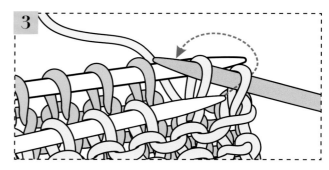

A LITTLE CROCHET

Sometimes basic crochet skills can be useful to improve knitted pieces. The crochet stitches most often used for this purpose are chain, slip stitch, and single crochet.

CHAIN

Chains can be used, for instance, to crochet short belt loops.

1

Arrange the working yarn into a loop shape and hold it in place using your thumb and index finger.

2

Insert the crochet hook into the center of the loop and pull the working yarn through.

3

Pull the resulting loop tighter on the crochet hook by pulling at the beginning tail and the working yarn. A beginning slipknot has been placed on the crochet hook.

4

Grasp the working yarn with the crochet hook and pull it through the loop to form a new chain, with another loop sitting on the crochet hook now. Repeat these steps for as many chains as needed.

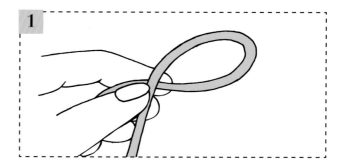

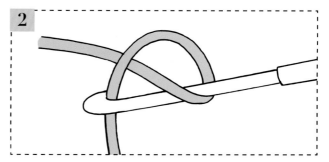

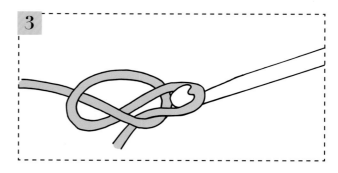

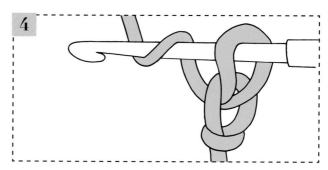

SLIP STITCH

Slip stitches can be used to improve an edge that has turned out too loose or looks untidy. When stitches are to be picked up from a rounded neckline, it can be helpful to first work a round of slip stitches—this makes picking up the stitches much easier.

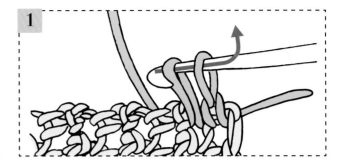

Insert the crochet hook into a stitch at the edge to be crocheted into and pull the working yarn through to the front of the work so that a loop has been placed on the crochet hook.

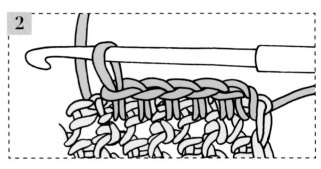

Insert the crochet hook into the next stitch and pull the working yarn through the fabric and through the loop on the crochet hook at once. Repeat this step to the end of the row or round.

SINGLE CROCHET

The edge of a collar or the side edge of a piece can be reinforced with a single-crochet edging. Moreover, a row of single crochet looks very tidy and makes for a neat finish.

Insert the crochet hook into a stitch at the edge to be crocheted into and pull the working yarn through so that a loop has been placed on the crochet hook. Chain 1. Insert the crochet hook into the next stitch and pull the working yarn through so there are two loops on the crochet hook now. Grasp the working yarn and pull it through both loops at once. One loop remains on the crochet hook. Work all following stitches as follows: Insert the hook into the next stitch and pull the working yarn through, so there are two loops on the hook. Now, pull the working yarn through both loops at once. Repeat these steps continuously until you have crocheted around the whole edge of the piece.

COLOR CHANGE AND JOINING NEW WORKING YARN

COLOR CHANGE IN ROUNDS

Changing color in rounds can create unsightly color steps called "jogs." To camouflage these steps, a smart trick can be applied: After the first round in the new color has been completed and the first stitch in the new color has been reached again, this stitch is just slipped with yarn in back of work. This way, the last stitch of the previous round and the first stitch of the current round end at the same height, and there is no offset. For a sweater worked in a pattern of not-too-wide stripes, the working yarn in the unused color can be carried in back of the work and does not need to be cut. It is recommended to cross the current and the carried color once in the heightwise middle of the stripe, so the float is less likely to be caught when the garment is worn.

COLOR CHANGE IN ROWS

When changing color in rows, the working yarn in the old color can just be left hanging while knitting with the working yarn in the new color. Here, too, the working yarn in the old color does not need to be cut, but can be carried up along the edge of the piece. The strands should then be crossed once at the beginning of every right-side row. A drawback of this is that the color change will be somewhat noticeable, but having to weave in countless ends can be skipped.

JOINING NEW WORKING YARN

When a new skein of yarn needs to be joined, and it is possible to do this at the edge of the piece, then it should be joined there. In this spot, weaving in ends is especially easy. With very long rows or when knitting in the round, this is, of course, not possible. For those cases, there are many different ways to join a new ball of yarn.

KNITTING IN THE TAILS

For this, a few stitches are worked with two strands of yarn held together. One of the strands is the end of the old working yarn, the other the beginning of the new skein. This will cause the knitted piece to be slightly thicker over a small area. For this reason, this method should only be applied in less conspicuous spots. The tails still need to be woven in.

A slightly more elegant way is to split in half both the outgoing working yarn and the yarn from the new skein. Then, work with half the old working yarn and half the new working yarn held together, so that the knitted fabric in the joining area will have the same thickness as the whole piece throughout. However, this yields four ends to be woven in instead of just two, and this method can only be used if the yarn is splittable; this cannot, for example, be done with unplied yarns or chainette-type yarns.

WEAVING IN THE TAILS

In this method, the new working yarn is used to weave in a length of the old working yarn. For this, the current stitches are worked alternatingly over or under the ending tail of the old yarn. This technique produces just a small nub on the wrong side of the fabric and is therefore relatively inconspicuous.

LEAVING THE TAILS HANGING

The easiest method and, at the same time, one of the less noticeable ones, is to just leave the old working yarn hanging for the time being and join the new working yarn. This creates a small hole. When hiding the ends later, the hole will be closed by using a yarn needle to inconspicuously weave in the tail.

FINISHING

GRAFTING

Grafting is used to join two edges to each other, creating a nearly invisible transition. It can be worked on already bound-off edges or live stitches, and with knit as well as purl stitches.

1

On already bound-off edges, grafting is worked from right to left. For this, the little V of the stitches in the top and bottom row must be alternatingly picked up. First, insert the needle into the stitch of the bottom row from back to front, then pass the needle under both legs of the stitch of the top row. Now, in the bottom row, insert the needle into the same stitch as before and grasp the next two legs of the stitch from the back, then exit to the front of the work. In the top row, at the stitch directly above it, grasp both legs of the stitch from the back again. Repeat this procedure until the edges have been grafted.

2

Two edges with live stitches are also grafted from right to left. Alternating between top and bottom edges, lead the tapestry needle through two adjoining stitches by inserting it at the top edge into the stitch to the right of the current one, and at the bottom edge, into the stitch to the left of the current one. Repeat until the edges have been grafted.

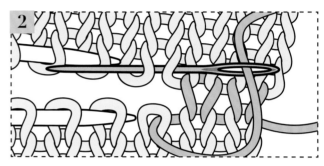

MATTRESS STITCH

The mattress stitch is used to join side edges; it works especially well with stockinette stitch or garter stitch fabric. The selvedge stitches are hidden within the seam, and a neat edge is created.

To join pieces worked in stockinette stitch, place the edges of the pieces to be joined next to each other. It is recommended to temporarily pin the edges together in a sufficient number of spots using tailor pins. Start at the bottom and work your way toward the top. Using a tapestry needle, beginning with the piece at the left, first grasp two bars between stitches of the same column between the selvedge stitch and the first stitch in. Now, on the piece at the right, likewise grasp the two bars between stitches in the corresponding row from bottom to top. Return to the piece at the left, grasp the bars above the previous ones in the same manner and continue in this way to the top, until the edges have been seamed. Gently tighten the working yarn from time to time.

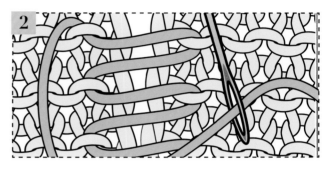

To join pieces worked in garter stitch, place the edges of the pieces to be joined next to each other. It is recommended to temporarily pin the edges together in a sufficient number of spots using tailor pins. Start at the bottom and work your way toward the top. Insert the tapestry needle from bottom to top into the purl bumps of the stitches alternatingly on the left and right piece. On the piece at right, grasp the purl bumps arched downward with the tapestry needle, and on the piece at left, use the purl bumps arched upward.

HIDING THE ENDS

At the end of knitting, all ends resulting from joining new colors or skeins or due to the construction of the piece must be hidden. It is important that these ends are not too short. They should be at least 4 inches (10 cm) long to be properly woven in. Extra thick yarns can be split to make the woven-in ends less noticeable. Generally, ends are always woven in on the wrong side of the fabric (i.e., the side not visible when the garment is being worn).

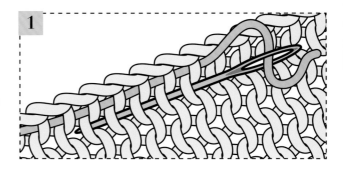

Ends hanging at side edges should be woven in as close to the edge as possible. For this, thread the tapestry needle with the yarn tail through the stitches along the edge. To better secure the end, first thread in one direction, then in the opposite direction.

When a tail needs to be woven in the middle of a knitted piece, care should be taken that it follows a meandering path. If possible, insert the needle through the strand of yarn to better secure the end in place.

WASHING

Yarn bands contain information from the manufacturer about the fiber content of the yarn and the recommended washing method. If a specific cycle for the washing machine is mentioned, it should be used; most modern washing machines have a hand-washing cycle. This hand-washing cycle is in most cases even gentler to the knitted item than actual washing by hand. Generally, all knitted items, including those made of pure cotton yarns, should be dried spread out horizontally—when the fiber is wet, the garment can become heavily stretched by its own weight.

When choosing a detergent, the fiber content of the yarn should be the key factor. For fibers of animal origin, except silk, it is recommended to use a detergent containing lanolin. This natural wool oil is refatting and protects the yarn from pilling.

For silk and rayon/viscose, however, detergents with lanolin should be avoided since they would leave the fibers dull and flat. Special detergents formulated to care for protein-containing fibers like these are a better choice.

Cotton and linen fibers as well as synthetic fibers are relatively undemanding and can be washed with regular detergent.

For fiber blends, a detergent that best cares for the most delicate fiber should always be chosen.

A miracle cure for heavy pilling, which happens especially with unplied yarns, is the lint shaver. It makes knits look like new again in no time.

By the way, purely natural wool fibers have a self-cleaning effect. Often they don't even need to be washed; it will be sufficient to let them hang outside in the fresh air.

DAMPENING AND PULLING INTO SHAPE

Before the first wearing, the fit of sweaters and cardigans is usually not yet optimal. To improve their fit, garments should be dampened and pulled into shape. This will often also improve the stitch definition, since the moisture causes the stitches to relax and become more evenly sized. For this, dampen the knitted piece using a spray bottle, gently pull the garment into the desired shape, and let it dry on an even horizontal surface. A clothes-drying rack covered with a towel on which the knitted piece can rest will do well.

STEAM BLOCKING

Sometimes, dampening and pulling into shape is not sufficient to open up a stitch pattern or achieve the desired fit. In these cases, steam blocking is recommended. For this, the lightly dampened knitted piece is pulled into shape and pinned to a blocking mat with tailor pins or special blocking pins. Then it is covered with a wet cloth and gently steamed with a hovering iron without touching the surface of the knitting.

WET BLOCKING

Especially for lace patterns, it is sometimes necessary to thoroughly soak the knitted piece and subsequently block it. When sleeves have turned out half an inch too short, blocking can adjust the length after the fact. For this, the knitted piece must be thoroughly wet. First, it should be washed according to the instructions on the yarn wrapper using a fiber-appropriate detergent. Then the wet piece should be pinned to a blocking mat with the help of T-pins, tailor pins, or blocking wires in the desired shape to the required dimensions. The dimensions should be checked using a measuring tape.

GAUGE SWATCHES

Correct gauge is the be-all and end-all for sweaters and cardigans. Even if your gauge differs by just one stitch from the one listed, it could mean that the garment fits quite differently than expected or, in the worst case, won't fit at all. For this reason, it is truly important to take the time to prepare a proper gauge swatch, even if you'd prefer to delve into the actual project right away. What to consider when making a gauge swatch is explained below.

1. What is the right size for a gauge swatch?

The gauge swatch for a sweater should be slightly larger than 4 x 4 inches (10 x 10 cm). Only then can the stitches be counted accurately enough. Some experienced knitters even advise a gauge swatch as large as a letter-sized sheet of paper. Obviously, this is really on the safe side! Many knitters, when starting a project, first work a little tighter and then become looser, or the other way around. For this reason, I recommend making a gauge swatch of at least 4 x 4 inches (10 x 10 cm). It is also important to both measure and count the stitches in at least three places in the swatch (and average the results), ideally once at the beginning, once in the middle, and once toward the end of the gauge swatch.

2. What stitch pattern should the gauge swatch be worked in?

At the beginning of every pattern, the appropriate gauge will be listed as well as information about the stitch pattern in which the gauge swatch should be worked. There may also be additional information, such as "when holding several strands of yarn together." It is important to work the swatch in the exact stitch pattern given, and it is a good idea to cast on ten stitches more than listed in the gauge. This way, a garter stitch edge can be worked over the first and last five stitches of every row (knit all stitches of this edge in right-side and wrong-side rows), which prevents the edges from curling and makes measuring easier.

3. What type of yarn will be used for the project?

The fiber content of the project yarn is very important. Does the yarn, for instance, contain merino? If yes, then the gauge swatch should be washed before measuring since merino wool can significantly grow. If, on the other hand, the yarn has a high cotton or linen content, the knitted piece, depending on the stitch pattern, could be expected to shrink somewhat. To prevent unpleasant surprises when your new favorite sweater doesn't fit after the first wash, it is essential to wash the gauge swatch prior to measuring.

4. What to do if the gauge doesn't match?

If using the same yarn as listed in the pattern, or a very similar substitute, and the gauge swatch still doesn't match, this is not a problem. Every knitter knits differently, some somewhat tighter, some somewhat more loosely. For this reason, the needle size listed for the gauge swatch should be understood as a negotiable recommendation only. If your gauge swatch contains too many stitches in 4 inches (10 cm), start over using needles one or two sizes smaller. Should your gauge swatch have fewer stitches in 4 inches (10 cm), begin again using needles one or two sizes larger.

If your gauge swatch has a different row count, this is not a big deal. It happens often and, as almost all patterns contain measurements for the length, you can adjust the number of rows as needed.

5. What do I do if I want to use a completely different yarn weight?

If you plan to use a completely different yarn, it is, of course, possible to do so. You should, however, take into account that this will significantly change the appearance of the knitted piece. Additionally, it will be necessary to recalculate all stitch counts. For this, the ratio between the gauge swatches needs to be figured. Example: According to the gauge listed in the pattern, 16 stitches per 4 inches (10 cm) are needed, but the yarn you intend to use is significantly thinner, so your own gauge swatch yields 28 stitches in 4 inches (10 cm). In this case, your own gauge needs to be divided by the gauge listed in the pattern (i.e., 28/16 = 1.75). All stitch counts listed in the pattern need to be multiplied by the resulting factor—in this example, 1.75.

Row counts are calculated the same way, however, this will often not be necessary since many patterns contain references to length rather than row counts. The rule is: When your gauge swatch has more stitches than listed in the pattern, then the factor will be larger than 1, and you will always need to work more stitches than indicated in the instructions. When your gauge swatch contains fewer stitches than listed in the pattern, then the calculated factor will be smaller than 1, and you will need to work fewer stitches than indicated in the instructions.

Generally, this method is only recommended for experienced knitters who have already knitted garments of a similar construction without performing any conversions, since often other things, such as the number and ratio of increases, need to be recalculated, or the ratio of repeats for increases or decreases in rows will be different and need to be recalculated.

ATTENTION

When using a different yarn than stated in the pattern, the total amount of yarn needed for the project can change. Even if the gauge matches, the yardage per skein should be double-checked. If your yarn has fewer yards per skein than that of the yarn recommended in the pattern, you will need more skeins. On the other hand, it can happen that you need fewer skeins than specified if your yarn has more yards than the original yarn.

TIP

If you want to make absolutely sure that the knitted garment will fit well, you should wash your gauge swatch the same way the finished garment will be washed later. It should also be lightly blocked. This way, you will be able to enjoy a well-fitting garment in the end.

FINDING THE CORRECT SIZE

To determine which size is right for you, you should first take accurate measurements of yourself. The most important measurement of all is the chest circumference, which is an important indicator for the clothing size. The sizes in this book are based on the following chest circumferences:

Size	Chest Circumference	Sleeve Length from Armhole
XS	33.8 in (86 cm)	13.4 in (34 cm)
S	35.4 in (90 cm)	14.2 in (36 cm)
M	39.0 in (99 cm)	15.7 in (40 cm)
L	42.9 in (109 cm)	17.3 in (44 cm)
XL	46.9 in (119 cm)	18.9 in (48 cm)
XXL	50.8 in (129 cm)	20.5 in (52 cm)

The tables shown at the beginning of every pattern provide the actual chest circumference of the garment. This means that if the numbers in the table in a pattern are smaller than those in the table above, this garment will have a closer fit. If the numbers for the appropriate size are larger in the pattern, the garment will have a loose fit; some of them are even designed to have an oversized fit. You should also think about how you normally like to wear your sweaters or cardigans. If, for instance, you generally prefer a looser fit, you can opt to work one size larger for garments designed with a close fit. It works the other way around as well—if you prefer to wear everything figure-hugging, then choose one or two clothing sizes smaller for the garments that are cut more loosely or designed with an oversized fit.

Another important measurement is the sleeve length. At the same body height, sleeve length can vary greatly among women, therefore almost all patterns in this book are designed so that the sleeve length can be easily adjusted. The table at the beginning of every pattern indicates the sleeve length used in the pattern. It is always measured from the lowest point of the armhole to the edge of the garment's bottom ribbing or hem. However, personal taste also matters here. Some women like to wear their sleeves ending at the base of the hand, others ending in the middle of the hand, while yet others prefer extra-long sleeves. Most of the patterns in this book are constructed top-down, which has the big advantage that the garment-in-progress can be tried on any time to check and adjust the fit and sleeve length.

Another measurement that can be adjusted easily is the overall garment length. Here, too, there are two reasons why it is important to be able to adjust the body length. First, like sleeve length, women with the same chest circumference can have significantly different body and torso lengths. Second, individual tastes vary. Do you like to wear your sweaters and cardigans short or rather long? Therefore, all patterns are equipped with measurements for the body length, so that each garment can be easily adjusted to your preferences.

My Measurements

Chest circumference: _____

Sleeve length from armhole: _____

Preferred garment length from armhole:

_____

BO = bind off

BOR = beginning of the round

CC = contrasting color

CDD = centered double decrease: slip 2 sts together knitwise, knit the next stitch, then pass the slipped stitches over the knitted one (2 sts decreased)

CO = cast on

DPN(s) = double-pointed needle(s)

inc = increase(d)

k2tog = knit 2 stitches together (1 st decreased)

k3tog = knit 3 stitches together (2 sts decreased)

kfslb = make 2 sts from 1 knitwise: knit the front leg of the stitch, then slip the back leg of the same stitch (1 st increased)

m = stitch marker

M1L = increase 1 stitch left-leaning knitwise from the bar between sts (1 st increased)

M1L-p = increase 1 stitch left-leaning purlwise from the bar between sts (1 st increased)

M1R = increase 1 stitch right-leaning knitwise from the bar between sts (1 st increased)

M1R-p = increase 1 stitch right-leaning purlwise from the bar between sts (1 st increased)

MC = main color

p2tog = purl 2 stitches together (1 st decreased)

pfb = purl front and back: purl the same stitch through the front and through the back leg (1 st increased)

pfkb = purl front, knit back: purl the stitch through the front and knit the same stitch through the back leg (1 st increased)

rep = repeat

rnd(s) = round(s)

sc = single crochet

selv st(s) = selvedge stitch(es)

skp = slip, knit, pass: decrease 1 stitch left-leaning knitwise—slip 1 stitch to the left needle, knit the next stitch, then pass the slipped stitch over the knitted one (1 st decreased)

sl = slip

sl1-w/yo = slip 1 stitch with accompanying yarn over

ssk = slip, slip, knit: decrease 1 stitch left-leaning knit-wise—slip 2 stitches individually knitwise to the right needle, return them to the left needle, then knit them together through the back loop (1 st decreased)

ssp = slip, slip, purl: decrease 1 stitch left-leaning purlwise—slip 2 stitches individually knitwise to the right needle, return them to the left needle, then purl them together through the back loop (1 st decreased)

sssk = slip, slip, slip, knit: decrease 2 stitches left-leaning knitwise—slip 3 stitches individually knitwise to the right needle, return them to the left needle, then knit them together through the back loop (2 sts decreased)

st(s) = stitch(es)

-tbl = through the back loop

tog = (knit or purl # of sts) together

t-st = turning stitch(es) or double stitch in German short rows

yo = yarn over

POSSIBLE COMBINATIONS

With the immense variety of available construction methods for pullovers and cardigans, the most important decision will first be whether to work in pieces and seam or to work seamlessly in one piece.

While knitting in pieces has a few advantages (see "Traditional Seamed Constructions," page 49), for those like me who dread sewing, seamless knitting clearly outweighs the advantages of knitting in pieces. The greatest advantage (apart from not having to sew anything together) is that garments worked seamlessly are much easier to try on or to hold up to measure at any stage of completion, such as adjusting the length.

For this reason, only three patterns in this book require seaming, and all are to be found in the chapter "Traditional Seamed Constructions." These are the designs Giselle, Ille, and Elisabeth.

The next decision is whether to work from the bottom up or from the top down. I prefer working from the top to the bottom, since here, too, the garment-in-progress can be easily tried on during the process. Additionally, after completion of the shoulder section, you can still change your mind about the body shape.

Designs Giselle, Ille, Elisabeth, Stefanie, and Dorita are worked from the bottom up; all others from the top down.

Beginning knitters should always stay with the instructions in the book, and work only with yarn that matches the gauge; advanced knitters will be able to work many of the garments in other yarns as well.

SHOULDER SECTION AND UPPER BODY

The most prominent feature on a sweater is often the region of the shoulders and upper body. It has the most profound effect on the overall fit, therefore it makes sense to think about which shoulder shape you like to wear yourself or which you want to knit next. In this book, six different shoulder shapes will be explored: with sleeve cap, raglan, circular yoke, dropped shoulders with angled sleeve top, dropped shoulders with straight sleeve top, and Dolman sleeve.

With Sleeve Cap	Raglan	Circular Yoke	Dropped Shoulders with Angled Sleeve Top	Dropped Shoulders with Straight Sleeve Top	Dolman Sleeve
Ille (pg. 54)	Roncita (pg. 72)	Sophia (pg. 106)	Irma (pg. 138)	Giselle (pg. 50)	Allegra (pg. 184)
Elisabeth (pg. 62)	Tiana (pg. 76)	Emma (pg. 110)	Olivia (pg. 144)	Stefanie (pg. 130)	
Dorita (pg. 166)	Ulla (pg. 82)	Marie (pg. 116)	Paola (pg. 160)	Elise (pg. 134)	
Elisa (pg. 174)	Ellen (pg. 88)	Elaine (pg. 122)			
	Daniela (pg. 94)				
	Noemi (pg. 152)				

SPECIAL BODY SHAPES

For all top-down garments, body shapes can be easily switched out. All garments worked from the bottom up have a straight body shape. The overall length can be easily adjusted for all designs. The following patterns in this book feature special body shapes:

Shaped waist: Ellen

Curved hem: Paola

Curved sides and side tails: Tiana

A-line: Tiana, Daniela

Longer in the back than in the front: Noemi (this effect is created by the way the shoulder section is constructed)

Notched/side slits: Elise

SLEEVE SHAPES

Different sleeve shapes, too, can quickly lend a new character to a garment. This is easiest to accomplish for sweaters knitted from the top to the bottom. In addition to traditional tapered sleeves, for which a new look can be conjured up very quickly through different lengths or cuffs, the following sleeve shapes are included in this book:

Trumpet sleeve: Daniela

Wide-cuffed sleeve: Giselle

Dolman sleeve with lace insert: Allegra

Balloon sleeve: Stefanie, Ulla

Extra-long cuff: Elise

Foldover cuff with decorative tie: Dorita

Short sleeve: Elaine, Ille

7/8-sleeve: Noemi

RIBBING AS SLEEVE CUFF AND HEM FINISHING

Different sleeve cuffs and hem ribbing can easily and quickly change the character of a garment. By modifying the length or the stitch pattern, a completely new look can be quickly achieved. Some of the designs can do without any cuffs at all, so the cuffs can just be omitted. This is especially appropriate for stitch patterns with an inherent stability, such as ribbing patterns, moss and seed stitch, or classic brioche. For pieces worked in stockinette stitch, edges automatically curl, and the rolled edges can be used as a deliberate feature.

In this book, a total of nine cuff varieties are introduced. In the table below, all patterns are listed with page numbers, so it will be easy to compare how different the same cuff can appear through changing lengths.

Cardigan designs Noemi, Ulla, and Elisa are worked with knitted-on front bands. Experienced knitters can easily switch out different stitch patterns for the bands. Noemi features an all-around cable as combined front band and collar, Ulla a combined front band and collar in 1x1 ribbing, and Elisa uses slipped stitches to create stockinette stitch fabric on both sides, which prevents curling of the edges.

1x1-Ribbing	1x1-Twisted Ribbing	2x2-Ribbing	Garter Stitch	Rolled Edge	No Ribbing	I-cord	Stockinette Brioche	Classic Brioche
Ulla (pg. 82)	Roncita (pg. 72)	Ille (pg. 54)	Marie (pg. 116)	Emma (pg. 110)	Giselle (pg. 50)	Daniela (pg. 94)	Elisa (pg. 174)	Olivia (pg. 144)
Ellen (pg. 88)		Tiana (pg. 76)		Elaine (pg. 122)	Elisabeth (pg. 62)			
Sophia (pg. 106)		Dorita (pg. 166)			Noemi (pg. 152)			
Elise (pg. 134)					Paola (pg. 160)			
Irma (pg. 138)								
Stefanie (pg. 130)								
Allegra (pg. 184)								

NECKBANDS AND COLLARS

Neckbands and collars, too, are interchangeable in many of the designs. To be able to delay the decision for the neckband design until the end of the garment even in top-down constructions, the neckband is almost always knitted on afterwards. In addition to the possibility to decide on a different ribbing pattern or neckband later, this has two more advantages: First, picking up stitches for the neckband at the end reinforces the neckline, and second, this allows one to better adjust the size of the neck opening. If it, for instance, is larger than it should be, fewer stitches need to be picked up than stated in the instructions. Or the other way around, you can pick up a few more stitches for the neckband when the neck opening seems rather small.

For some of the designs, however, owing to the construction, the neckline finishing cannot be swapped out for a different type. This is the case with the following patterns:

— In Giselle, an open-front cardigan, the side parts simply abut against each other in the back.
— Elisabeth's stand-up collar is directly worked at the same time as and in one piece with the body.
— Ulla and Noemi start with an all-around collar in the center back and are then continued in both directions together with the body.
— Elise features a boatneck, which is set up directly at the beginning.

For some of the designs, variations are possible by changing the stitch pattern for the ribbing:

— Ille and Irma have a somewhat deeper, round neckline and can be modified by exchanging the stitch pattern for the neckline ribbing.
— Paola, too, features a deep, round neckline and, because of the stitch pattern, does not need ribbing. If exchanging the stitch pattern anyway, any ribbing pattern would be suitable, such as that used in Ille or Irma.

— Ellen has a V-neck; the ribbing pattern can be exchanged. However, you must always work a decrease in the lowest point of the V.
— Olivia is a cardigan with all-around combined front band/collar, which can be changed as desired as it can be knitted on afterwards.

For the following patterns, it is not only possible to change the ribbing pattern without any difficulty, but the whole construction is interchangeable between these garments. In addition to conventional ribbing, you can also find different shapes:

— Stefanie, Daniela, Allegra, and Elise feature simple 1x1 ribbing.
— Roncita uses a 1x1 ribbing, but with stitches knitted through the back loop.
— Sophia, too, features a regular 1x1 ribbing pattern, but it is folded to the inside and sewn on, producing two layers of fabric.
— Emma features a rolled neckline edge.
— Marie features a neckband in reverse stockinette.
— Tiana and Elisa both have a hood. In Tiana, the hood is finished with a ribbing pattern; in Elisa, an I-cord is threaded through a drawstring channel.
— Dorita has a turtleneck collar.

STITCH PATTERNS

For all garments, stitch patterns can be exchanged 1:1 for a different pattern with the same gauge. If the desired stitch pattern has a different gauge than that listed in the pattern, stitch and row counts need to be recalculated as described in "Gauge Swatches" (see page 38) to adjust the stitch pattern. In this book, mainly basic stitch patterns were used to emphasize and differentiate the construction and shape of each garment. I would like for you to view the minimal colors and patterns from the book as a starting point for knitting your own sweaters and cardigans as colorful and patterned as you wish.

PROJECTS

LET'S GET STARTED

CHAPTER 1

Most traditional seamed constructions are worked from the bottom to the top and in pieces. This has the advantage of providing instant gratification, since individual parts will knit up quickly most of the time. Furthermore, usually only a minimal weight will be resting in your lap during knitting. Sweaters, such as those worked in one piece on US size 10 (6.0 mm) needles, can sometimes add up to quite a weight, and the heat generated by having that much wool resting on the lap can be quite substantial as well. Traditionally constructed garments often feature a sleeve cap, allowing for an exact fit in the shoulder area, which is a distinctive advantage.

The biggest drawback in my opinion is that garments worked this way can't be tried on and adjusted during knitting. For this reason, taking correct measurements of the body of the intended wearer is very important, since with this construction method, it won't be possible to just add some length to the body or the sleeves after an initial try-on.

Many knitters have an aversion to sewing, but the seams serve a reinforcing function and ensure the proper fit of the garment.

I prefer to use traditional seamed constructions for designs worked in garter stitch, since purling large numbers of stitches can be avoided, which would have to be done when working in the round.

In this chapter, three designs are presented as examples—a super-easy one made up of just rectangles, a summer top, and a cardigan.

LET'S GET STARTED

GISELLE

THE EASIEST CARDIGAN IN THE WORLD

SIZES
XS, S, M, L, XL, XXL

Numbers for size XS are listed before the parentheses, numbers for sizes S through XXL within parentheses. If only one number is listed, it applies to all sizes.

Size	Chest Circum-ference	Sleeve Length from Armhole (with cuff folded)	Garment Length from Armhole
XS	35.4 in (90 cm)	19.7 in (50 cm)	19.7 in (50 cm)
S	37.6 in (95.5 cm)	19.7 in (50 cm)	19.7 in (50 cm)
M	39.8 in (101 cm)	19.7 in (50 cm)	21.6 in (55 cm)
L	45.7 in (116 cm)	19.7 in (50 cm)	21.6 in (55 cm)
XL	49.6 in (126 cm)	19.7 in (50 cm)	23.6 in (60 cm)
XXL	52.8 in (134 cm)	19.7 in (50 cm)	23.6 in (60 cm)

MATERIALS AND TOOLS
— Rico Design Essentials Mega Wool Chunky; 55% wool, 45% acrylic; 136.7 yd (125 m) per 3.5 oz (100 g): #13 Gray, 10 (10/11/14/17/19) skeins
— Circular knitting needle, US size 10 (6.0 mm), length 32 in (80 cm)
— Tapestry needle

GAUGE
In horizontal ridge pattern on US size 10 (6.0 mm) needles: 15.5 sts and 20 rows = 4 x 4 in (10 x 10 cm)

CONSTRUCTION NOTES
The cardigan is worked in pieces from the bottom up. Every one of these pieces is a rectangle; these rectangles are seamed together at the end. Thanks to this, the cardigan is a great beginner project, since only knit and purl stitches need to be mastered. For the experienced knitters wanting to knit something simple, it also makes a great side project.

HORIZONTAL RIDGE PATTERN
Row 1 (RS): Knit all stitches.
Row 2 (WS): Work the same as Row 1.
Row 3 (RS): Purl all stitches.
Row 4 (WS): Work the same as Row 3.
Repeat Rows 1–4.

TIP

For a more refined edge, a crocheted edging can be added afterwards as described in Elisabeth (see page 62).

CONTINUED

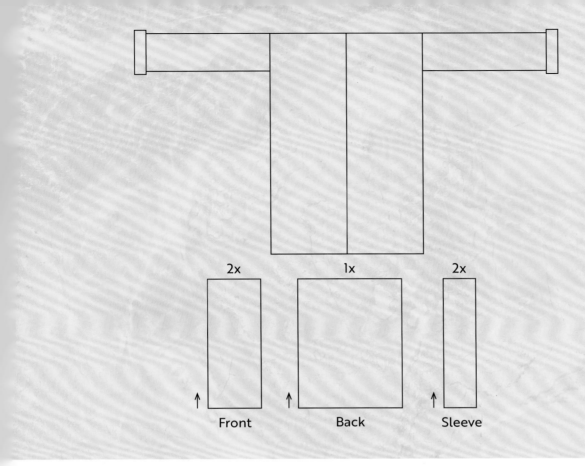

2x — Front

1x — Back

2x — Sleeve

INSTRUCTIONS

BACK

Using US size 10 (6.0 mm) needles, cast on 70 (74/78/90/98/104) sts. Work in horizontal ridge pattern until piece has reached a height of 27.5 (27.5/29.5/31.5/33.5/35.5) in [70 (70/75/80/85/90) cm], ending after having just completed a Row 4. In the following Row 1 of the stitch pattern, bind off all sts.

FRONT

The Front is worked twice, to make right and left sides. Using US size 10 (6.0 mm) needles, cast on 35 (37/39/45/49/52) sts. Work in horizontal ridge pattern until piece has reached a height of 27.5 (27.5/29.5/31.5/33.5/35.5) in [70 (70/75/80/85/90) cm], ending after having just completed a Row 4. In the following Row 1 of the stitch pattern, bind off all sts.

SLEEVES

Both Sleeves are worked the same. For the Sleeves, using US size 10 (6.0 mm) needles, cast on 62 (62/62/76/76/94) sts. Work in horizontal ridge pattern until piece has reached a height of 24.8 in (63 cm), ending after having just completed a Row 4. In the following Row 1 of the stitch pattern, bind off all sts. The Sleeves are sewn onto the body from right to left, therefore, make sure that tails are located at the right edge of the knitted piece.

FINISHING

First, graft the Fronts to the Back at the top, thus closing the shoulder seams. After this, sew on the Sleeves, with right sides held together, in mattress stitch. Finally, close Sleeve seams and side seams in mattress stitch. Fold over the Sleeves generously, hide all ends, dampen the cardigan, and pull it into the desired shape.

ILLE

SHORT-SLEEVED NARROW SUMMER TOP, WORKED IN GARTER STITCH

SIZES
XS, S, M, L, XL, XXL

Numbers for size XS are listed before the parentheses, numbers for sizes S through XXL within parentheses. If only one number is listed, it applies to all sizes.

Size	Chest Circum-ference	Sleeve Length from Armhole	Garment Length from Armhole
XS	32.3 in (82 cm)	2.4 in (6 cm)	14.2 in (36 cm)
S	33.5 in (85 cm)	2.4 in (6 cm)	14.6 in (37 cm)
M	36.6 in (93 cm)	2.8 in (7 cm)	14.6 in (37 cm)
L	39.4 in (100 cm)	3.1 in (8 cm)	15 in (38 cm)
XL	42.1 in (107 cm)	3.5 in (9 cm)	15 in (38 cm)
XXL	46.5 in (118 cm)	4 in (10 cm)	15.7 in (40 cm)

MATERIALS AND TOOLS
— Wolle Rödel Mille Fili; 100% cotton; 131.2 yd (120 m) per 1.75 oz (50 g): #17 Anthracite, 6 (7, 8, 9, 10, 12) skeins
— Circular knitting needle, US size 4 (3.5 mm), length 32 in (80 cm)
— Tapestry needle

GAUGE
In garter stitch on US size 4 (3.5 mm) needles: 22 sts and 40 rows = 4 x 4 in (10 x 10 cm)

CONSTRUCTION NOTES
The sweater is worked traditionally in pieces, in turned rows; the neckline and armholes are shaped with decreases. The sweater can also be worked in stockinette stitch, if desired, as long as gauge matches. At the end, individual parts are grafted and sewn together in mattress stitch. Stitches for the neckband are picked up from the neckline edge at the end, then the neckband is worked in the round. The sweater has a narrow silhouette and is comfortable on balmy summer evenings or in the mild spring or fall. If you prefer a looser fit, work one size larger.

GARTER STITCH
Knit all sts in RS and WS rows.

RIBBING
2x2 ribbing: * K2, p2 *, rep from * to * continuously.

CONTINUED

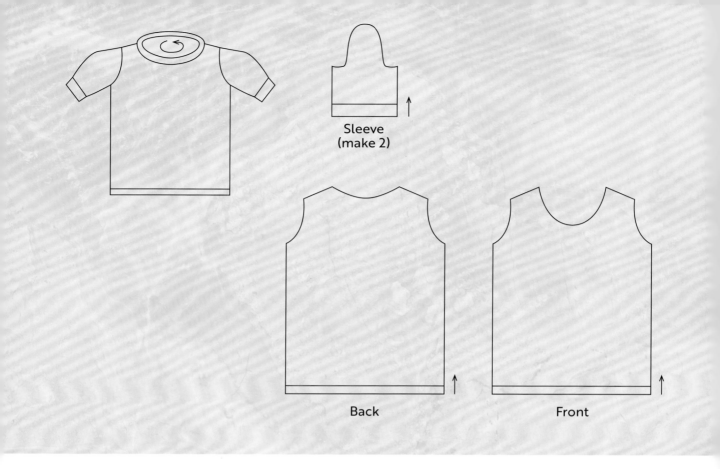

Sleeve
(make 2)

Back

Front

INSTRUCTIONS

BACK

Using US size 4 (3.5 mm) needles, cast on 90 (94/102/110/118/130) sts, and work ribbing as follows:

Row 1 (WS): K1, * p2, k2 *, rep from * to * to last stitch of this row, k1.

Rows 2–5: Repeat Row 1 four times.

Now, work in garter stitch until the knitted piece has reached a length of 14.2 (14.6/14.6/15/15/15.8) in [36 (37/37/38/38/40) cm], ending having just completed a WS row.

ARMHOLES

Row 1 (RS): BO 4 (4/5/6/6/8) sts, knit to end of row. You should now have 86 (90/97/104/112/122) sts on the needles.

Row 2 (WS): Work the same as Row 1. You should now have 82 (86/92/98/106/114) sts on the needles.

Row 3 (RS): K2, sssk, knit to last 5 sts, k3tog, k2. You should now have 78 (82/88/94/102/110) sts on the needles.

Row 4 (WS): Knit all stitches.

Rows 5–8: Repeat Rows 3 and 4 twice. You should now have 70 (74/80/86/94/102) sts on the needles.

Row 9 (RS): K2, skp, knit to last 4 sts, k2tog, k2. You should now have 68 (72/78/84/92/100) sts on the needles.

Row 10 (WS): Knit all stitches.

Sizes XS (S/M/L/-/-)

Rows 11–14: Repeat Rows 9 and 10 twice. You should now have 64 (68/74/80/-/-) sts on the needles.

Rows 15 and 16: Knit all stitches.

Rows 17 and 18: Repeat Rows 9 and 10 once. You should now have 62 (66/72/78/-/-) sts on the needles.

Rows 19–22: Knit all stitches.

Rows 23 and 24: Repeat Rows 9 and 10 once. You should now have 60 (64/70/76/-/-) sts on the needles.

Rows 25 and 26: Knit all stitches.

Sizes - (-/-/-/XL/XXL)

Rows 11–18: Repeat Rows 9 and 10 four times. You should now have - (-/-/-/84/92) sts on the needles.

Rows 19 and 20: Knit all stitches.

Rows 21 and 22: Repeat Rows 9 and 10 once. You should now have - (-/-/-/82/90) sts on the needles.

Rows 23–26: Knit all stitches.

Rows 27 and 28: Repeat Rows 9 and 10 once. You should now have - (-/-/-/80/88) sts on the needles.

Rows 29 and 30: Knit all stitches.

All Sizes

Work in garter stitch until the Back measures 6.3 (6.3/7.1/7.9/8.7/9.5) in [16 (16/18/20/22/24) cm] from beginning of armhole, ending having just completed a WS row.

BACK NECKLINE

Row 1 (RS): BO 6 (6/7/9/11/12) sts knitwise, k8 (10/12/12/12/14), BO 32 (32/32/34/34/36) sts knitwise, k14 (16/19/21/23/26). You should now have 14 (16/19/21/23/26) sts for the left half of the Back, and 8 (10/12/12/12/14) sts for the right half of the Back on the needles.

First, continue working over the stitches of the left half of the Back only, beginning with a WS row.

LEFT HALF OF THE BACK

Row 1 (WS): BO 6 (6/7/9/11/12) sts knitwise, knit to last 4 sts, k2tog, k2. You should now have 7 (9/11/11/11/13) sts on the needles.

Row 2 (RS): BO all stitches knitwise.

RIGHT HALF OF THE BACK

Row 1 (WS): K2, skp, knit to end of row. You should now have 7 (9/11/11/11/13) sts on the needles.

Row 2 (RS): BO all stitches knitwise.

FRONT

Using US size 4 (3.5 mm) needles, cast on 90 (94/102/110/118/130) sts. First, work hem ribbing as follows:

Row 1 (WS): K1, * p2, k2 *, rep from * to * to last stitch of this row, k1.

Rows 2–5: Repeat Row 1 four times.

Now, work in garter stitch until the knitted piece has reached a length of 14.2 (14.6/14.6/15/15/15.8) in [36 (37/37/38/38/40) cm], ending having just completed a WS row.

ARMHOLES

Row 1 (RS): BO 4 (4/5/6/6/8) sts, knit to end of row. You should now have 86 (90/97/104/112/122) sts on the needles.

Row 2 (WS): Work the same as Row 1. You should now have 82 (86/92/98/106/114) sts on the needles.

Row 3 (RS): K2, sssk, knit to last 5 sts, k3tog, k2. You should now have 78 (82/88/94/102/110) sts on the needles.

Row 4 (WS): Knit all stitches.

Rows 5–8: Repeat Rows 3 and 4 twice. You should now have 70 (74/80/86/94/102) sts on the needles.

Row 9 (RS): K2, skp, knit to last 4 sts, k2tog, k2. You should now have 68 (72/78/84/92/100) sts on the needles.

Row 10 (WS): Knit all stitches.

Sizes XS (S/M/L/-/-)

Rows 11–14: Repeat Rows 9 and 10 twice. You should now have 64 (68/74/80/-/-) sts on the needles.

Rows 15 and 16: Knit all stitches.

Rows 17 and 18: Repeat Rows 9 and 10 once. You should now have 62 (66/72/78/-/-) sts on the needles.

Rows 19–22: Knit all stitches.

Rows 23 and 24: Repeat Rows 9 and 10 once. You should now have 60 (64/70/76/-/-) sts on the needles.

Rows 25 and 26: Knit all stitches.

Sizes - (-/-/-/XL/XXL)

Rows 11–18: Repeat Rows 9 and 10 four times. You should now have - (-/-/-/84/92) sts on the needles.

Rows 19 and 20: Knit all stitches.

Rows 21 and 22: Repeat Rows 9 and 10 once. You should now have - (-/-/-/82/90) sts on the needles.

Rows 23–26: Knit all stitches.

Rows 27 and 28: Repeat Rows 9 and 10 once. You should now have - (-/-/-/80/88) sts on the needles.

Rows 29 and 30: Knit all stitches.

All Sizes

Work in garter stitch until the Back measures 4.7 (4.7 /5.5/6.3/7.1/7.9) in [12 (12/14/16/18/20) cm] from begin of armhole, ending having just completed a WS row.

NECKLINE SHAPING

Row 1 (RS): K22 (24/27/29/31/34), BO 16 (16/16/18/18/20) sts, k22 (24/27/29/31/34).

You should have 22 (24/27/29/31/34) sts each for the Fronts on the needles. First, work over the stitches of the Right Front only, beginning with a WS row.

RIGHT FRONT

Row 1 (WS): Knit all stitches.

Row 2 (RS): K2, sssk, knit to end of row. You should now have 20 (22/25/27/29/32) sts on the needles.

Row 3 (WS): Knit all stitches.

Rows 4–7: Repeat Rows 2 and 3 twice. You should now have 16 (18/21/23/25/28) sts on the needles.

Row 8 (RS): K2, skp, knit to end of row. You should now have 15 (17/20/22/24/27) sts on the needles.

Row 9 (WS): Knit all stitches.

Rows 10 and 11: Repeat Rows 8 and 9 once. You should now have 14 (16/19/21/23/26) sts on the needles.

Rows 12 and 13: Knit all stitches.

Rows 14 and 15: Repeat Rows 8 and 9 once. You should now have 13 (15/18/20/22/25) sts on the needles.

Rows 16 and 17: Knit all stitches.

Repeat Rows 16 and 17 until the Front measures 6.3 (6.3/7.1/7.9/8.7/9.5) in [16 (16/18/20/22/24) cm] from armhole, ending having just completed a RS row.

Continue as follows:

Row 1 (WS): BO 6 (6/7/9/11/12) sts knitwise, knit to end of row. You should now have 7 (9/11/11/11/13) sts on the needles.

Row 2 (RS): BO all stitches knitwise.

LEFT FRONT

Row 1 (WS): Knit all stitches.

Row 2 (RS): Knit to last 5 sts, k3tog, k2. You should now have 20 (22/25/27/29/32) sts on the needles.

Row 3 (WS): Knit all stitches.

Rows 4–7: Repeat Rows 2 and 3 twice. You should now have 16 (18/21/23/25/28) sts on the needles.

Row 8 (RS): Knit to last 4 sts, k2tog, k2. You should now have 15 (17/20/22/24/27) sts on the needles.

Row 9 (WS): Knit all stitches.

Rows 10 and 11: Repeat Rows 8 and 9 once. You should now have 14 (16/19/21/23/26) sts on the needles.

Rows 12 and 13: Knit all stitches.

Rows 14 and 15: Repeat Rows 8 and 9 once. You should now have 13 (15/18/20/22/25) sts on the needles.

Rows 16 and 17: Knit all stitches.

Repeat Rows 16 and 17 until the Front measures 6.3 (6.3/7.1/7.9/8.7/9.5) in [16 (16/18/20/22/24) cm] from armhole, ending having just completed a WS row.

Continue as follows:

Row 1 (RS): BO 6 (6/7/9/11/12) sts knitwise, knit to end of row. You should now have 7 (9/11/11/11/13) sts on the needles.

Row 2 (WS): Knit all stitches.

Row 3 (RS): BO all stitches knitwise.

SLEEVES

Both Sleeves are worked the same. Using US size 4 (3.5 mm) needles, cast on 66 (66/70/82/86/90) sts.

Row 1 (WS): K1, * p2, k2 *, rep from * to * to last st, k1.

Rows 2–5: Repeat Row 1 four times.

Now, work in garter stitch until the knitted piece has reached a length of 2.4 (2.4/2.4/2.8/2.8/3.2) in [6 (6/6/7/7/8) cm], ending having just completed a WS row.

Continue as follows:

Row 1 (RS): BO 4 (4/5/6/6/8) sts knit-wise, knit to end of row. You should now have 62 (62/65/76/80/82) sts on the needles.

Row 2 (WS): Work the same as Row 1. You should now have 58 (58/60/70/74/74) sts on the needles.

Row 3 (RS): K2, sssk, knit to last 5 sts, k3tog, k2. You should now have 54 (54/56/66/70/70) sts on the needles.

Row 4 (WS): Knit all stitches.

Sizes XS (S/M/-/-/-)

Rows 5–10: Repeat Rows 3 and 4 three times. You should now have 42 (42/44/-/-/-) sts on the needles.

Row 11 (RS): K2, skp, knit to last 4 sts, k2tog, k2. You should now have 40 (40/42/-/-/-) sts on the needles.

Row 12 (WS): Knit all stitches.

Rows 13–24: Repeat Rows 11 and 12 six times. You should now have 28 (28/30/-/-/-) sts on the needles.

Rows 25 and 26: Knit all stitches.

Rows 27 and 28: Repeat Rows 11 and 12 once. You should now have 26 (26/28/-/-/-) sts on the needles.

Rows 29–32: Knit all stitches.

Rows 33 and 34: Repeat Rows 11 and 12 once. You should now have 24 (24/26/-/-/-) sts on the needles.

Rows 35 and 36: Knit all stitches.

Sizes - (-/-/L/XL/XXL)

Rows 5–14: Repeat Rows 3 and 4 five times. You should now have - (-/-/46/50/50) sts on the needles.

Row 15 (RS): K2, skp, knit to last 4 sts, k2tog, k2. You should now have - (-/-/44/48/48) sts on the needles.

Row 16 (WS): Knit all stitches.

Rows 17–30: Repeat Rows 15 and 16 seven times. You should now have - (-/-/30/34/34) sts on the needles.

Rows 32 and 33: Knit all stitches.

Rows 34 and 35: Work the same as Rows 15 and 16. You should now have - (-/-/28/32/32) sts on the needles.

Rows 36 and 37: Knit all stitches.

Rows 38 and 39: Work the same as Rows 15 and 16. You should now have - (-/-/26/30/30) sts on the needles.

Rows 40 and 41: Knit all stitches.

All Sizes

Work in garter stitch until piece has reached 6.3 (6.3/7.1/7.5/8.3/9.05) in [16 (16/18/19/21/23) cm], measured from cast-on edge, ending having just completed a WS row.

Row 1 (RS): K2, skp, knit to last 4 sts, k2tog, k2. You should now have 22 (22/24/24/28/28) sts on the needles.

Row 2 (RS): Knit all stitches.

Row 3: BO all stitches knitwise.

FINISHING

First, graft the Fronts to the Back at the top, thus closing the shoulder seams. Pin the Sleeves in a sufficient number of spots to the armhole to assure a correct fit. After this, sew the Sleeves into the armholes using mattress stitch. Finally, close Sleeve seams and side seams in mattress stitch.

RIBBED NECKBAND

Using US size 4 (3.5 mm) needles and beginning at the left shoulder, pick up and knit stitches around the edge as follows: On slanted sections, pick up at a ratio of 3 sts from every 4 sts, and from the bound-off stitches, pick up 1 stitch each. Make sure that the total number of stitches picked up is a multiple of 4. Mark the BOR with a marker, and work in the round as follows:

Rounds 1–5: * K2, p2 *, rep from * to * to end of round.

Round 6: Bind off all sts in pattern.

Weave in all ends. Dampen the sweater, and pull it into the desired shape.

ELISABETH

CARDIGAN IN A WRAPAROUND LOOK WITH BELT AND WING COLLAR

SIZES
XS, S, M, L, XL, XXL

Numbers for size XS are listed before the parentheses, numbers for sizes S through XXL within parentheses. If only one number is listed, it applies to all sizes.

Size	Chest Circum-ference	Sleeve Length from Armhole	Garment Length from Armhole
XS	38.6 in (98 cm)	22 in (56 cm)	18.1 in (46 cm)
S	40.2 in (102 cm)	22.3 in (58 cm)	18.9 in (48 cm)
M	41.8 in (106 cm)	23.6 in (60 cm)	19.7 in (50 cm)
L	44 in (112 cm)	24.4 in (62 cm)	19.7 in (50 cm)
XL	48 in (122cm)	24.4 in (62 cm)	20.5 in (52 cm)
XXL	51.2 in (130cm)	24.4 in (62 cm)	21.3 in (54 cm)

MATERIALS AND TOOLS
— Lang Yarns Cashmere Classic; 100% cashmere; 54.7 yd (50 m) per 0.9 oz (25 g): #03 Light Gray, 26 (28/30/30/32/36) skeins
— Circular knitting needle, US size 10 (6.0 mm), length 32 in (80 cm)
— Crochet hook, US size H-8 (5.0 mm)
— Tapestry needle

GAUGE
In garter stitch on US size 10 (6.0 mm) needles: 15 sts and 30 rows = 4 x 4 in (10 x 10 cm)

CONSTRUCTION NOTES
The cardigan is worked in turned rows in a traditional seamed construction in pieces; collar and sleeve caps are shaped through decreases. If desired, the cardigan can also be worked in stockinette stitch, as long as gauge matches. Individual parts are grafted together at the end. The completed cardigan is finished with an all-around edging in single crochet for a neat finish. The belt is worked separately in a slip-stitch pattern. Thanks to its belt and overlapping fronts, this cardigan fits a variety of body shapes. It can be worn either open or closed.

GARTER STITCH
Knit all sts in RS and WS rows.

CONTINUED

Model is
wearing size L

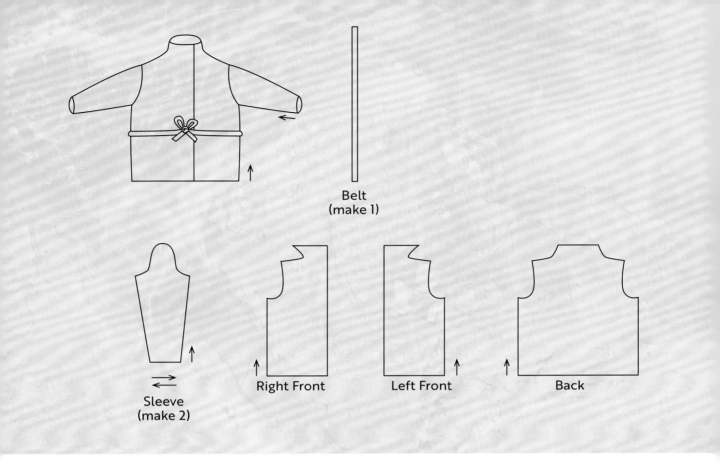

Belt
(make 1)

Sleeve
(make 2)

Right Front

Left Front

Back

INSTRUCTIONS

BACK

Using US size 10 (6.0 mm) needles, cast on 74 (76/80/84/92/98) sts. Beginning with a WS row, work in garter stitch until the piece has reached a length of 18.1 (18.9/19.7/19.7/20.5/21.3) in [46 (48/50/50/52/54) cm], ending having just completed a WS row.

ARMHOLES

Row 1 (RS): BO 3 (4/4/5/5/7) sts, knit to end of row. You should now have 71 (72/76/79/87/91) sts on the needles.

Row 2 (WS): Work the same as Row 1. You should now have 68 (68/72/74/82/84) sts on the needles.

Row 3 (RS): K2, sssk, knit to last 5 sts, k3tog, k2. You should now have 64 (64/68/70/78/80) sts on the needles.

Row 4 (WS): Knit all stitches.

Sizes XS (S/M/L/-/-)

Row 5 (RS): K2, skp, knit to last 4 sts, k2tog, k2. You should now have 62 (62/66/68/-/-) sts on the needles.

Row 6 (WS): Knit all stitches.

Rows 7–14: Repeat Rows 5 and 6 four times. You should now have 54 (54/58/60/-/-) sts on the needles.

Rows 15 and 16: Knit all stitches.

Rows 17 and 18: Repeat Rows 5 and 6 once. You should now have 52 (52/56/58/-/-) sts on the needles.

Rows 19 and 20: Knit all stitches.

Rows 21 and 22: Repeat Rows 5 and 6 once. You should now have 50 (50/54/56/-/-) sts on the needles.

Rows 23 and 24: Knit all stitches.

Rows 5 and 6: Repeat Rows 3 and 4 once. You should now have – (-/-/-/74/76) sts on the needles.

Row 7 (RS): K2, skp, knit to last 4 sts, k2tog, k2. You should now have – (-/-/-/72/74) sts on the needles.

Row 8 (WS): Knit all stitches.

Rows 9–16: Repeat Rows 7 and 8 four times. You should now have – (-/-/-/64/66) sts on the needles.

Rows 17 and 18: Knit all stitches.

Rows 19 and 20: Repeat Rows 7 and 8 once. You should now have – (-/-/-/62/64) sts on the needles.

Rows 21 and 22: Knit all stitches.

Rows 23 and 24: Repeat Rows 7 and 8 once. You should now have – (-/-/-/60/62) sts on the needles.

Rows 25 and 26: Knit all stitches.

All Sizes

Work in garter stitch until the Back measures 7.1 (7.1/7.9/8.3/8.7/9.5) in [18 (18/20/21/22/24) cm] from beginning of armhole, ending having just completed a WS row.

SLOPED SHOULDER WITH COLLAR

Row 1 (RS): BO 4 (4/4/5/5/5) sts knitwise, knit to end of row. You should now have 46 (46/50/51/55/57) sts on the needles.

Row 2 (WS): Work the same as Row 1. You should now have 42 (42/46/46/50/52) sts on the needles.

Rows 3 and 4: BO 4 (4/5/5/5/5) sts knitwise, knit to end of row. You should now have 34 (34/36/36/40/42) sts on the needles.

Rows 5 and 6: BO 4 (4/5/5/6/6) sts knitwise, knit to end of row. You should now have 26 (26/26/26/28/30) sts on the needles.

Row 7 (RS): K2, skp, knit to last 4 sts, k2tog, k2. You should now have 24 (24/24/24/26/28) sts on the needles.

Row 8 (WS): Knit all stitches.

Rows 9–22: Repeat Rows 7 and 8 seven times. You should now have 10 (10/10/10/10/12/14) sts on the needles.

Row 23 (RS): BO all stitches knitwise.

RIGHT FRONT

Using US size 10 (6.0 mm) needles, cast on 51 (52/54/56/62/65) sts. In the following WS row, knit all stitches. Now, work in garter stitch until the knitted piece has reached a length of 18.1 (18.9/19.7/19.7/20.5/21.3) in [46 (48/50/50/52/54) cm], ending having just completed a RS row.

Continue as follows:

Row 1 (WS): BO 3 (4/4/5/5/7) sts, knit to end of row. You should now have 48 (48/50/51/57/58) sts on the needles.

Row 2 (RS): Knit to last 5 sts, k3tog, k2. You should now have 46 (46/48/49/55/56) sts on the needles.

Row 3 (WS): Knit all stitches.

Sizes XS (S/M/L/-/-)

Row 4 (RS): Knit to last 4 sts, k2tog, k2. You should now have 45 (45/47/48/-/-) sts on the needles.

Row 5 (WS): Knit all stitches.

Rows 6–13: Repeat Rows 4 and 5 four times. You should now have 41 (41/43/44/-/-) sts on the needles.

Rows 14 and 15: Knit all stitches.

Rows 16 and 17: Repeat Rows 4 and 5 once. You should now have 40 (40/42/43/-/-) sts on the needles.

Rows 18–21: Repeat Rows 14–17 once. You should now have 39 (39/41/42/-/-) sts on the needles.

Rows 22 and 23: Knit all stitches.

Sizes - (-/-/-/XL/XXL)

Rows 4–7: Repeat Rows 2 and 3 twice. You should now have – (-/-/-/51/52) sts on the needles.

Row 8 (RS): Knit to last 4 sts, k2tog, k2. You should now have – (-/-/-/50/51) sts on the needles.

Row 9 (WS): Knit all stitches.

Rows 10–17: Repeat Rows 8 and 9 four times. You should now have – (-/-/-/46/47) sts on the needles.

Rows 18 and 19: Knit all stitches.

Row 20 (RS): Work the same as Row 8. You should now have – (-/-/-/45/46) sts on the needles.

Rows 21–23: Knit all stitches.

Rows 24 and 25: Work the same as Rows 8 and 9. You should now have – (-/-/-/44/45) sts on the needles.

Rows 26 and 27: Knit all stitches.

All Sizes

Work in garter stitch until the Right Front measures 7.1 (7.1/7.9/8.3/8.7/9.5) in [18 (18/20/21/22/24) cm] from armhole, ending having just completed a RS row.

SLOPED SHOULDER WITH COLLAR

Row 1 (WS): BO 4 (4/4/5/5/5) sts, knit to end of row. You should now have 35 (35/37/37/39/40) sts on the needles.

Row 2 (RS): Knit all stitches.

Row 3 (WS): BO 4 (4/5/5/5/5) sts, knit to end of row. You should now have 31 (31/32/32/34/35) sts on the needles.

Row 4: Knit all stitches.

Row 5 (WS): BO 4 (4/5/5/6/6) sts knitwise, then knit to end of row. You should now have 27 (27/27/27/28/29) sts on the needles.

Row 6 (RS): Knit to last 2 sts, M1L, k2. You should now have 28 (28/28 28/29/30) sts on the needles.

Row 7 (WS): Knit all stitches.

Rows 8–21: Repeat Rows 6 and 7 seven times. You should now have 35 (35/35/35/36/37) sts on the needles.

Row 22 (RS): BO all stitches knitwise.

LEFT FRONT

Using US size 10 (6.0 mm) needles, cast on 51 (52/54/56/62/65) sts. In the following WS row, knit all stitches. Now, work in garter stitch until the knitted piece has reached a length of 18.1 (18.9/19.7/19.7/20.5/21.3) in [46 (48/50/50/52/54) cm], ending having just completed a WS row.

Continue as follows:

Row 1 (RS): BO 3 (4/4/5/5/7) sts, knit to end of row. You should now have 48 (48/50/51/57/58) sts on the needles.

Row 2 (WS): Knit all stitches.

Row 3 (RS): K2, sssk, knit to end of row. You should now have 46 (46/48/49/55/56) sts on the needles.

Row 4 (WS): Knit all stitches.

Sizes XS (S/M/L/-/-)

Row 5 (RS): K2, skp, knit to end of row. You should now have 45 (45/47/48/-/-) sts on the needles.

Row 6 (WS): Knit all stitches.

Rows 7–14: Repeat Rows 5 and 6 four times. You should now have 41 (41/43/44/-/-) sts on the needles.

Rows 15 and 16: Knit all stitches.

Rows 17 and 18: Repeat Rows 5 and 6 once. You should now have 40 (40/42/43/-/-) sts on the needles.

Rows 19–22: Repeat Rows 15–18 once. You should now have 39 (39/41/42/-/-) sts on the needles.

Rows 23 and 24: Knit all stitches.

Sizes - (-/-/-/XL/XXL)

Rows 5–8: Repeat Rows 3 and 4 twice. You should now have – (-/-/-/51/52) sts on the needles.

Row 9 (RS): K2, skp, knit to end of row. You should now have – (-/-/-/50/51) sts on the needles.

Row 10 (WS): Knit all stitches.

Rows 11–18: Repeat Rows 9 and 10 four times. You should now have – (-/-/-/46/47) sts on the needles.

Rows 19 and 20: Knit all stitches.

Rows 21 and 22: Work the same as Rows 9 and 10. – (-/-/-/45/46) sts on the needles.

Rows 23 and 24: Knit all stitches.

Rows 25 and 26: Work the same as Rows 9 and 10. You should now have – (-/-/-/44/45) sts on the needles.

Rows 27 and 28: Knit all stitches.

All Sizes

Work in garter stitch until the Left Front measures 7.1 (7.1/7.9/8.3/8.7/9.5) in [18 (18/20/21/22/24) cm] from arm-hole, ending having just completed a WS row.

SLOPED SHOULDER WITH COLLAR

Row 1 (RS): BO 4 (4/4/5/5/5) sts, knit to end of row. You should now have 35 (35/37/37/39/40) sts on the needles.

Row 2 (WS): Knit all stitches.

Row 3 (RS): BO 4 (4/5/5/5/5) sts, knit to end of row. You should now have 31 (31/32/32/34/35) sts on the needles.

Row 4 (WS): Knit all stitches.

Row 5 (RS): BO 4 (4/5/5/6/6) sts knitwise, knit to end of row. You should now have 27 (27/27/27/28/29) sts on the needles.

Row 6 (WS): Knit all stitches.

Row 7 (RS): K2, M1L, knit to end of row. You should now have 28 (28/28/28/29/30) sts on the needles.

Row 8 (WS): Knit all stitches.

Rows 9–22: Repeat Rows 7 and 8 seven times. You should now have 35 (35/35/35/36/37) sts on the needles.

Row 23 (RS): BO all stitches knitwise.

SLEEVES

Both Sleeves are worked the same. Using US size 10 (6.0 mm) needles, cast on 28 (30/32/34/36/38) sts, then work in garter stitch until the knitted piece has reached a length of 22 (22.8/23.6/24.4/24.4/24.4) in [56 (58/60/62/62/62) cm], ending having just completed a WS row. During this, in every 10th (10th/12th/12th/12th/10th) row (RS), increase 2 sts each a total of 8 (8/9/11/11/12) times as follows: K2, M1R, knit to last 2 sts, M1L, k2. You should now have 44 (46/50/56/58/62) sts on the needles.

Now, the Sleeve Cap will be shaped.

Row 1 (RS): BO 3 (4/4/5/5/7) sts knitwise, knit to end of row. You should now have 41 (42/46/51/53/55) sts on the needles.

Row 2 (WS): Work the same as Row 1. You should now have 38 (38/42/46/48/48) sts on the needles.

Row 3 (RS): K2, sssk, knit to last 5 sts, k3tog, k2. You should now have 34 (34/38/42/44/44) sts on the needles.

Row 4 (WS): Knit all stitches.

Sizes XS (S/M/-/-/-)

Row 5 (RS): K2, skp, knit to last 4 sts, k2tog, k2. You should now have 32 (32/36/-/-/-) sts on the needles.

Row 6 (WS): Knit all stitches.

Rows 7–22: Repeat Rows 5 and 6 eight times. You should now have 16 (16/20/-/-/-) sts on the needles.

Rows 23 and 24: Knit all stitches.

Rows 25 and 26: Repeat Rows 5 and 6 once. You should now have 14 (14/18/-/-/-) sts on the needles.

Rows 27 and 28: Knit all stitches.

Sizes - (-/-/L/XL/XXL)

Rows 5 and 6: Repeat Rows 3 and 4 once. You should now have – (-/-/38/40/40) sts on the needles.

Row 7 (RS): K2, skp, knit to last 4 sts, k2tog, k2. You should now have – (-/-/36/38/38) sts on the needles.

Row 8 (WS): Knit all stitches.

Rows 9–24: Repeat Rows 7 and 8 eight times. You should now have – (-/-/20/22/22) sts on the needles.

Rows 25 and 26: Knit all stitches.

Rows 27 and 28: Repeat Rows 7 and 8 once. You should now have – (-/-/18/20/20) sts on the needles.

Rows 29 and 30: Knit all stitches.

All Sizes

Work in garter stitch until 5.1 (5.1/5.5/5.9 /6.3/7.1) in [13 (13/14/15/16/18) cm], measured from beginning of Sleeve Cap, have been reached, ending having just completed a WS row. You should now have 14 (14/18/18/20/20) sts on the needles.

Row 1 (RS): K2, skp, knit to last 4 sts, k2tog, k2. You should now have 12 (12/16/16/18/18) sts on the needles.

Row 2 (WS): Knit all stitches.

Row 3 (RS): BO all stitches knitwise.

FINISHING

First, graft the Fronts at the top to the Back, thus closing the shoulder seams. Pin the sleeves in a sufficient number of spots to the armhole to ensure a correct fit. After this, sew the sleeves into the armholes using mattress stitch. Finally, close sleeve seams and side seams in mattress stitch.

CROCHETED EDGING

Using US size H-8 (5.0 mm) crochet hook and beginning at the Right Front, work 1 single crochet each into every knot of the knotted selvedge until you've reached the top. Into the corner stitch of the collar, work 3 sc; along the edge of the collar, work 1 sc each into every bound-off stitch to the next side. Into the next corner stitch, work 3 sc again, and then along the knotted selvedge of the Left Front, work 1 sc each into every knot until you've reached the bottom. Break the working yarn and pull it through the working loop to secure.

BELT

Using US size 10 (6.0 mm) needles, cast on 7 sts.

Row 1 (WS): * K1, slip 1 st purlwise with yarn in front of work *, rep from * to * twice, k1.

Row 2 (RS): * Slip 1 st purlwise with yarn in front of work, k1 *, rep from * to * twice, slip 1 st purlwise with yarn in front of work.

Repeat Rows 1 and 2 until the Belt has reached a length of 88.5 (90.5/92.5/94.5/98.5/102.4) in [225 (230/235/240/250/260) cm]. BO all stitches in pattern.

FINISHING

Crochet two belt loops to thread the belt through. For each belt loop, using a crochet hook, chain 12, and sew these crocheted chains to the sides of the garment at waist level. Thread the belt through the two belt loops, hide all ends, dampen the cardigan, and pull it into the desired shape.

CHAPTER 2

The top-down raglan is one of the easiest constructions that can be worked. It is worked in the round with stitches increased in four spots, which creates the typical raglan lines running at an angle from the neckline to the armpits.

Generally, raglan constructions can also be worked from the bottom up with the sleeves and the body knitted separately and joined at the underarm, from where they are continued on one needle to the neckline. In this case, decreases will be worked instead of increases.

Top-down raglans have the advantage that both the length of the body as well as the sleeve length can be adjusted during knitting. The garment can be tried on at any stage of completion to check the fit. For this reason, this book contains only top-down raglans. There are five raglans in total; of these, three are sweaters and two are cardigans.

LET'S GET STARTED

RONCITA

NARROW TOP-DOWN RAGLAN SWEATER WITH SIMPLE STRANDED COLORWORK PATTERN

SIZES

XS, S, M, L, XL, XXL

Numbers for size XS are listed before the parentheses, numbers for sizes S through XXL within parentheses. If only one number is listed, it applies to all sizes.

Size	Chest Circum-ference	Sleeve Length from Armhole	Garment Length from Armhole
XS	31.5 in (80 cm)	18.9 in (48 cm)	15 in (38 cm)
S	33.1 in (84 cm)	18.9 in (48 cm)	15 in (38 cm)
M	37.0 in (94 cm)	19.3 in (49 cm)	16.1 in (41 cm)
L	41.3 in (105 cm)	19.3 in (49 cm)	18.1 in (46 cm)
XL	45.3 in (115 cm)	19.7 in (50 cm)	18.5 in (47 cm)
XXL	49.2 in (125 cm)	19.7 in (50 cm)	18.9 in (48 cm)

MATERIALS AND TOOLS

— GGH Maxima; 100% extrafine super-wash merino wool; 120 yd (110 m) per 1.75 oz (50 g): #62 Steel Gray, 8 (9/10/11/12/14) skeins; and #29 Black, 1 (2/2/2/2/3) skeins
— Circular knitting needle, US size 7 (4.5 mm), at least 32 in (80 cm) long
— Circular knitting needle, US size 6 (4.0 mm), 24 in (60 cm) long
— If desired, one DPN set each in sizes US 7 (4.5 mm) and US 6 (4.0 mm) for the sleeves
— 4 stitch markers
— Stitch holder or waste yarn
— Tapestry needle

GAUGE

In stockinette stitch on US size 7 (4.5 mm) needles: 22 sts and 27 rows = 4 x 4 in (10 x 10 cm)

COLOR KEY

MC = Steel Gray
CC = Black

CONSTRUCTION NOTES

The sweater is worked as a top-down raglan construction in one piece in stockinette stitch in the round in a stranded colorwork pattern. The ribbed neckband is knitted on afterwards. If omitting the stranded colorwork pattern, a simple basic raglan can be worked, which is also suitable as a unisex garment. For this, only Rows 2 and 3 must be repeated until the appropriate stitch count listed for the size worked has been reached. For the original design with stranded colorwork pattern, all stitches that are to be worked in contrasting color (CC) are marked "in CC" in the instructions; all stitches without this note are to be worked in main color (MC).

RIBBING PATTERN

Twisted 1x1 ribbing: * K1-tbl, p1 *, rep from * to * continuously.

STOCKINETTE STITCH

In the round: Knit all sts in all rounds.

STRANDED COLORWORK PATTERN

Rounds 1–3: Work in MC in stockinette stitch.
Round 4: * K3 in MC, k1 in CC *, rep from * to * to end of round.

Now, the stitch pattern will be staggered by 2 sts:
Rounds 5–7: Work in MC in stockinette stitch.
Round 8: K1, * k1 in CC, k3 in MC *, rep from * to * to 2 sts before end of round, k2.
Repeat Rounds 1–8 heightwise.

CONTINUED

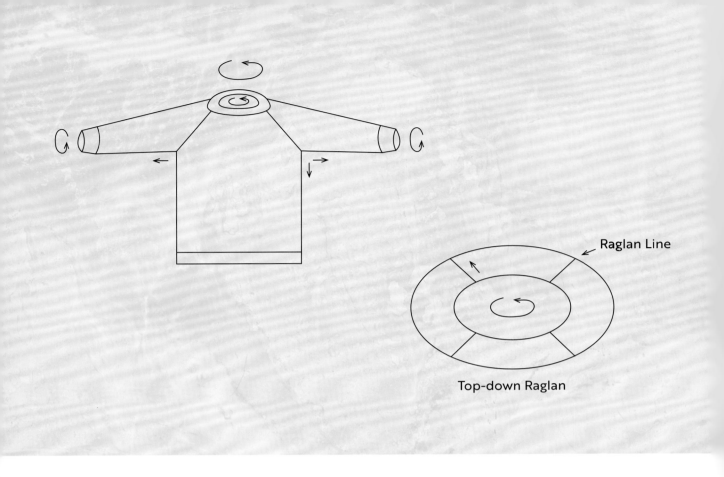

Raglan Line

Top-down Raglan

INSTRUCTIONS

Using US size 7 (4.5 mm) needles and MC, cast on 100 (100/108/116/116/124) sts, and join to work in the round, place a marker to denote the beginning of the round (= BOR).

Round 1: K15 (15/15/19/19/19), place m, k35 (35/39/39/39/43), place m, k15 (15/15/19/19/19), place m, k35 (35/39/39/39/43), slip BOR marker.

Round 2 (increase round): * K1, M1L, k to 1 st before next marker, M1R, k1, slip m *, rep from * to * 3 times more. You should now have 37 (37/41/41/41/45) sts each for Front and Back, and 17 (17/17/21/21/21) sts each for the Sleeves on the needles.

Round 3: Knit all stitches, slipping the markers as you come to them.

Round 4 (colorwork and increases): # K1, M1L, * k3, k1 in CC *, rep from * to * to 4 sts before next marker, k3, M1R, k1, slip m, k1, M1L, k1, ** k1 in CC, k3 **, rep from ** to ** 3 sts before next marker, k2, M1R, k1, slip m #, rep from # to # once more.

You should now have 39 (39/43/43/43/47) sts each for Front and Back, and 19 (19/19/23/23/23) sts each for the Sleeves on the needles.

Round 5: Knit all stitches, slipping the markers as you come to them.

Rounds 6 and 7: Work the same as Rounds 2 and 3. You should now have 41 (41/45/45/45/49) sts each for Front and Back, and 21 (21/21/25/25/25) sts each for the Sleeves on the needles.

Repeat Rounds 4–7 another 11 (12/14/16/18/20) times, ending having just completed a Round 7. You should now have 85 (89/101/109/117/129) sts each for Front and Back, and 65 (69/77/89/97/105) sts each for the Sleeves on the needles.

The sweater should now measure approximately 7.5 (7.9/9.0/10.2/11.4/12.6) in [19 (20/23/26/29/32) cm] from cast-on edge to separating round.

SLEEVE SEPARATION ROUND

Remove marker, transfer the following 65 (69/77/89/97/105) sts (sleeve) to next m to a stitch holder or a piece of waste yarn for holding, cast on 2 (2/2/4/4/4) new sts using backwards-loop CO, place m, cast on 1 (1/1/3/3/3) new st(s) using backwards-loop CO, k2, * k1 in CC, k3 *, rep from * to * to 3 sts before next marker, k1 in CC, k2 #, rep from # to # once more.

You should have a total of 176 (184/208/232/248/272) sts for the Body on the needles; continue to work in the round.

BODY

Rounds 1–3: Knit all stitches.

Round 4 (colorwork round): K1, * k1 in CC, k3 *, rep from * to * to 3 sts before BOR marker, k1 in CC, k2.

Rounds 5–7: Knit all stitches.

Round 8: * K3, k1 in CC *, rep from * to * to end of round.

Repeat Rounds 1–8 until the sweater has either reached a length of 13 (13/14.1/16.1/16.5/16.9) in [33 (33/36/41/42/43) cm], measured from the underarm, or is 2 in (5 cm) shorter than desired Body length to accommodate ribbing to be added, ending having just completed a Round 5 or 1 of the pattern.

RIBBING

Change to US size 6 (4.0 mm) needles.

Rounds 1–12: * K1-tbl, p1 *, rep from * to * to end of round.

Round 13: BO all sts in pattern.

SLEEVES

Both Sleeves are worked the same. For the Sleeve, first take up the 65 (69/77/89/97/105) formerly held sts, then using US size 7 (4.5 mm) needles, pick up and knit 2 (2/2/4/4/4) sts from the newly cast-on underarm sts, place m, pick up and knit an additional 1 (1/1/3/3/3) st(s), and join into the round. The Sleeve is worked in the round from here on; the marker indicates the BOR. There should be a total of 68 (72/80/96/104/112) sts on the needles.

Continue the Sleeve in stockinette stitch with the established stranded colorwork pattern, at the same time, in every 14th (11th/9th/7th/6th/5th) round, decrease as follows a total of 8 (10/12/16/18/22) times:

K2tog, work in pattern to 3 sts before m, skp, k1, slip m.

Work the Sleeve in the established pattern until the Sleeve has either reached a length of 16.9 (16.9/17.3/17.3/17.7/17.7) in [43 (43/44/44/45/45) cm] or is 2 in (5 cm) shorter than desired sleeve length to accommodate the sleeve cuff to be added.

SLEEVE CUFFS

Change to US size 6 (4.0 mm) needles.

Rounds 1–12: * K1-tbl, p1 *, rep from * to * to end of round.

Round 13: BO all sts in pattern.

RIBBED NECKBAND

Using US size 6 (4.0 mm) needles, pick up and knit stitches from the neckline edge at a rate of 9 sts picked up from every 10 sts, for a total of 90 (90/98/104/104/112) sts picked up for the neckline, and join into the round.

Rounds 1–7: * K1-tbl, p1 *, rep from * to * to end of round.

Round 8: BO all stitches.

FINISHING

Weave in all ends, dampen the sweater, and pull it into the desired shape.

TIANA

TOP-DOWN HOODED RAGLAN SWEATER
WITH A-LINE SHAPING AND SIDE TAILS

SIZES

XS, S, M, L, XL, XXL

Numbers for size XS are listed before the parentheses, numbers for sizes S through XXL within parentheses. If only one number is listed, it applies to all sizes.

Size	Chest Circum-ference	Sleeve Length from Armhole	Garment Length from Armhole
XS	35.4 in (90 cm)	17.3 in (44 cm)	16.5 in (42 cm)
S	37.4 in (95 cm)	17.3 in (44 cm)	16.5 in (42 cm)
M	39.4 in (100 cm)	17.7 in (45 cm)	17.3 in (44 cm)
L	43.3 in (110 cm)	17.7 in (45 cm)	19.7 in (50 cm)
XL	47.2 in (120 cm)	18.1 in (46 cm)	20.1 in (51 cm)
XXL	51.2 in (130 cm)	18.1 in (46 cm)	20.5 in (52 cm)

MATERIALS AND TOOLS

— Lana Grossa Ecopuno; 72% cotton, 17% merino wool, 11% alpaca; 235.1 yd (215 m) per 1.75 oz (50 g): #15 Dark Gray, 6 (7/8/8/9/10) skeins
— Circular knitting needle, US size 6 (4.0 mm), at least 32 in (80 cm) long
— Circular knitting needle, US size 4 (3.5 mm), 24 in (60 cm) long
— If desired, one DPN set each in sizes US 6 (4.0 mm) and US 4 (3.5 mm) for the sleeves
— 6 stitch markers
— Stitch holder or waste yarn
— Tapestry needle

GAUGE

In stockinette stitch on US size 6 (4.0 mm) needles: 23 sts and 34 rows = 4 x 4 in (10 x 10 cm)

CONSTRUCTION NOTES

The sweater is worked as a top-down raglan construction in one piece in stockinette stitch in the round. After having divided for the sleeves, increases are worked at the sides to create an A-line shape. To form the tips at the sides, short-row shaping is worked. The hood is knitted on afterwards.

RIBBING

2x2 ribbing: * K2, p2 *, rep from * to * continuously.

STOCKINETTE STITCH

In the round: Knit all sts in all rounds.

TURNING STITCHES (T-ST)

Place the working yarn behind work, turn work, slip 1 stitch purlwise, move the working yarn over the right needle from front to back and pull up on the stitch. This creates a turning stitch with two legs sitting on the needle. The resulting "double stitch" will be worked and counted as one stitch further on. Knit stitches can be worked immediately; for purl stitches, the working yarn first needs to be moved to the front of the work between the needles.

SELVEDGE STITCHES

In RS and WS rows, always knit the first and last stitch of the row (= selv st).

CONTINUED

Model is
wearing size M

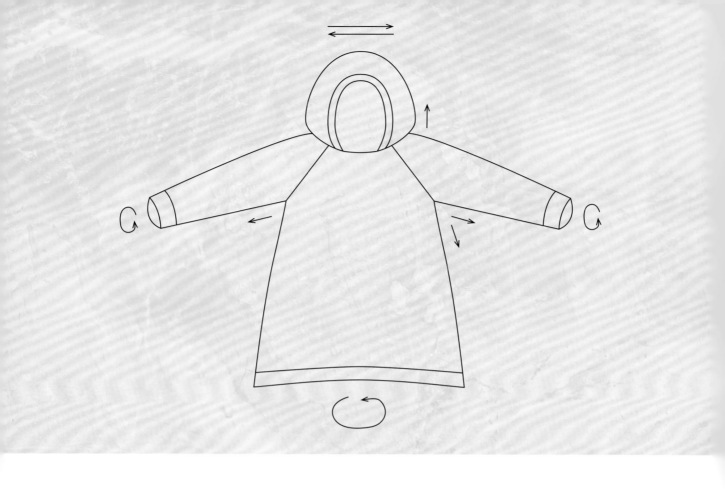

INSTRUCTIONS

Using US size 6 (4.0 mm) needles, cast on 112 (112/120/124/128/132) sts, place a BOR marker, and join in the round without twisting.

Round 1: K14 (14/16/16/16/18), place m, k42 (42/44/46/48/48), place m, k14 (14/16/16/16/18), place m, k42 (42/44/46/48/48), slip BOR marker.

Round 2 (increase round): * K1, M1L, k to 1 st before next marker, M1R, k1, slip m *, rep from * to * 3 times more. You should now have 44 (44/46/48/50/50) sts each for Front and Back, and 16 (16/18/18/18/20) sts each for the Sleeves on the needles.

Round 3: Knit all stitches, slipping the markers when you encounter them.

Repeat Rows 2 and 3 another 27 (29/31/35/40/45) times, ending having just completed a Round 3. You should now have 98 (102/108/118/130/140) sts each for Front and Back, and 70 (74/80/88/98/110) sts each for the Sleeves on the needles.

SLEEVE SEPARATION ROUND

* Remove marker, transfer the next 70 (74/80/88/98/110) sts (Sleeve) to next m to a stitch holder or a piece of waste yarn for holding (keep m in place), cast on 3 (3/3/4/4/5) new sts using backwards-loop CO, place m, cast on 3 (3/3/4/4/5) new sts using backwards-loop CO, knit to next m *, rep from * to* once more.

You should now have a total of 208 (216/228/252/276/300) sts for the body on the needles, continue to work in the round.

BODY: A-LINE

The body is worked in stockinette stitch until it has either reached a length of 12.5 (12.5/13.3/15.7/16.1/16.5) in [32 (32/34/40/41/42) cm], measured from the underarm, or is 4 in (10 cm) shorter than desired body length to accommodate the tails and ribbing, increasing 4 sts each in every 16th row as follows: * K1, M1L, k to 1 st before next marker, M1R, k1, slip m *, rep from * to * 3 times more.

SIDE TAILS

To keep the instructions for the tails usable with all body options, including straight shapes, specific stitch counts will not be listed, but the method is described in general terms. First, place a marker at each side, dividing the Front and Back evenly, and removing other markers. Now, count the stitches of the Front, then divide by 3 and place 2 markers to divide Front into thirds; repeat for the Back. If your division does not result in a whole number, make sure that the stitch counts between the side marker and the markers to each side of it match. You should now have 6 markers: 2 side markers, and 2 each on Front and Back. The stitch markers are numbered from 1 through 6, beginning with the first at the beginning of the round (BOR marker). Between the 6th and 2nd marker, short rows are worked around the first marker (BOR marker). Another set of short rows will later be worked between the 5th and 3rd marker around the 4th marker. For the option with A-line body, increases are continued as established in every 16th row around the side markers.

Row 1 (RS): Knit all stitches to the 2nd marker, turn work.

Row 2 (WS): T-st, purl to 6th marker, turn work.

Row 3 (RS): T-st, knit to 6 sts before the previous t-st, turn work.

Row 4 (WS): T-st, purl to 6 sts before the previous t-st, turn work.

Row 5 (RS): T-st, knit to 5 sts before the previous t-st, turn work.

Row 6 (WS): T-st, purl to 5 sts before the previous t-st, turn work.

Row 7 (RS): T-st, knit to 4 sts before the previous t-st, turn work.

Row 8 (WS): T-st, purl to 4 sts before the previous t-st, turn work.

Row 9 (RS): T-st, knit to 3 sts before the previous t-st, turn work.

Row 10 (WS): T-st, purl to 3 sts before the previous t-st, turn work.

Row 11 (RS): T-st, knit to 2 sts before the previous t-st, turn work.

Row 12 (WS): T-st, purl to 2 sts before the previous t-st, turn work.

Row 13 (RS): T-st, knit to 1 st before the previous t-st, turn work.

Row 14 (WS): T-st, purl to 1 st before the previous t-st, turn work.

Repeat Rows 13 and 14 until you have reached the first marker (BOR marker).

Next RS row: T-st, knit to 5th marker, turn work.

Next WS row: T-st, purl to 3rd marker, turn work.

After this, work Rows 3–14 around the 4th marker.

Then, repeat only Rows 13 and 14 until the the 4th marker has been reached.

Next RS row: T-st, knit to BOR marker.

Now, the ribbing will be added, working in the round again. Remove all markers except BOR marker before you begin.

RIBBING

Change to US size 4 (3.5 mm) needles. If the stitch count is not a multiple of 4, increase 2 sts total, evenly distributed, during the first round.

Rounds 1–7: * K2, p2 *, rep from * to * to end of round.

Round 8: BO all sts in pattern.

SLEEVES

Both Sleeves are worked the same. To work the Sleeve, first take up the 70 (74/80/88/98/110) formerly held sts with US size 6 (4.0 mm) needles, pick up and knit 3 (3/3/4/4/5) sts from the newly cast-on underarm sts, place m, pick up and knit 3 (3/3/4/4/5) more sts from the newly cast-on underarm sts, and join in the round. The Sleeve is worked in the round from here on; the marker indicates the BOR. You should now have a total of 76 (80/86/96/106/120) sts on the needles. Continue, working the Sleeve in stockinette stitch, at the same time decreasing as follows in every 14th (12th/12th/8th/6th/6th) round a total of 8 (8/10/14/18/22) times:

K1, k2tog, work in pattern to 3 sts before m, skp, k1, slip m.

Work the Sleeve in the established pattern until the Sleeve has either reached a length of 16.5 (16.5/16.9/16.9/17.3/17.3) in [42 (42/43/43/44/44) cm] or is 0.8 in (2 cm) shorter than desired sleeve length to accommodate the ribbed cuff to be added.

SLEEVE CUFF

Change to US size 4 (3.5 mm) needles. If the stitch count is not a multiple of 4, decrease 2 sts total, evenly distributed, during the first round.

Rounds 1–7: * K2, p2 *, rep from * to * to end of round.

Round 8: BO all sts in pattern.

HOOD

To keep the Hood instructions usable for any stitch count, specific stitch counts will not be listed, but the method is described in general terms. First, find the center front on the Front neckline, skip the next 5 sts, then pick up and knit stitches all around to 5 sts before the center front. 10 sts in all have been excluded from picking up.

Row 1 (WS): Selv st, purl to last stitch, placing a marker after half of the stitches, selv st.

Row 2 (RS): Knit all stitches.

Row 3 (WS): Selv st, purl to last stitch, selv st.

Rows 4 and 5: Work the same as Rows 2 and 3.

Row 6 (RS): Knit to 1 st before marker, M1R, k1, slip m, k1, M1L, knit to last st, selv st.

Row 7 (WS): Work the same as Row 3.

Repeat Rows 2–7 another 6 times, then repeat only Rows 2 and 3, until the hood measures 13.4 in (34 cm). 14 sts have been increased in all. Now, stitches will be decreased again; for this, row counting starts anew with Row 1, beginning with a RS row.

Row 1 (RS): Knit to 4 sts before marker, sssk, k1, slip m, k1, k3tog, knit to end of row.

Row 2 (WS): Selv st, purl to last stitch, selv st.

Repeat Rows 1 and 2 another 12 times; 52 sts total have been decreased. Now, distribute the stitches evenly on two needles, and graft them together.

HOOD RIBBING

Using US size 4 (3.5 mm) needles, pick up stitches from the edge of the Hood at a rate of 3 sts picked up from every 4 sts. The stitch count should be a multiple of 2, but not of 4.

Row 1 (WS): * P2, k2 *, rep from * to * to last 2 sts of this row, purl 2.

Row 2 (RS): * K2, p2 *, rep from * to * to last 2 sts of this row, k2.

Row 3 (WS): Work the same as Row 1.

Rows 4–7: Repeat Rows 2 and 3 twice.

Round 8: BO all sts in pattern.

Sew the side edges of the ribbing to the 10 unused stitches in the center front.

FINISHING

To finish, weave in all ends, dampen the sweater, and pull it into the desired shape.

ULLA

TOP-DOWN CARDIGAN WITH GARTER RIDGES AND INCORPORATED ALL-AROUND RIBBED EDGING

SIZES
XS, S, M, L, XL, XXL

Numbers for size XS are listed before the parentheses, numbers for sizes S through XXL within parentheses. If only one number is listed, it applies to all sizes.

Size	Chest Circumference	Sleeve Length from Armhole	Garment Length from Armhole
XS	35.4 in (90 cm)	18.9 in (48 cm)	20.5 in (52 cm)
S	37.4 in (95 cm)	18.9 in (48 cm)	21.6 in (55 cm)
M	39.4 in (100 cm)	19.3 in (49 cm)	22.4 in (57 cm)
L	43.3 in (110 cm)	19.3 in (49 cm)	22.4 in (57 cm)
XL	47.2 in (120 cm)	19.7 in (50 cm)	23.6 in (60 cm)
XXL	51.2 in (130 cm)	19.7 in (50 cm)	23.6 in (60 cm)

MATERIALS AND TOOLS
— Lana Grossa Lovely Cotton Lala Berlin; 75% virgin wool, 25% cotton; 98 yd (90 m) per 1.75 oz (50 g): #05 Light Gray, 8 (9, 10, 12, 13, 15) skeins
— Circular knitting needle, US size 11 (8.0 mm), at least 32 in (80 cm) long
— Circular knitting needle, US size 11 (8.0 mm), 24 in (60 cm) long
— If desired, a DPN set in US size 11 (8.0 mm) for the sleeves
— 6 stitch markers
— Stitch holder or waste yarn
— Tapestry needle

GAUGE
In stockinette stitch on US size 11 (8.0 mm) needles: 12 sts and 16 rows = 4 x 4 in (10 x 10 cm)

CONSTRUCTION NOTES
The cardigan is worked as a top-down raglan construction in one piece in stockinette stitch in turned rows. Work starts with the ribbed neckband in the back, from which stitches for the body are then picked up. The ribbing is worked at the same time as the main part of the cardigan. Delicate garter ridges give the knitted fabric a light and interesting texture. If they are omitted, a simple plain cardigan can be worked. The sleeves are worked without tapering decreases down to the cuff, where many stitches are decreased over the course of 2 rows, creating a moderate balloon sleeve.

RIBBING
1x1 ribbing: * K1, p1 *, rep from * to * continuously.

STOCKINETTE STITCH
In rows: Knit on RS, purl on WS.

SELVEDGE STITCHES
Work all sts listed as "selv st" in the instructions as follows: In RS and WS rows, slip the selvedge stitch purlwise with yarn in front of work.

CONTINUED

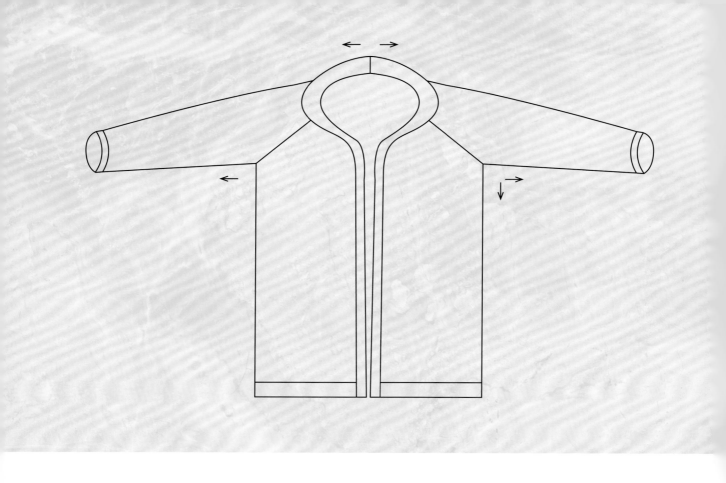

INSTRUCTIONS

First, the ribbed neckband in the Back is worked, beginning in the middle; for this, using US size 11 (8.0 mm) needles, cast on 8 sts.

Row 1 (RS): * K1, p1 *, rep from * to * to last 2 sts of this row, k2.

Row 2 (WS): * K1, p1 *, rep from * to * to last 2 sts of this row, k1, selv st.

Repeat Rows 1 and 2 another 17 (17/18/20/21/23) times, do not break the working yarn, transfer all stitches to a stitch holder or piece of waste yarn for holding.

Pick up and knit a total of 8 sts from the cast-on edge. Now the ribbed neckband will be worked in the opposite direction.

Row 1 (WS): K2, * p1, k1 *, rep from * to * to end of row.

Row 2 (RS): K1, * k1, p1 *, rep from * to * to last stitch of this row, selv st.

Row 3 (WS): Work the same as Row 1.

Repeat Rows 2 and 3 another 16 (16/17/19/20/22) times, then break the working yarn. Now, all stitches are combined on one needle, and additional stitches for Back and Sleeves

are picked up. For this, place the formerly held sts on the needle again and continue, using the working yarn previously left hanging. In the following WS row, stitch markers will be placed to denote the sections for the Fronts, the Sleeves, and the Back. After this, raglan increases as well as neckline shaping increases will begin.

Row 1 (RS): * K1, p1 *, rep from * to * twice, k1, place m, M1L, k1, place m, rotate the knitted piece by 90 degrees, and pick up and knit a total of 52 (52/54/58/60/64) stitches from the knotted selvedge at a rate of 3 sts picked up from every 4 sts, then rotate the knitted piece again by 90 degrees, now the stitches worked last will be worked once more, k1, place m, M1R, place m, * k1, p1 *, rep from * to * 2 times more, selv st.

Row 2 (WS): K1, * k1, p1 *, rep from * to * 2 times more, slip m, p3, place m, k14 (14/14/16/16/18), place m, k24 (24/26/26/28/28), place m, k14 (14/14/16/16/18), place m, k3, slip m, * p1, k1 *, rep from * to * 2 times more, selv st.

Now, raglan increases as well as neck-line shaping increases will be worked.

Row 3 (RS, increase row): * K1, p1 *, rep from * to * twice, k1, slip m, M1R, ** knit to 1 st before next marker, M1L, k1, slip m, k1, M1R **, repeat from ** to ** another 3 times, knit to next marker, M1L, slip m, *** k1, p1 ***, re-peat from *** to *** 2 times more, selv st. You should now have 12 sts each for the Fronts, 16 (16/16/18/18/20) sts each for the Sleeves, and 26 (26/28/28/30/30) sts for the Back on the needles.

Row 4 (WS): K1, * k1, p1 *, rep from * to * 2 times more, slip m, purl to last marker, slip m, ** p1, k1 **, repeat from ** to ** 2 times more, selv st.

Row 5 (RS, increase row): Work the same as Row 3. You should now have 14 sts each for the Fronts, 18 (18/18/20/20/22) sts each for the Sleeves, and 28 (28/30/30/32/32) sts for the Back on the needles.

Row 6 (WS): K1, * k1, p1 *, rep from * to * 2 times more, slip m, knit to last marker, slip m, ** p1, k1 **, repeat from ** to ** 2 times more, selv st.

Row 7 (RS, increase row): Work the same as Row 3. You should now have 16 sts each for the Fronts, 20 (20/20/22/22/24) sts each for the Sleeves,

and 30 (30/32/32/34/34) sts for the Back on the needles.

Row 8 (WS): Work the same as Row 4.

Rows 9 and 10: Repeat Rows 7 and 8 once. You should now have 18 sts each for the Fronts, 22 (22/22/24/24/26) sts each for the Sleeves, and 32 (32/34/34/36/36) sts for the Back on the needles.

Rows 11 and 12: Repeat Rows 5 and 6 once. You should now have 20 sts each for the Fronts, 24 (24/24/26/26/28) sts each for the Sleeves, and 34 (34/36/36/38/38) sts for the Back on the needles.

Work 6 (6/8/8/10/10) more rows, re-peating Rows 7–12. After Row 12 has been worked, begin again with Row 7 (if needed for size). After this, only raglan increases will be worked, but no more increases for the ribbed neckband. You should now have 26 (26/28/28/30/30) sts each for the Fronts, 30 (30/32/34/36/38) sts each for the Sleeves, and 40 (40/44/44/48/48) sts for the Back on the needles.

Row 1 (RS, increase row): * K1, p1 *, rep from * to * twice, k1, slip m, ** knit to 1 st before next marker, M1L, k1, slip m, k1, M1R **, repeat from ** to ** another 3 times, knit to next marker, slip m, *** k1, p1 ***, repeat from *** to *** 2 times more, selv st. You should now have 27 (27/29/29/31/31) sts each for the Fronts, 32 (32/34/36/38/40) sts each for the Sleeves, and 42 (42/46/46/50/50) sts for the Back on the needles.

Row 2 (WS): K1, *k1, p1 *, rep from * to * 2 times more, slip m, purl to last marker, slip m, ** p1, k1 **, repeat from ** to ** 2 times more, selv st.

Rows 3 and 4: Work the same as Rows 1 and 2. You should now have 28 (28/30/30/32/32) sts each for the Fronts, 34 (34/36/38/40/42) sts each for the Sleeves, and 44 (44/48/48/52/52) sts for the Back on the needles.

Row 5 (RS, increase row): Work the same as Row 1. You should now have 29 (29/31/31/33/33) sts each for the Fronts, 36 (36/38/40/42/44) sts each for the Sleeves, and 46 (46/50/50/54/54) sts for the Back on the needles.

Row 6 (WS): K1, * k1, p1 *, rep from * to * 2 times more, slip m, knit to last marker, slip m, ** p1, k1 **, repeat from ** to ** 2 times more, selv st.

Work 12 (16/16/18/20/24) rows in all, repeating Rows 1–6, keeping the stripe sequence in pattern.

You should now have 32 (34/36/37/40/42) sts each for the Fronts, 42 (46/48/52/56/62) sts each for the Sleeves, and 52 (56/60/62/68/72) sts for the Back on the needles.

SLEEVE SEPARATION ROUND

Next RS row: Selv st, * k1, p1 *, rep from * to * twice, k1, slip m, ** knit to next m, remove m, transfer the next 42 (46/48/52/56/62) sts (Sleeve) to the next m to a stitch holder or a piece of waste yarn for holding, cast on 1 (1/1/2/2/3) new underarm st(s), place m, cast on 1 (1/1/2/2/3) new underarm st(s) **, rep from ** to ** once more, knit to next m, slip m, *** k1, p1 *** repeat from *** to *** 2 times more, selv st. You should now have a total of 120 (128/136/144/156/168) sts on the needles.

BODY

The Body is continued in the established pattern. For clarification, the stitch pattern is again written out here, beginning with a RS row after having completed a garter ridge. After the setup round, you will need to begin with the appropriate WS row to correctly stay in the pattern sequence for your size.

Row 1 (RS): * K1, p1 *, rep from * to * twice, k1, slip m, knit to last m, slip m, ** k1, p1 ** repeat from ** to ** 2 times more, selv st.

Row 2 (WS): K1, * k1, p1 *, rep from * to * 2 times more, slip m, purl to last m, slip m, ** p1, k1 **, repeat from ** to ** 2 times more, selv st.

Rows 3 and 4: Work the same as Rows 1 and 2.

Row 5 (RS): Work the same as Row 1.

Row 6 (WS): K1, *k1, p1 *, rep from * to * 2 times more, slip m, knit to last m, slip m, ** p1, k1 **, repeat from ** to ** 2 times more, selv st.

Repeat Rows 1–6 until the cardigan has either reached a length of 18.5 (19.7/20.5/20.5/21.7/23.6) in [47 (50/52/52/55/60) cm], measured from the underarm, or is 2 in (5 cm) shorter than desired body length, to accommodate ribbing to be added, ending after having just completed a Row 4.

RIBBING

Row 1 (RS): * K1, p1 *, rep from * to * to 2 sts before the last m, p2tog, slip m, ** k1, p1 **, repeat from ** to ** 2 times more, selv st.

Row 2 (WS): K1, * k1, p1 *, rep from * to * to last 2 sts of this row, k1, selv st.

Row 3 (RS): * K1, p1 *, rep from * to * to last stitch of this row, selv st.

Row 4 (WS): Work the same as Row 2.

Rows 5–8: Repeat Rows 3 and 4 twice.

Row 9 (RS): BO all sts in pattern.

SLEEVES

Both Sleeves are worked the same. For the Sleeve, first take up the 42 (46/48/52/56/62) formerly held sts with US size 11 (8.0 mm) needles, pick up and knit 1 (1/1/2/2/3) st(s) of the cast-on underarm sts, place m, pick up and knit another 1 (1/1/2/2/3) st(s) of the cast-on underarm sts, and join in the round. The Sleeve is worked in the round from here on; the marker indicates the BOR. You should now have a total of 44 (48/50/56/60/68) sts on the needles.

Continue in the already established pattern in stockinette stitch with garter ridges, and work until the Sleeve has either reached a length of 16.9 (16.9/17.3/17.3/17.7/17.7) in [43

(43/44/44/45/45) cm] or is 2 in (5 cm) shorter than desired Sleeve length, to accommodate ribbing to be added, ending having just completed a Round 6 (= purl round). For better understanding, here again is the pattern in written-out form:

Rounds 1–5: Knit all stitches.

Round 6: Purl all stitches.

SLEEVE CUFF

Round 1: * K4 (4/4/3/3/3), k2tog *, rep from * to * to end of round, knitting rem sts.

Round 2: Knit all stitches.

Round 3: * K3 (3/3/2/2/2), k2tog *, rep from * to * to end of round, knitting rem sts.

Round 4: * K1, p1 *, rep from * to * to end of round; should the stitch count be an odd one, work ssp over the last 2 sts.

Rounds 5–9: Repeat Round 4 five times.

Round 10: BO all sts in pattern.

FINISHING

To finish, weave in all ends, dampen the cardigan, and pull it into the desired shape.

ELLEN

TOP-DOWN RAGLAN SWEATER WITH V-NECK AND SLIGHT WAIST SHAPING

SIZES

XS, S, M, L, XL, XXL

Numbers for size XS are listed before the parentheses, numbers for sizes S through XXL within parentheses. If only one number is listed, it applies to all sizes.

Size	Chest Circumference	Sleeve Length from Armhole	Garment Length from Armhole
XS	35.4 in (90 cm)	17.7 in (45 cm)	15.7 in (40 cm)
S	37.4 in (95 cm)	17.7 in (45 cm)	15.7 in (40 cm)
M	39.4 in (100 cm)	18.1 in (46 cm)	16.5 in (42 cm)
L	43.3 in (110 cm)	18.1 in (46 cm)	18.5 in (47 cm)
XL	47.2 in (120 cm)	18.5 in (47 cm)	18.9 in (48 cm)
XXL	51.2 in (130 cm)	18.5 in (47 cm)	18.9 in (48 cm)

MATERIALS AND TOOLS

— ITO Rakuda; 70% wool, 30% camel hair; 231 yd (212 m) per 1.4 oz (40 g): #654 White, 5 (5/6/6/7/8) skeins
— ITO Sensai; 60% mohair, 40% silk; 262 yd (240 m) per 0.7 oz (20 g): #330 White, 5 (5/6/6/7/8) skeins
— Circular knitting needle, US size 6 (4.0 mm), at least 32 in (80 cm) long
— Circular knitting needle, US size 4 (3.5 mm), 24 in (60 cm) long
— If desired, one DPN set each in sizes US 6 (4.0 mm) and US 4 (3.5 mm) for the sleeves
— 4 stitch markers
— Stitch holder or waste yarn
— Tapestry needle

GAUGE

In stockinette stitch with 2 strands of yarn (= 1 strand Sensai and 1 strand Rakuda) held together on US size 6 (4.0 mm) needles: 23 sts and 34 rows = 4 x 4 in (10 x 10 cm)

CONSTRUCTION NOTES

The sweater is worked as a top-down raglan construction in one piece in stockinette stitch with 2 strands of yarn (= 1 strand Sensai and 1 strand Rakuda) held together. To shape the V-neck, work begins in turned rows. After completion of the neckline, the main part is worked in the round. After having divided for the sleeves, decreases and subsequent increases are worked at the sides for waist shaping. The ribbed neckband is knitted on afterwards.

RIBBING

1x1 ribbing: * K1, p1 *, rep from * to * continuously.

STOCKINETTE STITCH

In the round: Knit all sts in all rounds.

SELVEDGE STITCHES

In RS and WS rows, always knit the first and the last stitch of the row (= selv st).

CONTINUED

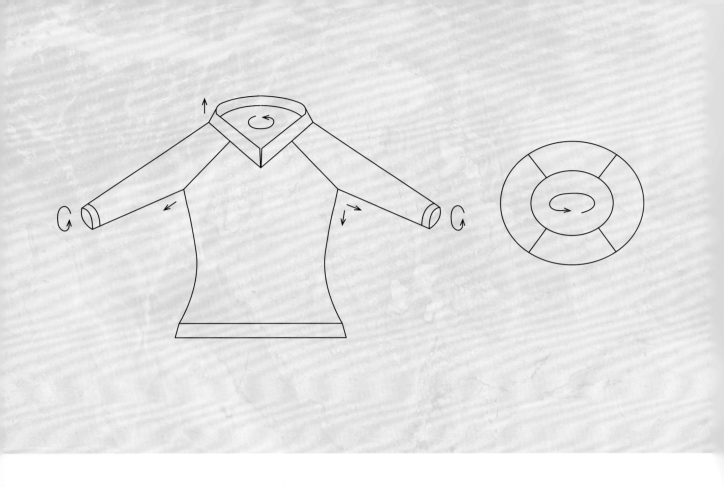

INSTRUCTIONS

Using US size 6 (4.0 mm) needles and 2 strands of yarn (= 1 strand Sensai and 1 strand Rakuda) held together, cast on 54 (54/58/60/64/70) sts, then first work V-neck shaping in turned rows:

Row 1 (WS): Selv st, p2, place m, p6 (6/8/8/10/12), place m, p36 (36/36/38/38/40), place m, p6 (6/8/8/10/12), place m, p2, selv st.

Row 2 (RS, increase row): K1, M1R, * knit to 1 st before next m, M1L, k1, slip m, k1, M1R *, rep from * to * 3 times more, knit to last 2 sts, M1L, k1, selv st.

You should now have 5 sts each for the Fronts, 8 (8/10/10/12/14) sts each for the Sleeves, and 38 (38/38/40/40/42) sts for the Back on the needles.

Row 3 (WS): Selv st, purl to last stitch, selv st.

Repeat Rows 2 and 3 another 14 (14/14/15/15/16) times more, ending having just completed a Row 3. You should now have a total of 33 (33/33/35/35/37) sts each for the Fronts, 36 (36/38/40/42/46) sts each for the Sleeves, and 66 (66/66/70/70/74) sts for the Back on the needles.

In the following RS row, pieces are joined and continued in the round, then the garment will be worked in the round. For this, * knit to 1 st before next m, M1L, k1, slip m, k1, M1R *, rep from * to * 3 times more, knit to end of row, join in the round, and continue, working to the first marker. This marker, positioned at the raglan line on the Left Front, marks the new beginning of the round (BOR). You should now have 38 (38/40/42/44/48) sts each for the Sleeves, and 68 (68/68/72/72/76) sts each for Front and Back on the needles. For ease of counting, round numbers start anew with Round 1 from here on.

Round 1: Knit all stitches, slipping markers as you encounter them.

Round 2 (increase round): * K1, M1L, k to 1 st before next m, M1R, k1, slip m *, rep from * to * 3 times more. You should now have 40 (40/42/44/46/50) sts each for the Sleeves, and 70 (70/70/74/74/78) sts each for Front and Back on the needles.

Round 3: Work the same as Round 1.

Repeat Rounds 2 and 3 14 (16/18/21/27/30) times more, ending having just completed a Round 3. You should now have 68 (72/78/86/100/110) sts each for the Sleeves, and 98 (102/106/116/128/138) sts each for Front and Back on the needles.

SLEEVE SEPARATION ROUND

* Remove marker, transfer the next 68 (72/78/86/100/110) sts (Sleeve) to next m to a stitch holder or a piece of waste yarn for holding, cast on 3 (3/4/5/5/6) new underarm sts using backwards-loop CO, place m, cast on 3 (3/4/5/5/6) new underarm sts using backwards CO, knit to next m *, rep from * to* once more.

You should have a total of 208 (216/228/252/276/300) sts for the body on the needles, continue to work in the round.

BODY: WAIST SHAPING

The Body is worked in stockinette stitch, with waist-shaping decreases beginning after the first 10 rounds. Work 10 rounds in stockinette stitch; on last round stop 3 sts before the BOR marker, then work as follows:

Round 1: * Skp, k1, slip m, k1, k2tog, knit to 3 sts before the next marker *, rep from * to* once more, k3. You should now have a total of 204 (212/224/248/272/296) sts for the Body on the needles.

Rounds 2 and 3: Knit all stitches.

Round 4: Knit to 3 sts before the BOR marker.

Round 5: Work the same as Round 1. You should now have a total of 200 (208/220/244/268/292) sts for the Body on the needles.

Rounds 6–9: Repeat Rounds 4 and 5 twice.

You should now have a total of 192 (200/212/236/260/284) sts for the Body on the needles.

Work 4 (4.3/4.3/4.7/4.7/5.1) in [10 (11/11/12/12/13) cm] in stockinette stitch.

Now, waist-shaping increases will be worked; for this, in the last round, stop 1 st before the BOR marker.

Round 1: * M1R, k1, slip m, k1, M1L, knit to 1 st before the next m *, rep from * to* once more, k1. You should now have a total of 196 (204/216/240/264/288) sts for the Body on the needles.

Round 2: Knit to 1 st before the BOR marker.

Round 3: Work the same as Round 1. You should now have a total of 200 (208/220/244/268/292) sts for the Body on the needles.

Rounds 4 and 5: Repeat Rounds 2 and 3 once. You should now have a total of 204 (212/224/248/272/296) sts for the Body on the needles.

Rounds 6 and 7: Knit all stitches.

Round 8: Work the same as Round 2.

Round 9: Work the same as Round 1. You should now have a total of 208 (216/228/252/276/300) sts for the Body on the needles.

Continue the sweater in stockinette stitch until it has either reached a length of 13.8 (13.8 /14.5/16.5/16.9/16.9) in [35 (35/37/42/43/43) cm], measured from the armhole, or is 2 in (5 cm) shorter than desired Body length to accommodate ribbing to be added.

RIBBING

Change to US size 4 (3.5 mm) needles.

Rounds 1–20: * K1, p1 *, rep from * to * to end of round.

Round 21: BO all sts in pattern.

SLEEVES

Both Sleeves are worked the same. To work the Sleeve, first take up the formerly held 68 (72/78/86/100/110) sts using US size 6 (4.0 mm) needles, then pick up and knit 3 (3/4/5/5/6) sts from the newly cast-on underarm sts, place m, pick up and knit 3 (3/4/5/5/6) more sts from the newly cast-on underarm sts, and join in the round. The Sleeve is worked in the round from here on; the marker indicates the BOR. You should now have a total of 74 (78/86/96/110/122) sts on the needles.

Continue, working the Sleeve in stockinette stitch, at the same time, in every 14th (12th/12th/12th/6th/6th) round, decreasing as follows a total of 8 (8/10/11/18/22) times: K1, k2tog, work in pattern to 3 sts before m, skp, k1, slip m.

Work the Sleeve in stockinette stitch until the sleeve has either reached a length of 15.7 (15.7/16.1/16.1/16.5/16.5) in [40 (40/41/41/42/42) cm] or is 2 in (5 cm) shorter than desired Sleeve length to accommodate the ribbed cuff to be added.

SLEEVE CUFF

Change to US size 4 (3.5 mm) needles. First, knit 1 round, at the same time decreasing 10 sts evenly distributed.

Rounds 1–20: * K1, p1 *, rep from * to * to end of round.

Round 21: BO all sts in pattern.

RIBBING FOR V-NECK

For the ribbing instructions to work with any number of stitches, no specific stitch counts are given in the following part, but the method is described in general terms. First, using US size 4 (3.5 mm) needles and beginning at the Back Left Shoulder, pick up and knit stitches at a rate of 1 st picked up from every shoulder stitch, 3 sts picked up from every 4 sts along the knotted selvedge of the neckline, picking up 1 additional stitch at the tip of the V (in the spot where work had been joined in the round), and marking this stitch with a stitch marker. Then, along the sloped section of the Right Front, again at a rate of 3 sts picked up from every 4 sts, 1 st picked up from

every shoulder stitch and from the Back neckline. Make sure that the total number of stitches picked up is an even number. Place a BOR marker and join in the round without twisting.

Now, count the stitches up to the marked stitch (without counting the marked stitch itself). If this number is even, begin the ribbing pattern with a knit stitch, if this number is odd, begin it with a purl stitch, so that the marked stitch will be a knit stitch.

Round 1: Work 1x1 ribbing.

Round 2: Work 1x1 ribbing to 2 sts before the marked stitch, work a single left-leaning decrease, keeping in ribbing pattern (either ssk or ssp), k1, work a single right-leaning decrease, keeping in ribbing pattern (either k2tog or p2tog), work 1x1 ribbing to end of round. 2 sts have been decreased.

Round 3: Work the same as Round 1.

Rounds 4 and 5: Repeat Rounds 2 and 3 once. 2 sts have been decreased.

Round 6: Bind off in pattern while working a Round 2, removing the marker when you come to it. 2 sts have been decreased.

FINISHING

To finish, weave in all ends, dampen the sweater, and pull it into the desired shape.

DANIELA

TOP-DOWN CARDIGAN WITH CABLES

SIZES
XS, S, M, L, XL, XXL

Numbers for size XS are listed before the parentheses, numbers for sizes S through XXL within parentheses. If only one number is listed, it applies to all sizes.

Size	Chest Circum-ference	Sleeve Length from Armhole	Garment Length from Armhole
XS	33.5 in (85 cm)	18.5 in (47 cm)	14.2 in (36 cm)
S	35.8 in (91 cm)	18.5 in (47 cm)	14.2 in (36 cm)
M	38.2 in (97 cm)	18.9 in (48 cm)	14.6 in (37 cm)
L	42.5 in (108 cm)	18.9 in (48 cm)	15.4 in (39 cm)
XL	47.2 in (120 cm)	19.3 in (49 cm)	16.1 in (41 cm)
XXL	52 in (132 cm)	19.3 in (49 cm)	17.7 in (45 cm)

MATERIALS AND TOOLS
— Lamana Premia; 60% mohair, 40% silk; 328 yd (300 m) per 0.9 oz (25 g): #05 Silver Gray, 3 (4/4/5/6/6) skeins
— Lamana Como; 100% merino su-perfine wool; 131 yd (120 m) per 0.9 oz (25 g): #05 Silver Gray, 8 (10/11/13/15/17) skeins
— Circular knitting needle, US size 9 (5.5 mm), at least 32 in (80 cm) long
— Circular knitting needle, US size 7 (4.5 mm), 24 in (60 cm) long
— If desired, a DPN set in US size 9 (5.5 mm) for the sleeves

— 7 mother-of-pearl buttons, approx. 18 mm (Union Knopf: https://unionknopf.pl/en)
— 4 stitch markers
— Cable needle or auxiliary needle
— Stitch holder or waste yarn
— Tapestry needle

GAUGE
In ribbing pattern (2x1 ribbing) on US size 9 (5.5 mm) needles with 2 strands of yarn held together (= 1 strand Como and 1 strand Premia): 21 sts and 26 rows = 4 x 4 in (10 x 10 cm)

CONSTRUCTION NOTES
The cardigan is worked in one piece in a top-down raglan construction using two strands of yarn (= 1 strand Como and 1 strand Premia) held together. First, the neckline is shaped with short rows, then the button band is knitted on. The upper part of the cardigan is worked in a ribbing pattern. The knit-purl columns of the ribbing pattern transition to a simple cable pattern in the bottom part of the sleeves and the body, which is additionally shaped into a slight A-line with increases. The sleeves are given a slight trumpet shape through increases. The body and the sleeves are finished with narrow I-cord edging.

RIBBING PATTERN
2x1 ribbing: * K2, p1 *, rep from * to * all the time.

BINDING OFF WITH APPLIED I-CORD
Stitches are bound off with applied I-cord edging. For this, cast on 1 stitch to the left needle using the backwards-loop cast-on method, * k1, skp, slip 2 sts from the right needle to the left one *, rep from * to * until all stitches have been bound off.

CONTINUED

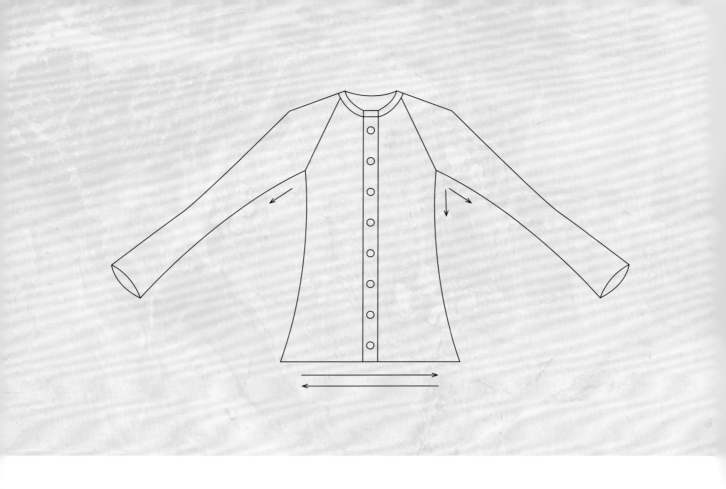

TURNING STITCHES (T-ST)

Place the working yarn behind the work, turn the work, slip 1 stitch purlwise, move the working yarn over the right needle from front to back and pull up on the stitch. This creates a turning stitch with two legs sitting on the needle. The "double stitch" will be worked and counted as one stitch further on. Knit stitches can be worked immediately, for purl stitches, the working yarn first needs to be moved to the front of work between the needles.

SELVEDGE STITCHES

In RS and WS rows, always knit the first and the last stitch of the row (= selv st).

MAKING 2 STITCHES FROM 1 (PFKB)

Purl the next stitch, but leave the old stitch on the left needle, then move the working yarn to the back, insert the right needle once again into the back leg of the same stitch and knit this loop. Then, let the old stitch slip from the left needle.

RIBBING

1x1 ribbing: * K1, p1 *, rep from * to * continuously.

STOCKINETTE STITCH

In the round: Knit all sts in all rounds.

INSTRUCTIONS

With US size 7 (4.5 mm) needles and 2 strands of yarn (= 1 strand Como and 1 strand Premia) held together, cast on 71 (71/83/95/95/95) sts, then work a WS row as follows:

Selv st, work 12 (12/15/18/18/18) sts in ribbing pattern, beginning with a purl stitch, place m, work 7 sts in ribbing pattern, place m, work 31 (31/37/43/43/43) sts in ribbing pattern, place m, work 7 sts in ribbing pattern, place m, work 12 (12/15/18/18/18) sts in ribbing pattern, selv st.

You now have 13 (13/16/19/19/19) sts each for the Fronts, 7 sts each for the Sleeves, and 31 (31/37/43/43/43) sts for the Back on the needles.

Rows 1–8: Work in ribbing pattern with selv st, slipping the markers when you come to them.

Change to US size 9 (5.5 mm) needles; the smaller needles will not be needed anymore after the short row section, but for the time being, the unworked stitches can be held on the smaller needle. In Rows 9–14, the Back neckline is shaped with the help of short rows with double stitches (t-st). As an alternative, you can work without short rows, which will create a wider neckline in the back; for this, begin at Row 21, then work Row 22, then jump back to Row 17. In every RS row, 8 sts in all are increased; stitch counts listed at the end of the row apply only to the option of working short rows.

Row 9 (RS): Selv st, * k2, p1 *, rep from * to * to 3 sts before next m, k2, M1R, k1, slip m, k1, M1L, ** k2, p1 **, rep from ** to ** to 3 sts before next m, k2, M1R, k1, slip m, k1, M1L, *** k2, p1

***, rep from *** to *** to 3 sts before next m, k2, M1R, k1, slip m, k1, M1L, # k2, p1 #, rep from # to # to 3 sts before next m, k2, M1R, k1, slip m, k1, M1L, k1, t-st. You should now have 14 (14/17/20/20/20) sts each for the Fronts, 9 sts each for the Sleeves, and 33 (33/39/45/45/45) sts for the Back on the needles.

Row 10 (WS): K1, p1, slip m, p1, k1, * p2, k1 *, rep from * to * to 1 st before next m, p1, slip m, p1, k1, ** p2, k1 **, rep from ** to ** to 1 st before next m, p1, slip m, p1, k1, *** p2, k1 ***, rep from *** to *** to 1 st before next m, p1, slip m, p1, k1, p1, t-st.

Row 11 (RS): P1, M1R, k1, slip m, k1, M1L, p1, * k2, p1 *, rep from * to * to 1 st before next m, M1R, k1, slip m, k1, M1L, p1, ** k2, p1 **, rep from ** to ** to 1 st before next m, M1R, k1, slip m, k1, M1L, p1, *** k2, p1 ***, rep from *** to *** to 1 st before next m, M1R, k1, slip m, k1, M1L, p1, k2, t-st. You should now have 15 (15/18/21/21/21) sts each for the Fronts, 11 sts each for the Sleeves, and 35 (35/41/47/47/47) sts for the Back on the needles.

Row 12 (WS): P1, k1, p2, slip m, * p2, k1 *, rep from * to * to 2 sts before next m, p2, slip m, ** p2, k1 **, rep from ** to ** to 2 sts before next m, p2, slip m, *** p2, k1 ***, rep from *** to *** to 2 sts before next m, p2, slip m, p2, k1, p2, t-st.

Row 13 (RS): K1, p1, k1, M1R, k1, slip m, k1, M1L, k1, p1, * k2, p1 *, rep from * to * to 2 sts before next m, k1, M1R, k1, slip m, k1, M1L, k1, p1, ** k2, p1 **, rep from ** to ** to 2 sts before next m, k1, M1R, k1, slip m, k1, M1L, k1, p1, *** k2, p1 ***, rep from *** to *** to 2 sts before next m, k1, M1R, k1, slip m, k1, M1L, k1, p1, k2, p1, t-st. You should now have 16 (16/19/22/22/22) sts

each for the Fronts, 13 sts each for the Sleeves, and 37 (37/43/49/49/49) sts for the Back on the needles.

Row 14 (WS): P2, k1, p3, slip m, p1, * p2, k1 *, rep from * to * to 3 sts before next m, p3, slip m, p1, ** p2, k1 **, rep from ** to ** to 3 sts before next m, p3, slip m, p1, *** p2, k1 ***, rep from *** to *** to 3 sts before next m, p3, slip m, p3, k1, p2, k1, t-st.

Now, the short row section has been completed, and regular increase rows will be worked; in every RS row, 8 sts total will be increased.

Row 15 (RS): * K2, p1 *, rep from * to * to 3 sts before next m, k2, M1R, k1, slip m, k1, pfkb (=inc 1 purlwise), ** k2, p1 **, rep from ** to ** to 3 sts before next m, k2, M1R, k1, slip m, k1, M1L, *** k2, p1 ***, rep from *** to *** to 3 sts before next m, k2, M1R, k1, slip m, k1, M1L, # k2, p1 #, rep from # to # to 3 sts before next m, k2, M1R, k1, slip m, k1, M1L, ## k2, p1 ##, rep from ## to ## to last 3 sts of the row, k2, selv st. You should now have 17 (17/20/23/23/23) sts each for the Fronts, 15 sts each for the Sleeves, and 39 (39/45/51/51/51) sts for the Back on the needles.

Row 16 (WS): Selv st, * p2, k1 *, rep from * to * to 1 st before next m, p1, slip m, p1, k1, ** p2, k1 **, rep from ** to ** to 1 st before next m, p1, slip m, p1, k1, *** p2, k1 ***, rep from *** to *** to 1 st before next m, p1, slip m, p1, k1, # p2, k1 #, rep from # to # to 1 st before next m, p1, slip m, p1, k1, ## p2, k1 ##, rep from ## to ## to last 3 sts of the row, p2, selv st.

Row 17 (RS): Selv st, * k2, p1 *, rep from * to * to 1 st before next m, M1R, k1, slip m, k1, M1L, p1, ** k2, p1 **, rep from ** to ** to 1 st before next m,

M1R, k1, slip m, k1, M1L, p1, *** k2, p1 ***, rep from *** to *** to 1 st before next m, M1R, k1, slip m, k1, M1L, p1, # k2, p1 #, rep from # to # to 1 st before next m, M1R, k1, slip m, k1, M1L, p1, ## k2, p1 ##, rep from ## to ## to last 3 sts of the row, k2, selv st. You should now have 18 (18/21/24/24/24) sts each for the Fronts, 17 sts each for the Sleeves, and 41 (41/47/53/53/53) sts for the Back on the needles.

Row 18 (WS): Selv st, * p2, k1 *, rep from * to * to 2 sts before next m, p2, slip m, ** p2, k1 **, rep from ** to ** 2 sts before next m, p2, slip m, *** p2, k1 ***, rep from *** to *** to 2 sts before next m, p2, slip m, # p2, k1 #, rep from # to # to 2 sts before next m, p2, slip m, ## p2, k1 ##, rep from ## to ## to last 3 sts of this row, p2, selv st.

Row 19 (RS): Selv st, * k2, p1 *, rep from * to * to 2 sts before next m, k1, M1R, k1, slip m, k1, M1L, k1, p1, ** k2, p1 **, rep from ** to ** to 2 sts before next m, k1, M1R, k1, slip m, k1, M1L, k1, p1, *** k2, p1 ***, rep from *** to *** to 2 sts before next m, k1, M1R, k1, slip m, k1, M1L, k1, p1, # k2, p1 #, rep from # to # to 2 sts before next m, k1, M1R, k1, slip m, k1, M1L, k1, k1, p1, ## k2, p1 ##, rep from ## to ## to last 3 sts of the row, k2, selv st. You should now have 19 (19/22/25/25/25) sts each for the Fronts, 19 sts each for the Sleeves, and 43 (43/49/55/55/55) sts for the Back on the needles.

Row 20 (WS): Selv st, * p2, k1 *, rep from * to * to 3 sts before next m, p3, slip m, p1, ** p2, k1 **, rep from ** to ** to 3 sts before next m, p3, slip m, p1, *** p2, k1 ***, rep from *** to *** to 3 sts before next m, p3, slip m, p1, # p2, k1 #, rep from # to # to 3 sts before next marker, p1, slip m, ## p2, k1 ##, rep from ## to ## to last 3 sts of the row, p2, selv st.

Row 21 (RS): Selv st, * k2, p1 *, rep from * to * to 3 sts before next m, k2, M1R, k1, slip m, k1, M1L, ** k2, p1 **, rep from ** to ** to 3 sts before next m, k2, M1R, k1, slip m, k1, M1L, *** k2, p1 ***, rep from *** to *** to 3 sts before next m, k2, M1R, k1, slip m, k1, M1L, # k2, p1 #, rep from # to # to 3 sts before next m, k2, M1R, k1, slip m, k1, M1L, ## k2, p1 ##, rep from ## to ## to last 3 sts of the row, k2, selv st. You should now have 20 (20/23/26/26/26) sts each for the Fronts, 21 sts each for the Sleeves, and 45 (45/51/57/57/57) sts for the Back on the needles.

Row 22 (WS): Work the same as Row 16.

You will work a total of 44 (50/50/62/68/72) rows, repeating Rows 17–22 continuously. When Row 22 has been worked, begin again with Row 17. For the version without short rows, a total of 50 (56/56/68/74/78) rows will be worked, repeating Rows 17–22, beginning with Row 21. When the appropriate number of rows for the respective size has been completed, you will have worked a total of 25 (28/28/34/37/40) increase rows.

Before dividing for the sleeves, you have 38 (41/44/50/56/62) sts each for the Fronts, 57 (63/63/75/87/99) sts each for the Sleeves, and 81 (87/93/105/117/129) sts for the Back on the needles. From the cast-on row to the sleeve division row, the cardigan should now measure approximately 8.7 (9.6/9.6/11.4/12.2/13.4) in [22 (24.5/24.5/29/31/34) cm]—if it doesn't, continue in pattern, working even without increases until the listed measurements have been reached.

Sleeve division row (RS): Selv st, * k2, p1 *, rep from * to * to 1 st before m, k1, remove m, transfer the following 57 (63/63/75/87/99) sts (Sleeve) to next m to a stitch holder or a piece of waste yarn for holding, cast on 9 new underarm sts, k1, ** k2, p1 **, rep from ** to ** to 1 st before m, k1, remove m, transfer the following 57 (63/63/75/87/99) sts (Sleeve) to next m to a stitch holder or a piece of waste yarn for holding, cast on 9 new underarm sts, k1, *** k2, p1 ***, rep from *** to *** to 3 sts before m, k2, selv st.

You should now have a total of 175 (187/199/223/247/271) sts for the Body on the needles.

First, work a WS row as follows: Selv st, * p2, k1 *, rep from * to * to last 3 sts of this row, p2, selv st.

BODY

Row 1 (RS): Selv st, * k2, p1*, rep from * to * to last 3 sts of this row, k2, selv st.

Row 2 (WS): Selv st, * p2, k1 *, rep from * to * to last 3 sts of this row, p2, selv st.

Repeat Rows 1 and 2 until the cardigan has either reached a length of 7.1 (7.1/7.5/8.3/9/10.6) in [18 (18/19/21/23/27) cm], measured from the underarm, or is 7.1 in [18 cm] shorter than desired Body length to accommodate the following cable section. For ease of counting, row counting starts anew from here with Row 1:

Row 1 (RS): Selv st, * k5, pfb *, rep from * to * to last 6 sts, k5, selv st. You should now have a total of 203 (217/231/259/287/315) sts on the needles.

Row 2 (WS): Selv st, * p5, k2 *, rep from * to * to last 6 sts of this row, p5, selv st.

Row 3 (RS): Selv st, * k5, p2 *, rep from * to * to last 6 sts of this row, k5, selv st.

Row 4 (WS): Work the same as Row 2.

Row 5 (RS): Selv st, * hold 3 sts on a cable needle in front of work, k2, then knit the 3 sts from the cable needle, p2 *, rep from * to * to last 6 sts, hold 3 sts on a cable needle in front of work, k2, then knit the 3 sts from the cable needle, selv st.

Row 6 (WS): Work the same as Row 2.

Rows 7–10: Repeat Rows 3 and 4 twice.

Rows 11–22: Repeat Rows 5–10 twice.

Row 23 (RS): Selv st, * hold 3 sts on a cable needle in front of work, k2, then knit the 3 sts from the cable needle, p1, pfb, hold 3 sts on a cable needle in front of work, k2, then knit the 3 sts from the cable needle, p2 *, rep from * to * to last 6 sts of this row, hold 3 sts on a cable needle in front of work, k2, then knit the 3 sts from the cable needle, selv st. You should now have a total of 217 (232/247/277/307/337) sts on the needles.

Row 24 (WS): Selv st, * p5, k2, p5, k3 *, rep from * to * to last 6 sts of this row, p5, selv st.

Row 25 (RS): Selv st, * k5, p3, k5, p2 *, rep from * to * to last 6 sts of this row, k5, selv st.

Row 26 (WS): Work the same as Row 24.

Rows 27 and 28: Work the same as Rows 25 and 26.

Row 29 (RS): Selv st, * hold 3 sts on a cable needle in front of work, k2, then knit the 3 sts from the cable needle, p3, hold 3 sts on a cable needle in front of work, k2, then knit the 3 sts from the cable needle, p2 *, rep from * to * to last 6 sts of this row, hold 3 sts on a cable needle in front of work, k2, then knit the 3 sts from the cable needle, selv st.

Rows 30–34: Work the same as Rows 24–28.

Rows 35–40: Work the same as Rows 29–34.

Row 41 (RS): Selv st, * hold 3 sts on a cable needle in front of work, k2, then knit the 3 sts from the cable needle, p3, hold 3 sts on a cable needle in front of work, k2, then knit the 3 sts from the cable needle, p1, pfb *, rep from * to * to last 6 sts of this row, hold 3 sts on a cable needle in front of work, k2, then knit the 3 sts from the cable needle, selv st. You should now have a total of 231 (247/253/295/327/359) sts on the needles.

Row 42 (WS): Selv st, * p5, k3 *, rep from * to * to last 6 sts of this row, p5, selv st.

Row 43 (RS): Selv st, * k5, p3 *, rep from * to * to last 6 sts of this row, k5, selv st.

Row 44 (WS): Work the same as Row 42.

Rows 45 and 46: Work the same as Rows 43 and 44.

Row 47 (RS): Selv st, * hold 3 sts on a cable needle in front of work, k2, then knit the 3 sts from the cable needle, p3 *, rep from * to * to last 6 sts, hold 3 sts on a cable needle in front of work, k2, then knit the 3 sts from the cable needle, selv st.

Rows 48–50: Work the same as Rows 42–44.

Row 51 (RS): Bind off all sts, using applied I-cord BO.

SLEEVES

Both Sleeves are worked the same. For the Sleeve, first take up the 57 (63/63/75/87/99) formerly held sts using US size 9 (5.5 mm) needles, pick up and knit 5 sts from the newly cast-on underarm sts, place m, pick up and knit another 4 sts, and join in the round. The Sleeve is worked in the round from here on; the marker indicates the BOR. You should now have a total of 66 (72/72/84/96/108) sts on the needles.

Rounds 1–9: * K2, p1 *, rep from * to * to end of round, slip m.

Round 10: K2tog, p1, * k2, p1 *, rep from * to * to 3 sts before m, skp, p1, slip m. You should have a total of 64 (70/70/82/94/106) sts on the needles.

Rounds 11–19: K1, p1, * k2, p1 *, rep from * to * to 2 sts before m, k1, p1, slip m.

Round 20: P2tog, * k2, p1 *, rep from * to * to 5 sts before m, k2, ssp, p1, slip m. You should now have a total of 62 (68/68/80/92/104) sts on the needles.

Rounds 21–29: P1, * k2, p1 *, rep from * to * to 1 st before m, p1, slip m.

Round 30: K2tog, k1, p1, * k2, p1 *, rep from * to * to 4 sts before m, k1, skp,

p1, slip m. You should now have a total of 60 (66/66/78/90/102) sts on the needles.

Rounds 31–60: Rep Rounds 1–30 once. You should have a total of 54 (60/60/72/84/96) sts on the needles.

Round 61: Work the same as Round 1.

Rep Round 61 until the sleeve has either reached a length of 13.8 (13.8/14.2/14.2/14.6/14.6) in [35 (35/36/36/37/37) cm] or is 4.7 in [12 cm] shorter than desired sleeve length to accommodate the following cable section.

For ease of counting, counting starts anew from here with Round 1.

Round 1: * K5, pfb *, rep from * to * to m, slip m. You should now have a total of 63 (70/70/84/98/112) sts on the needles.

Rounds 2–4: * K5, p2 *, rep from * to * to m, slip m.

Round 5: * Hold 3 sts on a cable needle in front of work, k2, then knit the 3 sts from the cable needle, p2 *, rep from * to * to m, slip m.

Rounds 6–10: * K5, p2 *, rep from * to * to m, slip m.

Rounds 11–28: Repeat Rounds 5–10 3 times.

Round 29: Work the same as Round 5.

Rounds 30–32: Repeat Rounds 2–4 once.

Round 33: Bind off all sts, using applied I-cord BO.

FRONT BANDS

Both Fronts are finished with a Front Band in 1x1 ribbing. For this, pick up and knit stitches from the edge at a rate of 3 sts picked up from every 4 sts, and work 8 rows heightwise. In Row 8 (RS), bind off all sts in pattern. On the Right Front Band, in Row 4 (RS), work 7 buttonholes, evenly spaced. For each buttonhole, work "k2tog, yo." This Front Band (buttonhole band) will later cover the other Front Band. Sew the buttons to the corresponding spots on the Left Front Band (button band).

FINISHING

To finish, weave in all ends, dampen the cardigan, and pull it into the desired shape.

CHAPTER 3

CIRCULAR YOKES

Circular yokes are very similar to raglan constructions. Generally speaking, a raglan is a circular yoke with only four increase spots, which creates a trapezoid shape. Circular yokes have a significantly larger number of increase spots; in principle, any number is possible. As a rule, the number of increase spots will usually be an even one, and the following rule of thumb can be applied: Half the number of increase spots equals the number of rows or increase rows or rounds. Another rule applies, too: The more increase spots there are, the higher the number of rows worked in between increase rows or rounds.

In this chapter, you'll find circular yoke sweaters with 8, 12, and 16 increase spots—one of each, as well as a cardigan with 20 increase spots.

Circular yoke sweaters lend themselves to colorwork and stitch patterns incorporated in the yoke. Increases are symmetrical everywhere so that a pattern can be distributed evenly over the whole sweater. Especially well suited are raised textured patterns, lace patterns, or stranded colorwork patterns—for this reason, all garments in this book feature simple patterns: a simple stripe pattern, bobbles, an eyelet pattern, and a cable pattern. Omitting these patterns will give you wonderful basic circular yoke sweaters.

LET'S GET STARTED

SOPHIA

CIRCULAR YOKE SWEATER WITH SIMPLE BOBBLE PATTERN

SIZES

XS, S, M, L, XL, XXL

Numbers for size XS are listed before the parentheses, numbers for sizes S through XXL within parentheses. If only one number is listed, it applies to all sizes.

Size	Chest Circum- ference	Sleeve Length from Armhole	Garment Length from Armhole
XS	33.1 in (84 cm)	18.9 in (48 cm)	15 in (38 cm)
S	35.4 in (90 cm)	18.9 in (48 cm)	15 in (38 cm)
M	38.6 in (98 cm)	19.3 in (49 cm)	16.1 in (41 cm)
L	44.1 in (112 cm)	19.3 in (49 cm)	18.1 in (46 cm)
XL	47.2 in (120 cm)	19.7 in (50 cm)	18.5 in (47 cm)
XXL	50 in (127 cm)	19.7 in (50 cm)	18.9 in (48 cm)

MATERIALS AND TOOLS

— Lang Yarns Jawoll Superwash; 75% virgin wool superwash, 25% nylon; 230 yd (210 m) per 1.75 oz (50 g): #03 Dark Gray Heathered, 4 (4/5/5/6/7) skeins
— Lang Yarns Lace; 58% mohair, 42% silk; 339 yd (310 m) per 0.9 oz (25 g): #26 Beige, 3 (3/4/4/5/5) skeins
— Circular knitting needle, US size 6 (4.0 mm), at least 32 in (80 cm) long
— Circular knitting needle, US size 4 (3.5 mm), 24 in (60 cm) long
— If desired, one DPN set each in sizes US 6 (4.0 mm) and US 4 (3.5 mm) for the sleeves
— 13 stitch markers
— Stitch holder or waste yarn
— Tapestry needle

GAUGE

In stockinette stitch with 2 strands of yarn held together (= 1 strand Jawoll and 1 strand Lace) on US size 6 (4.0 mm) needles: 22 sts and 32 rows = 4 x 4 in (10 x 10 cm)

CONSTRUCTION NOTES

The sweater is worked in a circular yoke construction from the top to the bottom in one piece in stockinette stitch in the round with a bobble pattern. It is worked with 2 strands of yarn held together (= 1 strand Jawoll and 1 strand Lace) throughout, with a total of 12 increase spots. The ribbed neckband is knitted on afterwards, folded over, and sewn down on the inside. When omitting the bobble pattern, a simple basic circular yoke sweater suitable as unisex wear can be made. For this modification, the bobble rounds in the pattern should be worked as Round 2. Sleeve cuffs and hem ribbing are long and lend the sweater a special touch.

RIBBING

1x1 ribbing: * K1, p1 *, rep from * to * continuously.

BOBBLES

Make 5 sts from 1 as follows (kfbfbf): * K1, leaving the old st on the left needle, then knit the same st through the back loop, again leaving the old st on the left needle *, rep from * to*, then knit once more through the front loop and let the old st slip from the left needle. You should now have created a total of 5 new sts out of the old one. Turn work, p5, turn work, k5, turn work, p5, turn work, k5. Now, pass the 4 previously worked sts one after another over the stitch worked last. Now, only 1 stitch remains.

STOCKINETTE STITCH

In the round: Knit all sts in all rounds.

CONTINUED

Model is
wearing size M

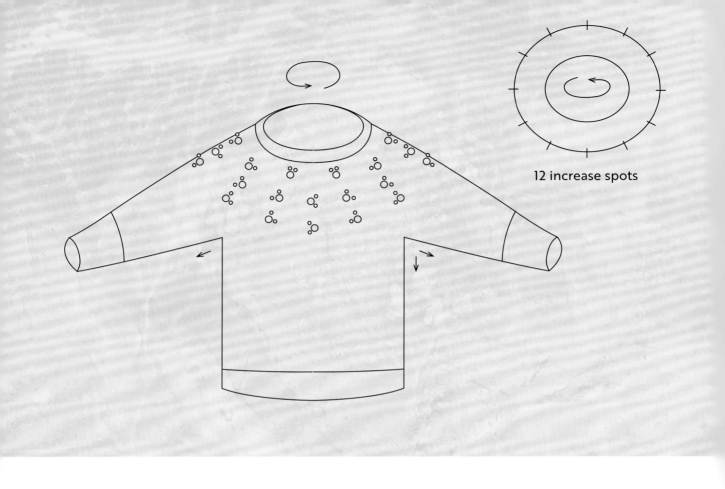

12 increase spots

INSTRUCTIONS

With US size 6 (4.0 mm) needles and 2 strands of yarn held together (= 1 strand Jawoll and 1 strand Lace), cast on 108 (108/108/132/132/132) sts, place a BOR marker, and join in the round without twisting.

Round 1: * K9 (9/9/11/11/11), place m *, rep from * to * 11 times more., slip BOR marker.

Round 2: Knit all stitches, slipping the markers when you come to them.

Round 3 (increase round): * K1, M1L, k to 1 st before next m, M1R, k1, slip m *, rep from * to * 11 times more. You should now have a total of 132 (132/132/156/156/156) sts on the nee-

dles, 11 (11/11/13/13/13) sts each for the 12 sections.

Round 4: Work the same as Round 2.

Round 5 (bobble rnd): * K5 (5/5/6/6/6), 1 bobble, k5 (5/5/6/6/6), slip m *, rep from * to * 11 times more, slip BOR marker

Round 6: Work the same as Round 2.

Round 7 (bobble rnd): *K4 (4/4/5/5/5), 1 bobble, k1, 1 bobble, k4 (4/4/5/5/5), slip m *, rep from * to * 11 times more, slip BOR marker.

Round 8: Work the same as Round 2.

Round 9 (increase round): Work the same as Round 3. You should now have a total of 156 (156/156/180/

180/180) sts on the needles, 13 (13/13/15/15/15) sts each for the 12 sections.

Rounds 10–14: Work the same as Round 2.

Round 15 (increase round): Work the same as Round 3. You should now have a total of 180 (180/180/204/204/204) sts on the needles, 15 (15/15/17/17/17) sts each for the 12 sections.

Round 16: Work the same as Round 2.

Round 17 (bobble rnd): * K7 (7/7/8/8/8), 1 bobble, k7 (7/7/8/8/8), slip m *, rep from * to * 11 times more, slip BOR marker.

Round 18: Work the same as Round 2.

Round 19 (bobble rnd): * K6 (6/6/7/7/7), 1 bobble, k1, 1 bobble, k6 (6/6/7/7/7), slip m *, rep from * to * 11 times more, slip BOR marker.

Round 20: Work the same as Round 2.

Round 21 (increase round): Work the same as Round 3. You should now have a total of 204 (204/204/228/228/228) sts on the needles, 17 (17/17/19/19/19) sts each for each one of the 12 sections.

Rounds 22–26: Work the same as Round 2.

Round 27 (increase round): Work the same as Round 3. You should now have a total of 228 (228/228/252/252/252) sts on the needles, 19 (19/19/21/21/21) sts each for the 12 sections.

Round 28: Work the same as Round 2.

Round 29 (bobble rnd): * K9 (9/9/10/10/10), 1 bobble, k9 (9/9/10/10/10), slip m *, rep from * to * 11 times more, slip BOR marker.

Round 30: Work the same as Round 2.

Round 31 (bobble rnd): * K8 (8/8/9/9/9), 1 bobble, k1, 1 bobble, k8 (8/8/9/9/9), slip m *, rep from * to * 11 times more, slip BOR marker.

Round 32: Work the same as Round 2.

Round 33 (increase round): Work the same as Round 3. You should now have a total of 252 (252/252/276/276/276) sts on the needles, 21 (21/21/23/23/23) sts each for the 12 sections.

Rounds 34–38: Work the same as Round 2.

Repeat Rounds 33–38 another 1 (2/3/4/5/6) time(s), in the last repeat of Round 38, remove all markers, and stop 4 (4/5/5/6/6) sts before the BOR marker. You should now have 276 (300/324/372/396/420) sts on the needles, 23 (25/27/31/33/35) sts each for the 12 sections.

SLEEVE SEPARATION ROUND

* Transfer the next 54 (58/64/72/78/82) sts (Sleeve) to a stitch holder or a piece of waste yarn for holding, cast on 4 (4/5/5/6/6) new underarm sts using backwards-loop CO, place m, cast on 4 (4/5/5/6/6) new underarm sts using backwards-loop CO, k84 (92/98/114/120/128) *, rep from * to* once more, join in the round, knit the following 4 (4/5/5/6/6) newly cast-on underarm sts to the next marker, now the new BOR marker.

You should have a total of 184 (200/216/248/264/280) sts for the Body on the needles. Continue to work in the round.

BODY

The Body is worked in stockinette stitch until the sweater has either-reached a length of 11.4 (11.4/12.6/14.6/15/15.4) in [29 (29/32/37/38/39) cm], measured from the underarm, or is 3.5 in (9 cm) shorter than desired body length to accommodate ribbing to be added, ending having just worked a Round 1 or Round 5.

RIBBING

Change to US size 4 (3.5 mm) needles.

Rounds 1–28: * K1, p1 *, rep from * to * to end of round.

Round 29: BO all sts in pattern.

SLEEVES

Both Sleeves are worked the same. For the Sleeve, take up the 54 (58/64/72/78/82) formerly held sts using US size 6 (4.0 mm) needles, pick up and knit 4 (4/5/5/6/6) sts from the newly cast-on underarm sts, place m, pick up and knit another 4 (4/5/5/6/6) sts from the newly cast-on underarm sts, and join in the round. The Sleeve is worked in the round from here on; the marker indicates the BOR. You should now have a total of 62 (66/74/82/90/94) sts on the needles.

Work the Sleeve in stockinette stitch in the round, at the same time, in every 18th (18th/12th/10th/8th/8th) round, decrease as follows a total of 4 (4/7/9/11/13) times:

K2tog, work in stockinette stitch to 3 sts before m, skp, k1, slip m.

Work the Sleeve in stockinette stitch in the round until the Sleeve has either reached a length of 15.4 (15.4/15.8/15.8/16.2/16.2) in [39 (39/40/40/41/41) cm] or is 3.5 in (9 cm) shorter than desired Sleeve length to accommodate the sleeve cuff to be added.

SLEEVE CUFF

Change to US size 4 (3.5 mm) needles.

Rounds 1–28: * K1, p1 *, rep from * to * to end of round.

Round 29: BO all sts in pattern.

RIBBED NECKBAND

Using US size 4 (3.5 mm) needles, pick up and knit stitches around the neckline edge at a rate of 4 sts picked up from every 5 sts, for a total of 86 (86/86/106/106/106) neckline sts on the needles; join in the round.

Rounds 1–25: * K1, p1 *, rep from * to * to end of round.

Round 26: BO all stitches.

Fold the bound-off edge to the wrong side and sew it on along the picked up and knitted stitches, creating a double-layered neckband.

FINISHING

Weave in all ends, dampen the sweater, and pull it into the desired shape.

EMMA

CIRCULAR YOKE SWEATER WITH SIMPLE CABLES

SIZES
XS, S, M, L, XL, XXL

Numbers for size XS are listed before the parentheses, numbers for sizes S through XXL within parentheses. If only one number is listed, it applies to all sizes.

Size	Chest Circum- ference	Sleeve Length from Armhole	Garment Length from Armhole
XS	36.2 in (92 cm)	18.9 in (48 cm)	15 in (38 cm)
S	39 in (99 cm)	18.9 in (48 cm)	15 in (38 cm)
M	41.7 in (106 cm)	19.3 in (49 cm)	16.1 in (41 cm)
L	44.9 in (114 cm)	19.3 in (49 cm)	18.1 in (46 cm)
XL	48 in (122 cm)	19.7 in (50 cm)	18.5 in (47 cm)
XXL	50.8 in (129 cm)	19.7 in (50 cm)	18.9 in (48 cm)

MATERIALS AND TOOLS
— We Are Knitters The Meriwool; 100% merino wool; 149 yd (136 m) per 3.5 oz (100 g): Natural White, 7 (7/7/7/8/9) skeins
— Circular knitting needle, US size 10 (6.0 mm), at least 32 in (80 cm) long
— Circular knitting needle, US size 8 (5.0 mm), 24 in (60 cm) long
— If desired, one DPN set each in sizes US 10 (6.0 mm) and US 8 (5.0 mm) for the sleeves
— 17 stitch markers
— Stitch holder or waste yarn

— Cable needle
— Tapestry needle

GAUGE
In stockinette stitch on US size 10 (6.0 mm) needles: 16 sts and 24 rows = 4 x 4 in (10 x 10 cm)

CONSTRUCTION NOTES
The sweater is worked in a circular yoke construction from the top down in one piece in stockinette stitch in the round with eight cables. The circular yoke is divided into eight sections, the increases are first within the cable stitches and next to the cables, later only next to the cables. Neckline and sleeves are finished with a rolled edge; the body is finished with narrow ribbing. The rolled edge is knitted on afterwards. Working steps in the instructions are sometimes different for different sizes; for this reason, all sizes to which a particular step does not apply are marked with "–".

RIBBING
1x1 ribbing: * K1, p1 *, rep from * to * continuously.

STOCKINETTE STITCH
In the round: Knit all sts in all rounds.

CABLE PATTERN
See instructions.

MAKING 2 STITCHES FROM 1 KNITWISE (KFSLB)
Insert the right needle into the next stitch knitwise and pull the working yarn through. However, do not let the just-worked stitch slip off the left needle yet, but slip this stitch purlwise to the right needle.

CONTINUED

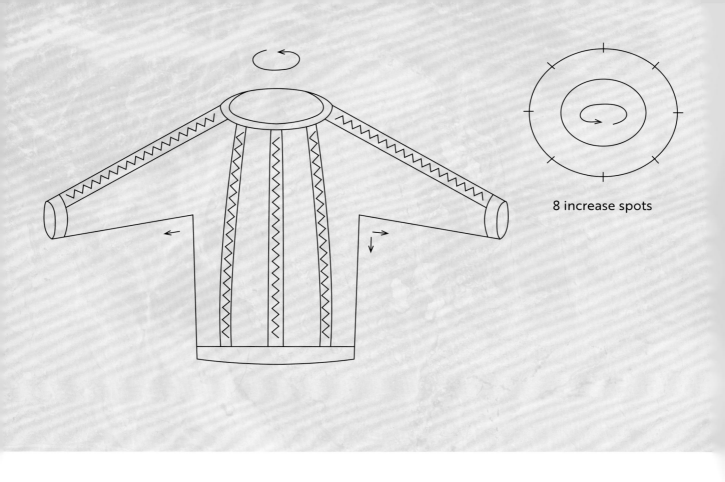

8 increase spots

INSTRUCTIONS

With US 10 (6.0 mm) needles, cast on 64 (64/64/80/80/80) sts, place a BOR marker, and join in the round without twisting.

Round 1: * K1 (1/1/2/2/2), place m, p1, k4, p1, k1 (1/1/2/2/2), place m *, rep from * to * 7 times more, slip BOR marker.

Round 2: * Knit to next m, slip m, p1, k4, p1, knit to next m, slip m *, rep from * to * 7 times more, slip BOR marker.

Round 3: Work the same as Round 2.

Round 4 (increase and cable-crossing round): * Knit to next m, slip m, M1L, p1, hold 2 sts on a cable needle in front of work, knit the next 2 sts, then knit the 2 sts from the cable needle, p1, M1R, knit to next m, slip m *, rep from * to * 7 times more, slip BOR marker. You should now have 80 (80/80/96/96/96) sts on the needles, 10 (10/10/12/12/12) sts for each of the 8 sections.

Rounds 5–7: Work the same as Round 2.

Round 8 (increase round): * Knit to next m, slip m, M1L, p1, k4, p1, M1R, knit to next m, slip m *, rep from * to * 7 times more, slip BOR marker. You

should now have 96 (96/96/112/112/112) sts on the needles, 12 (12/12/14/14/14) sts for each of the 8 sections.

Round 9: Work the same as Round 2.

Round 10 (cable-crossing round): * Knit to next m, slip m, p1, hold 2 sts on a cable needle in front of work, knit the next 2 sts, then knit the 2 sts from the cable needle, p1, knit to next m, slip m *, rep from * to * 7 times more, slip BOR marker.

Round 11: Work the same as Round 2.

Round 12 (increase round): Work the same as Round 8. You should now have 112 (112/112/128/128/128) sts on the needles, 14 (14/14/16/16/16) sts for each of the 8 sections.

Rounds 13–15: Work the same as Round 2.

Round 16 (increase within cable): * Knit to next m, slip m, p1, hold 2 sts on a cable needle in front of work, kfb, k1, then knit the first stitch from the cable needle, work kfb increase into the next stitch from the cable needle, p1, knit to next m, slip m *, rep from * to * 7 times more, slip BOR marker. You should now have 128 (128/128/144/144/144) sts on the needles, 16 (16/16/18/18/18) sts for each of the 8 sections.

Round 17: * Knit to next m, slip m, p1, k6, p1, knit to next m, slip m *, rep from * to * 7 times more, slip BOR marker.

Rounds 18 and 19: Work the same as Round 17.

Round 20 (increase round): * Knit to next m, slip m, M1L, p1, k6, p1, M1R, knit to next m, slip m *, rep from * to * 7 times more, slip BOR marker. You should now have 144 (144/144/160/160/160) sts on the needles, 18 (18/18/20/20/20) sts for each of the 8 sections.

Rounds 21–23: Work the same as Round 17.

Round 24 (increase and cable-crossing round): * Knit to next m, slip m, M1L, p1, hold 3 sts on a cable needle in front of work, knit the next 3 sts, then knit the 3 sts from the cable needle, p1, M1R, knit to next m, slip m *, rep from * to * 7 times more, slip BOR marker. You should now have 160 (160/160/176/176/176) sts on the needles, 20 (20/20/22/22/22) sts for each of the 8 sections.

Rounds 25–27: Work the same as Round 17.

Round 28 (increase round): Work the same as Round 20. You should now have 176 (176/176/192/192/192) sts on the needles, 22 (22/22/24/24/24) sts for each of the 8 sections.

Rounds 29–31: Work the same as Round 17.

Round 32 (increase within cable): * Knit to next m, slip m, p1, hold 3 sts on a cable needle in front of work, kfb, k2, then knit the first 2 sts from the cable needle, work kfb increase into the next stitch from the cable needle, p1, knit to next m, slip m *, rep from * to * 7 times more, slip BOR marker. You should now have 192 (192/192/208/208/208) sts on the needles, 24 (24/24/26/26/26) sts for each of the 8 sections.

Round 33: * Knit to next m, slip m, p1, k8, p1, knit to next m, slip m *, rep from * to * 7 times more, slip BOR marker.

Rounds 34 and 35: Work the same as Round 33.

Round 36 (increase round): * Knit to next m, slip m, M1L, p1, k8, p1, M1R, knit to next m, slip m *, rep from * to * 7 times more, slip BOR marker. You should now have 208 (208/208/224/224/224) sts on the needles, 26 (26/26/28/28/28) sts for each of the 8 sections.

Rounds 37–39: Work the same as Round 33.

Round 40 (increase round): Work the same as Round 36. You should now have 224 (224/224/240/240/240) sts on the needles, 28 (28/28/30/30/30) sts for each of the 8 sections.

Round 41: Work the same as Round 33.

Round 42 (cable-crossing round): * Knit to next m, slip m, p1, hold 4 sts on a cable needle in front of work, knit the next 4 sts, then knit the 4 sts from the cable needle, p1, knit to next m, slip m *, rep from * to * 7 times more, slip BOR marker.

Round 43: Work the same as Round 33.

For size XS: In Round 43, end 4 sts before the BOR marker, and proceed with Sleeve separation round.

All other sizes:

Round 44: Work the same as Round 36. You should now have - (240/240/256/256/256) sts on the needles, - (30/30/32/32/32) sts for each of the 8 sections.

Rounds 45–47: Repeat Round 33 three times.

For size S: In Round 47, end 4 sts before the BOR marker, and proceed with Sleeve separation round.

All other sizes:

Round 48: Work the same as Round 36. You should now have - (-/256/272/272/272) sts on the needles, - (-/32/34/34/34) sts for each of the 8 sections.

Rounds 49–51: Repeat Round 33 three times.

For sizes M and L: In Round 51, end 5 sts before the BOR marker, and proceed with Sleeve separation round.

All other sizes:

Round 52 (increase and cable-crossing round): * Knit to next m, slip m, M1L, p1, hold 4 sts on a cable needle in front of work, knit the next 4 sts, then knit the 4 sts from the cable needle, p1, M1R, knit to next m, slip m *, rep from * to * 7 times more, slip BOR marker. You should now have - (-/-/-/288/288) sts on the needles, - (-/-/-/36/36) sts for each of the 8 sections.

Rounds 53–55: Work the same as Round 33.

For size XL: In Round 55, end 6 sts before BOR marker, and proceed with Sleeve separation round.

Size XXL:

Rounds 56–58: Work the same as Rounds 44–47. You should now have - (-/-/-/-/304) sts on the needles, - (-/-/-/-/38) sts for each of the 8 sections.

Round 59: Work the same as Round 33, but end 6 sts before BOR marker.

SLEEVE SEPARATION ROUND FOR SIZES XS, S, XL, AND XXL

Transfer the next 36 (38/-/-/48/50) sts (Sleeve) including the stitch markers to a stitch holder or a piece of waste yarn for holding, cast on 4 (4/-/-/6/6) new underarm sts, place m, cast on 4 (4/-/-/6/6) new underarm sts, * knit to next m, slip m, p1, k8, p1, knit to next m, slip m *, rep from * to * once more, knit to next m, slip m, p1, k8, p1, k to 4 (4/-/-/6/6) sts before the next m [76 (82/-/-/102/108) sts should have been worked] #, rep from # to # once more. Join in the round, knit the 4 (4/-/-/6/6) newly cast-on sts to the next m; this marker is now the new BOR marker.

You should have a total of 168 (180/-/-/216/228) sts for the Body on the needles, 28 (30/-/-/36/38) sts for each of the 6 sections. Continue to work in the round.

SLEEVE SEPARATION ROUND FOR SIZES M AND L

Transfer the next - (-/42/44/-/-) sts (Sleeve) including the stitch markers to a stitch holder or a piece of waste yarn for holding, cast on - (-/5/5/-/-) new underarm sts, place m, cast on - (-/5/5/-/-) new underarm sts, * knit to next m, slip m, p1, hold 4 sts on a cable needle in front of work, knit the next 4 sts, then knit the 4 sts from the cable needle, p1, knit to next m, slip m *, rep from * to* once more, knit to next m, slip m, p1, hold 4 sts on a cable needle in front of work, knit the next 4 sts, then knit the 4 sts from the cable needle, p1, knit to - (-/5/5/-/-) sts before next m [- (-/86/92/-/-) sts should have been worked] #, rep from # to # once more. Join in the round, knit the - (-/5/5/-/-) newly cast-on sts to the next m; this marker is now the new BOR marker.

You should have a total of - (-/192/204/-/-) sts for the Body on the needles, - (-/32/34/-/-) sts for each of the 6 sections. Continue to work in the round.

BODY

The Body is continued in the already established cable pattern. For this, repeat Rounds 1–10 (as described below) until the sweater has either reached a length of 14.2 (14.2/15.3/17.3/17.7/18.1) in [36 (36/39/44/45/46) cm], measured from the underarm, or is 0.8 in (2 cm) shorter than desired body length to accommodate

ribbing to be added, ending having just worked a Round 7, 8, or 9.

Begin with a Round 3 (7/1/1/5/9).

Rounds 1–9: * Knit to next m, slip m, p1, k8, p1, knit to next m, slip m *, rep from * to * 5 times more, slip BOR marker.

Round 10 (cable-crossing round): * Knit to next m, slip m, p1, hold 4 sts on a cable needle in front of work, knit the next 4 sts, then knit the 4 sts from the cable needle, p1, knit to next m, slip m *, rep from * to * 5 times more, slip BOR marker.

RIBBING

Change to US size 8 (5.0 mm) needles.

Rounds 1–4: * K1, p1 *, rep from * to * to end of round.

Round 5: BO all sts in pattern.

SLEEVES

Both Sleeves are worked the same. For the Sleeve, first take up the 36 (38/42/44/48/50) formerly held sts using US size 10 (6.0 mm) needles, removing the 1st and 3rd markers, so that only the 2nd marker (from the cable) remains, pick up and knit 4 (4/5/5/6/6) sts from the newly cast-on underarm sts, place BOR marker, pick up and knit another 4 (4/5/5/6/6) sts from the newly cast-on underarm sts, and join in the round. The Sleeve is worked in the round from here on. You should now have a total of 44 (46/52/54/60/62) sts on the needles.

The Sleeve is continued in the already established cable pattern. For this, repeat Rounds 1–10 (as de-

scribed below) until the Sleeve has either reached a length of 18.5 (18.5/18.9/18.9/19.3/19.3) in [47 (47/48/48/49/49) cm] measured from the underarm or is 0.4 in (1 cm) shorter than desired sleeve length to accommodate ribbing to be added; at the same time, in every 24th (22nd/20th/18th/16th/14th) round, decrease as follows a total of 3 (4/5/6/7/8) times: K1, k2tog, work in pattern to 3 sts before m, skp, k1, slip m.

Begin with a Round 3 (7/1/1/5/9).

Rounds 1–9: * Knit to next m, slip m, p1, k8, p1, knit to end of round, slip BOR marker.

Round 10 (cable-crossing round): * Knit to next m, slip m, p1, hold 4 sts on a cable needle in front of work, knit the next 4 sts, then knit the 4 sts from the cable needle, p1, knit to end of round, slip BOR marker.

ROLLED SLEEVE EDGE

Change to US size 8 (5.0 mm) needles.

Rounds 1 and 2: Knit all stitches.

Round 3: BO all sts in pattern.

ROLLED NECKLINE EDGE

With US size 8 (5.0 mm) needles, pick up and knit all sts around the neckline edge, which should yield 64 (64/64/80/80/80) sts on the needles, and join in the round.

Rounds 1 and 2: Knit all stitches.

Round 3: BO all sts in pattern.

FINISHING

To finish, weave in all ends, dampen the sweater, and pull it into the desired shape.

MARIE

CIRCULAR YOKE SWEATER WITH SIMPLE EYELET PATTERN

SIZES
XS, S, M, L, XL, XXL

Numbers for size XS are listed before the parentheses, numbers for sizes S through XXL within parentheses. If only one number is listed, it applies to all sizes.

Size	Chest Circum-ference	Sleeve Length from Armhole	Garment Length from Armhole
XS	33.8 in (86 cm)	18.9 in (48 cm)	15 in (38 cm)
S	37 in (94 cm)	18.9 in (48 cm)	15 in (38 cm)
M	41 in (104 cm)	19.3 in (49 cm)	16.1 in (41 cm)
L	44.5 in (113 cm)	19.3 in (49 cm)	18.1 in (46 cm)
XL	48 in (122 cm)	19.7 in (50 cm)	18.5 in (47 cm)
XXL	51.6 in (131 cm)	19.7 in (50 cm)	18.9 in (48 cm)

MATERIALS AND TOOLS
— Lang Yarns Nova; 48% merino wool, 32% camel hair, 20% polyamide; 197 yd (180 m) per 0.9 oz (25 g): #96 Sand, 6 (7/8/9/10/11) skeins
— Circular knitting needle, US size 8 (5.0 mm), at least 32 in (80 cm) long
— Circular knitting needle, US size 7 (4.5 mm), 24 in (60 cm) long
— If desired, one DPN set each in sizes US 8 (5.0 mm) and US 7 (4.5 mm) for the sleeves
— 18 stitch markers
— Stitch holder or waste yarn
— Tapestry needle

GAUGE
In stockinette stitch on US size 8 (5.0 mm) needles: 25 sts and 40 rows = 4 x 4 in (10 x 10 cm)

CONSTRUCTION NOTES
The sweater is worked in a circular yoke construction from the top to the bottom in one piece in the round in stockinette stitch with an eyelet pattern; the circular yoke has a total of 16 increase spots. The ribbed neckband is knitted afterwards. All edges of the sweater are finished in garter stitch. Omitting the eyelet pattern produces a plain basic sweater with circular yoke, which is also suitable as a unisex garment. First, the same number of stitches is cast on for all sizes; only the increase repeats are different. For this reason, the instructions sometimes contain different steps for different sizes. All sizes to which a particular step does not apply are marked with "-".

STOCKINETTE STITCH
In the round: Knit all sts in all rounds.

GARTER STITCH
Garter stitch in the round: Alternate knit 1 round, purl 1 round.

EYELET PATTERN
See instructions.

CONTINUED

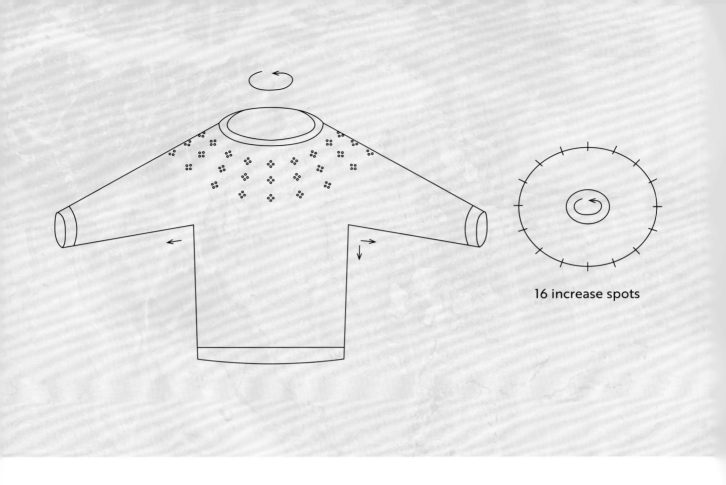

16 increase spots

INSTRUCTIONS

With US size 8 (5.0 mm) needles, cast on 96 (96/128/128/128/128) sts. Place a BOR marker and join in the round without twisting.

Round 1: * K6 (6/8/8/8/8), place m *, rep from * to * 15 times more, slip BOR marker.

Round 2: Knit all stitches, slipping the markers when you come to them.

Round 3 (increase round): * K1, M1L, knit to 1 st before next m, M1R, k1, slip m *, rep from * to * 15 times more. You should now have 128 (128/160/160/160 160) sts on the needles, 8 (8/10/10/10/10) sts for each of the 16 sections.

Round 4: Work the same as Round 2.

Round 5 (eyelet round): * K3 (3/4/4/4/4), k2tog, yo, k3 (3/4/4/4/4), slip m *, rep from * to * 15 times more, slip BOR marker.

Round 6: Work the same as Round 2.

Round 7 (eyelet round): * K2 (2/3/3/3/3), k2tog, yo, k1, yo, skp, k1 (1/2/2/2/2), slip m *, rep from * to * 15 times more, slip BOR marker.

Round 8: Work the same as Round 2.

Round 9 (eyelet round): Work the same as Round 5.

Round 10: Work the same as Round 2.

Round 11 (increase round): Work the same as Round 3. You should now have 160 (160/192/192/192/192) sts on the needles, 10 (10/12/12/12/12) sts for each of the 16 sections.

Rounds 12–18: Work the same as Round 2.

Round 19 (increase round): Work the same as Round 3. You should now have 192 (192/224/224/224/224) sts on the needles, 12 (12/14/14/14/14) sts for each of the 16 sections.

Round 20: Work the same as Round 2.

Round 21 (eyelet round): * K5 (5/6/6/6/6), k2tog, yo, k5 (5/6/6/6/6), slip m *, rep from * to * 15 times more, slip BOR marker.

Round 22: Work the same as Round 2.

Round 23 (eyelet round): * K4 (4/5/5/5/5), k2tog, yo, k1, yo, skp, k3 (3/4/4/4/4), slip m *, rep from * to * 15 times more, slip BOR marker.

Round 24: Work the same as Round 2.

Round 25 (eyelet round): Work the same as Round 21.

Round 26: Work the same as Round 2.

Round 27 (increase round): Work the same as Round 3. You should now have 224 (224/256/256/256/256) sts on the needles, 14 (14/16/16/16/16) sts for each of the 16 sections.

Rounds 28–34: Work the same as Round 2.

Round 35: Work the same as Round 3. You should now have 256 (256/288/288/288/288) sts on the needles, 16 (16/18/18/18/18) sts for each of the 16 sections.

Round 36: Work the same as Round 2.

Round 37 (eyelet round): * K7 (7/8/8/8/8), k2tog, yo, k7 (7/8/8/8/8), slip m *, rep from * to * 15 times more, slip BOR marker.

Round 38: Work the same as Round 2.

Round 39 (eyelet round): * K6 (6/7/7/7/7), k2tog, yo, k1, yo, skp, k5 (5/6/6/6/6), slip m *, rep from * to * 15 times more, slip BOR marker.

Round 40: Work the same as Round 2.

Round 41 (eyelet round): Work the same as Round 37.

Round 42: Work the same as Round 2.

Round 43 (increase round): Work the same as Round 3. You should now have 288 (288/320/320/320/320) sts on the needles, 18 (18/20/20/20/20) sts for each of the 16 sections.

Rounds 44–50: Work the same as Round 2.

Round 51: Work the same as Round 3. You should now have 320 (320/352/352/352/352) sts on the needles, 20 (20/22/22/22/22) sts for each of the 16 sections.

Round 52: Work the same as Round 2.

Round 53 (eyelet round): * K9 (9/10/10/10/10), k2tog, yo, k9 (9/10/10/10/10), slip m *, rep from * to * 15 times more, slip BOR marker.

Round 54: Work the same as Round 2.

Round 55 (eyelet round): * K8 (8/9/9/9/9), k2tog, yo, k1, yo, skp, k7 (7/8/8/8/8), slip m *, rep from * to * 15 times more, slip BOR marker.

Round 56: Work the same as Round 2.

Round 57 (eyelet round): Work the same as Round 53.

Round 58: Work the same as Round 2.

For size XS: End after having completed Round 58, and proceed with Sleeve separation round.

All other sizes:

Round 59 (increase round): Work the same as Round 3. You should now have - (352/384/384/384/384) sts on the needles, - (22/24/24/24/24) sts for each of the 16 sections.

Rounds 60–66: Work the same as Round 2.

For sizes S and M: End after having completed Round 66, and proceed with Sleeve separation round.

All other sizes:

Round 67 (increase round): Work the same as Round 3. You should now have - (-/-/416/416/416) sts on the needles, - (-/-/26/26/26) sts for each of the 16 sections.

Round 68: Work the same as Round 2.

Round 69 (eyelet round): * K - (-/-/12/12/12), k2tog, k - (-/-/12/12/12), slip m *, rep from * to * 15 times more, slip BOR marker.

Round 70: Work the same as Round 2.

Round 71 (eyelet round): * K - (-/-/11/11/11), k2tog, yo, k1, yo, skp, k - (-/-/10/10/10), slip m *, rep from * to * 15 times more, slip BOR marker.

Round 72: Work the same as Round 2.

Round 73 (eyelet round): Work the same as Round 69.

Round 74: Work the same as Round 2.

For size L: End after having completed Round 74, and proceed with Sleeve separation round.

All other sizes:

Round 75 (increase round): Work the same as Round 3. You should now have - (-/-/-/448/448) sts on the needles, - (-/-/-/28/28) sts for each of the 16 sections.

Rounds 76–82: Work the same as Round 2.

For size XL: End after having completed Round 82, and proceed with Sleeve separation round.

For size XXL:

Round 83 (increase round): Work the same as Round 3. You should now have - (-/-/-/-/480) sts on the needles, - (-/-/-/-/30) sts for each of the 16 sections.

Round 84: Work the same as Round 2.

Round 85 (eyelet round): * K - (-/-/-/-/14), k2tog, k - (-/-/-/-/14), slip m *, rep from * to * 15 times more, slip BOR marker.

Round 86: Work the same as Round 2.

Round 87 (eyelet round): * K - (-/-/-/-/13), k2tog, yo, k1, yo, skp, k - (-/-/-/-/12), slip m *, rep from * to * 15 times more, slip BOR marker.

Round 88: Work the same as Round 2.

Round 89 (eyelet round): Work the same as Round 85.

Round 90: Work the same as Round 2.

You should have 320 (352/384/416/448/480) sts on the needles, 20 (22/24/26/28/30) sts for each of the 16 sections.

SLEEVE SEPARATION ROUND

* Transfer the next 60 (66/72/78/84/90) sts (Sleeve) to a stitch holder or a piece of waste yarn for holding, cast on 3 (3/4/4/5/5) new underarm sts, place m, cast on 3 (3/4/4/5/5) new underarm sts, k100 (110/120/130/140/150) *, rep from * to* once more, join in the round, knit the 3 (3/4/4/5/5) newly cast-on underarm sts to next m; this marker is now the new BOR marker. You should have a total of 212 (232/256/276/300/320) sts for the Body on the needles; continue to work in the round.

BODY

The Body is worked in stockinette stitch until the sweater has either reached a length of 14.2 (14.2/15.3/17.3/17.7/18.1) in [36 (36/39/44/45/46) cm], measured from the underarm, or is 0.8 in (2 cm) shorter than desired body length to accommodate ribbing to be added.

GARTER STITCH HEM

Change to US size 7 (4.5 mm) needles.

Round 1: Purl all stitches.

Round 2: Knit all stitches.

Rounds 3 and 4: Work the same as Rounds 1 and 2.

Round 5: Work the same as Round 1.

Round 6: BO all stitches knitwise.

SLEEVES

Both Sleeves are worked the same. To work the Sleeve, first take up the formerly held 60 (66/72/78/84/90) sts using US size 8 (5.0 mm) needles, pick up and knit 3 (3/4/4/5/5) sts from the newly cast-on underarm sts, place m, pick up and knit another 3 (3/4/4/5/5) sts from the newly cast-on underarm sts, and join in the round. The Sleeve is worked in the round from here on; the marker indicates the beginning of the round. You should now have a total of 66 (72/80/86/94/100) sts on the needles.

Work the Sleeve in stockinette stitch, at the same time, in every 18th (18th/12th/10th/8th/8th) round, decrease as follows a total of 4 (4/7/9/11/13) times:

K1, k2tog, knit to 3 sts before m, skp, k1, slip m.

Work in stockinette stitch until the Sleeve has either reached a length of 18.1 (18.1/18.5/18.5/18.9/18.9) in [46 (46/47/47/48/48) cm] or is 0.8 in (2 cm) shorter than desired sleeve length to accommodate the sleeve cuff to be added.

SLEEVE CUFF

Change to US size 7 (4.5 mm) needles.

Round 1: Purl all stitches.

Round 2: Knit all stitches.

Rounds 3 and 4: Work the same as Rounds 1 and 2.

Round 5: Work the same as Round 1.

Round 6: BO all stitches knitwise.

NECKBAND

With US size 7 (4.5 mm) needles, pick up and knit stitches from the neckline edge at a rate of 4 (4/3/3/4/4) sts picked up from every 4 sts, for a total of 96 (96/96/96/128/128) sts on the needles, then join in the round.

Round 1: Purl all stitches.

Round 2: Knit all stitches.

Rounds 3 and 4: Work the same as Rounds 1 and 2.

Round 5: Work the same as Round 1.

Round 6: BO all stitches knitwise.

FINISHING

To finish, weave in all ends, dampen the sweater, and pull it into the desired shape.

ELAINE

NARROW JACKET WITH CIRCULAR YOKE AND SHORT SLEEVES IN PATTERNED GARTER STITCH

SIZES
XS, S, M, L, XL, XXL

Numbers for size XS are listed before the parentheses, numbers for sizes S through XXL within parentheses. If only one number is listed, it applies to all sizes.

Size	Chest Circum- ference	Sleeve Length from Armhole	Garment Length from Armhole
XS	31.5 in (80 cm)	4.7 in (12 cm)	10.2 in (26 cm)
S	34.6 in (88 cm)	4.7 in (12 cm)	10.6 in (27 cm)
M	38.6 in (98 cm)	5.1 in (13 cm)	11.4 in (29 cm)
L	42.5 in (108 cm)	5.1 in (13 cm)	12.2 in (31 cm)
XL	45.7 in (116 cm)	5.5 in (14 cm)	12.6 in (32 cm)
XXL	48.8 in (124 cm)	5.5 in (14 cm)	13.0 in (33 cm)

MATERIALS AND TOOLS
— Sandnes Garn Line; 53% cotton, 33% viscose, 14% linen; 120 yd (110 m) per 1.75 oz (50 g): #1099 Black, 6 (7/8/9/10/11) skeins
— Circular knitting needle, US size 6 (4.0 mm), at least 32 in (80 cm) long
— Circular knitting needle, US size 4 (3.5 mm), 24 in (60 cm) long
— If desired, one DPN set each in sizes US 6 (4.0 mm) and US 4 (3.5 mm) for the sleeves
— 2 stitch markers
— Stitch holder or waste yarn
— Tapestry needle

GAUGE
In garter stitch on US size 6 (4.0 mm) needles: 20 sts and 36 rows = 4 x 4 in (10 x 10 cm)

CONSTRUCTION NOTES
This narrow, short cardigan with circular yoke is worked from the top to the bottom in one piece in garter stitch in turned rows. In the top part of the yoke, a stripe pattern is created by working a few rows in stockinette stitch between garter ridges. The jacket is meant to be worn with open fronts. The yoke has a total of 20 evenly spaced increase spots. Ribbed neckband and Front bands are knitted on afterwards; both are worked in 1x1 ribbing. The short sleeves are finished with a rolled edge.

RIBBING
1x1 ribbing: * K1, p1 *, rep from * to * continuously.

GARTER STITCH
In rows: Knit all sts in RS and WS rows.
In rounds: Alternate knit 1 round, purl 1 round.

STOCKINETTE STITCH
In rows: Knit on RS, purl on WS.

KNIT INTO THE FRONT AND BACK OF STITCH (KFB)
Knit into the next stitch as normal, but do not slide it off the left needle yet. Insert the right needle into the back loop of the same stitch from right to left. Wrap the yarn around the needle counterclockwise and pull the yarn through the stitch. Now allow the old stitch to slip from the left needle. Two stitches have been made from one (one stitch increased).

CONTINUED

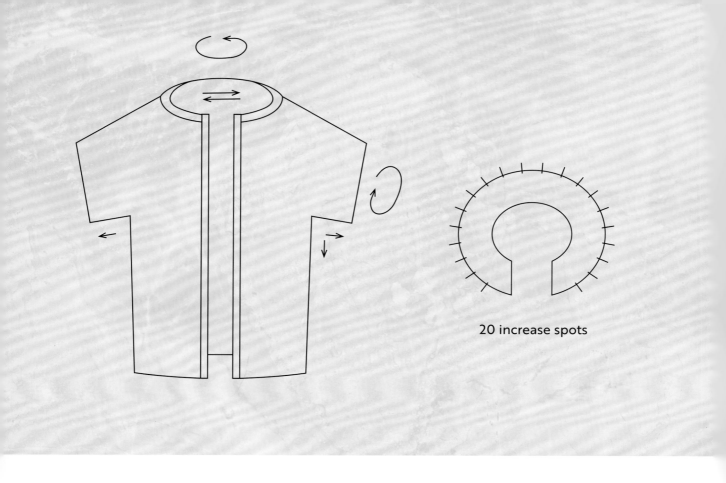

20 increase spots

INSTRUCTIONS

With US size 6 (4.0 mm) needles, cast on 100 (100/100/110/110/110) sts.

Row 1 (WS): K1, p4, place m, p 90 (90/90/100/100/100), place m, p4, k1.

Row 2 (RS): Knit all stitches, slipping the markers as you come to them.

Row 3 (WS): K1, purl to last stitch, slipping the markers as you come to them, k1.

Rows 4–7: Work the same as Rows 2 and 3.

Rows 8–13: Knit all stitches, slipping the markers as you come to them.

Row 14 (RS, increase row): K5, slip m, k2, * kfb, k3 (3/3/4/4/4), kfb, k4 *, rep from * to * 8 times more, kfb, k3 (3/3/4/4/4), kfb, k2, slip m, k5. You should now have 120 (120/120/130/130/130) sts on the needles.

Rows 15–25: Work the same as Rows 3–13.

Row 26 (RS, increase row): K5, slip m, k3, * kfb, k4 (4/4/5/5/5), kfb, k5 *, rep from * to * 8 times more, kfb, k4 (4/4/5/5/5), kfb, k2, slip m, k5. You should now have 140 (140/140/150/150/150) sts on the needles.

Rows 27–37: Work the same as Rows 3–13.

Row 38 (RS, increase row): K5, slip m, k3, * kfb, k5 (5/5/6/6/6), kfb, k6 *, rep from * to * 8 times more, kfb, k5 (5/5/6/6/6), kfb, k3, slip m, k5. You should now have 160 (160/160/170/170/170) sts on the needles.

Rows 39–49: Work the same as Rows 3–13.

Row 50 (RS, increase row): K5, slip m, k4, * kfb, k6 (6/6/7/7/7), kfb, k7 *, rep from * to * 8 times more, kfb, k6 (6/6/7/7/7), kfb, k3, slip m, k5. You should now have 180 (180/180/190/190/190) sts on the needles.

Rows 51–61: Work the same as Rows 3–13.

Row 62 (RS, increase row): K5, slip m, k4, * kfb, k7 (7/7/8/8/8), kfb, k8 *, rep from * to * 8 times more, kfb, k7 (7/7/8/8/8), kfb, k4, slip m, k5. You should now have 200 (200/200/210/210/210) sts on the needles.

Row 63 (WS): Knit all stitches, removing all stitch markers as you come to them.

For size XS: End after having completed Row 63, and proceed with separating row for sleeve division.

All other sizes:

Rows 64–75: Knit all stitches.

Row 76 (RS, increase row): K5, slip m, k5, *kfb, k - (8/8/9/9/9), kfb, k9 *, rep from * to * 8 times more, kfb, k - (8/8/9/9/9), kfb, k4, slip m, k5. You should now have - (220/220/230/230/230) sts on the needles.

Row 77 (WS): Knit all stitches.

For size S: End after having completed Row 77, and proceed with separating row for sleeve division.

All other sizes:

Rows 78–89: Knit all stitches.

Row 90 (RS, increase row): K5, slip m, k5, * kfb, k - (-/9/10/10/10), kfb, k10 *, rep from * to * 8 times more, kfb, k - (-/9/10/10/10), kfb, k5, slip m, k5. You should now have - (-/240/250/250/250) sts on the needles.

Row 91 (WS): Knit all stitches.

For size M: End after having completed Row 91, and proceed with separating row for sleeve division.

All other sizes:

Rows 92–103: Knit all stitches.

Row 104 (RS, increase row): K5, slip m, k6, * kfb, k11, kfb, k11 *, rep from * to * 8 times more, kfb, k11, kfb, k5, slip m, k5. You should now have - (-/-/270/270/270) sts on the needles.

Row 105 (WS): Knit all stitches.

For size L: End after having completed Row 105, and proceed with separating row for sleeve division.

All other sizes:

Rows 106–117: Knit all stitches.

Row 118 (RS, increase row): K5, slip m, k6, * kfb, k12, kfb, k12 *, rep from * to * 8 times more, kfb, k12, kfb, k6, slip m, k5. You should now have - (-/-/-/290/290) sts on the needles.

Row 119 (WS): Knit all stitches.

For size XL: End after having completed Row 119, and proceed with Separating row for sleeve division.

All other sizes:

Rows 120–131: Knit all stitches.

Row 132 (RS, increase row): K5, slip m, k7, *kfb, k13, kfb, k13*, rep from * to * 8 times more, kfb, k13, kfb, k6, slip m, k5. You should now have - (-/-/-/-/310) sts on the needles.

Row 133 (WS): Knit all stitches.

You should now have 200 (220/240/270/290/310) sts on the needles.

SEPARATING ROW

K25 (29/32/37/40/44), transfer the next 40 (42/46/51/55/57) sts (Sleeve) to a stitch holder or a piece of waste yarn for holding, cast on 5 (5/7/7/8/8) new underarm sts, place m, cast on 5 (5/7/7/8/8) new underarm sts, k70 (78/84/94/100/108), transfer the next 40 (42/46/51/55/57) sts (Sleeve) to a stitch holder or a piece of waste yarn for holding, cast on 5 (5/7/7/8/8) new underarm sts, place m, cast on 5 (5/7/7/8/8) new underarm sts, k25 (29/32/37/40/44).

You should have a total of 140 (156/176/196/212/228) sts for the Body on the needles.

BODY

The Body is worked in turned rows in garter stitch until the cardigan has either reached a length of 10 (10.4/11.2/12/12.4/12.8) in [25.5 (26.5/28.5/30.5/31.5/32.5) cm], measured from the underarm, or is 0.2 in (0.5 cm) shorter than desired Body length to accommodate rolled hem to be added.

ROLLED HEM

Change to US 4 (3.5 mm) needles.

Row 1 (RS): Knit all stitches.

Row 2 (WS): K1, purl to last stitch, k1.

Rows 3 and 4: Work the same as Rows 1 and 2.

Row 5: BO all sts in pattern.

SLEEVES

Both Sleeves are worked the same. For each Sleeve, first take up the 40 (42/46/51/55/57) formerly held sts using US size 6 (4.0 mm) needles, pick up and knit 5 (5/7/7/8/8) sts from the newly cast-on underarm sts, place m, pick up and knit another 5 (5/7/7/8/8) sts from the newly cast-on underarm sts, then join in the round. The Sleeve is worked in the round from here on; the marker indicates the BOR. You should now have a total of 50 (52/60/65/71/73) sts on the needles.

Work the Sleeve in garter stitch in the round until the Sleeve has either reached a length of 4.5 (4.5/4.9/4.9/5.3/5.3) in [12 (12/13/13/14/14) cm] or is 0.2 in (0.5 cm) shorter than desired sleeve length to accommodate rolled edge sleeve finishing to be added.

ROLLED EDGE SLEEVE FINISH

Change to US size 4 (3.5 mm) needles.

Rounds 1–4: Knit all stitches.

Round 5: BO all sts in pattern.

RIBBED NECKBAND

With US 4 (3.5 mm) needles, pick up and knit stitches from the neckline edge at a rate of 5 sts picked up from every 6 sts, for a total of 83 (83/83/91/91/91) sts picked up, then work 7 rows of 1x1 ribbing, always knitting the last stitch of every row regardless of ribbing sequence. In Row 8, bind off all sts in pattern.

FRONT BANDS

Both Fronts are finished with a Front Band in 1x1 ribbing. For this, with US size 4 (3.5 mm) needles, pick up and knit stitches from the edge at a rate of 2 sts picked up from every 3 rows, and work 9 rows in 1x1 ribbing, always knitting the last stitch of every row regardless of ribbing sequence. In Row 10, bind off all sts in pattern.

FINISHING

To finish, weave in all ends, dampen the cardigan, and pull it into the desired shape.

CHAPTER 4

In addition to the traditional constructions covered in the first three chapters, there are many other construction options that include a wide variety of shapes and techniques. In some of them, the design of the sleeve cap is combined with modern techniques, eliminating the need for seaming. Others feature a completely freestyled construction, such as Allegra, in which the contrasting-color lace strips running from the neckline over the length of the sleeve are worked first.

This chapter also features a number of designs with dropped shoulders, either with straight or slanted sleeve top, depending on the construction.

Before embarking on a project, it is well worth the effort to study the schematics as well as to read through the construction notes, which give a short overview of the general construction. This is the largest chapter, containing nine designs, three of them cardigans.

LET'S GET STARTED

STEFANIE

SWEATER IN SEED STITCH WITH CONTRASTING COLOR BLOCKS

SIZES

XS/S, M/L, XL/XXL

Numbers for size XS/S are listed before the parentheses, numbers for sizes M/L and XL/XXL within parentheses. If only one number is listed, it applies to all sizes.

Size	Chest Circum-ference	Sleeve Length from Armhole	Garment Length from Armhole
XS/S	39.4 in (100 cm)	18.5 in (47 cm)	15.7 in (40 cm)
M/L	45.3 in (115 cm)	18.5 in (47 cm)	16.5 in (42 cm)
XL/XXL	51.2 in (130 cm)	18.5 in (47 cm)	17.3 in (44 cm)

MATERIALS AND TOOLS

— Lang Yarns Wooladdicts Fire; 98% extrafine merino wool, 2% polyester; 82 yd (75 m) per 3.5 oz (100 g): #94 White, 5 (6/7) skeins; and #03 Gray, 1 (2/2) skeins
— Circular knitting needle, US size 17 (12.0 mm), 32 in (80 cm) long
— Circular knitting needle, US size 15 (10.0 mm), 32 in (80 cm) long
— Tapestry needle
— Stitch marker

GAUGE

In seed stitch on US size 17 (12.0 mm) needles: 8 sts and 12 rows = 4 x 4 in (10 x 10 cm)

CONSTRUCTION NOTES

This sweater is worked from the bottom up in the round in seed stitch up to the armholes, then Front and Back are worked separately in turned rows. Shoulder seams are joined using the three-needle bind-off method. The Sleeves and the ribbed Neckband are directly knitted on afterwards.

COLOR KEY

Color 1 = White
Color 2 = Gray

SEED STITCH IN ROUNDS

Round 1: * P1, k1 *, rep from * to * to end of round.
Round 2: * K1, p1 *, rep from * to * to end of round.
Repeat Rounds 1 and 2 all the time.

SEED STITCH IN ROWS FOR EVEN STITCH COUNTS

Row 1: * P1, k1 *, rep from * to * to end of row.
Row 2: * K1, p1 *, rep from * to * to end of row.
Repeat Rows 1 and 2 all the time.

SEED STITCH IN ROWS FOR ODD STITCH COUNTS

Row 1: * P1, k1 *, rep from * to * to end of round.
Row 2: Work the same as Row 1.
Repeat Rows 1 and 2 all the time.

CONTINUED

Model is
wearing size M/L

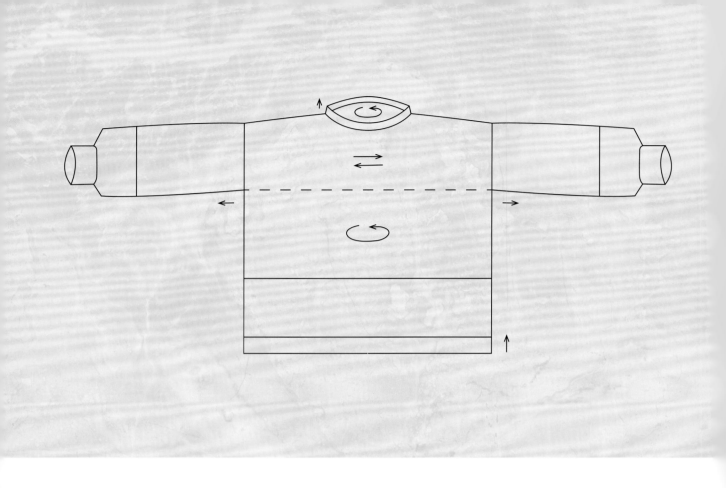

INSTRUCTIONS

With US size 15 (10.0 mm) needles and Color 2, cast on 80 (92/104) sts. Place BOR marker, join in the round, and work ribbing as follows:

Rounds 1–7: * K1, p1 *, rep from * to * to end of round, slip BOR marker.

Now, change to US size 17 (12.0 mm) needles, and continue in seed stitch as follows:

Round 8: * P1, k1 *, rep from * to * to end of round, slip BOR marker.

Round 9: * K1, p1 *, rep from * to * to end of round, slip BOR marker.

Rounds 10–15: Rep Rounds 8 and 9 another 3 times.

Change to Color 1, and continue as follows:

Round 16: Knit all sts, slip BOR marker.

Round 17: Work the same as Round 8.

Round 18: Work the same as Round 9.

Repeat Rounds 17 and 18 until the piece has reached a height of 15.8 (16.5/17.3) in [40 (42/44) cm], measured from the cast-on edge. From here on, continue Back and Front

separately in turned rows, each one over 40 (46/52) sts.

BACK

Rows 1–20: Work all sts in seed stitch, ending having just completed a RS row.

For sizes XL/XXL: Work an additional 4 rows in seed stitch.

Row 21 (RS): Work 12 (15/17) sts in seed stitch, BO the next 16 (16/18) sts in pattern, work 12 (15/17) sts in seed stitch. Transfer the 12 (15/17) shoulder sts each to a stitch holder or a piece of waste yarn for holding.

FRONT

Rows 1–16: Work all sts in seed stitch, beginning with a RS row.

For sizes XL/XXL: Work an additional 4 rows in seed stitch.

Row 17 (RS): Work 15 (18/20) sts in seed stitch, bind off 10 (10/12) sts in pattern, work 15 (18/20) sts in seed stitch.

RIGHT FRONT

Row 18 (WS): Work in seed stitch to last 3 sts of this row, work a single right-leaning decrease, keeping in seed stitch pattern (either k2tog or p2tog), k1. 14 (17/19) sts remain on the needles.

Row 19 (RS): K1, work a single left-leaning decrease, keeping in seed stitch pattern (either ssk or ssp); work in seed stitch to end of row. 13 (16/18) sts remain on the needles.

Row 20 (WS): Work the same as Row 18. 12 (15/17) sts remain on the needles.

Row 21 (RS): Work all sts in seed stitch.

Take up the formerly held sts of the Back right shoulder, and join them with the sts of the Front left shoulder using the three-needle bind-off method.

LEFT FRONT

Row 18 (WS): K1, work a single left-leaning decrease, keeping in seed stitch pattern (either ssk or ssp); work in seed stitch to end of row. 14 (17/19) sts remain on the needles.

Row 19 (RS): Work in seed stitch to last 3 sts of this row, work a single right-leaning decrease, keeping in seed stitch pattern (either k2tog or p2tog), k1. 13 (16/18) sts remain on the needles.

Row 20 (WS): Work the same as Row 18. 12 (15/17) sts remain on the needles.

Row 21 (RS): Work all sts in seed stitch.

Take up the formerly held sts of the Back left shoulder, and join them with the sts of the Front left shoulder using the three-needle bind-off method.

RIBBED NECKBAND

With US size 15 (10.0 mm) needles and Color 1, pick up stitches from the bound-off neckline edge at a rate of 1:1 on straight sections and 4 sts picked up from every 5 sts on slanted sections, making sure that the total number of stitches picked up is even. Place BOR marker, join in the round, and work ribbing as follows:

Rounds 1–5: * K1, p1 *, rep from * to * to end of round, slip BOR marker.

Round 6: BO all stitches in pattern.

SLEEVES

Both Sleeves are worked the same. Using US size 17 (12.0 mm) needles and Color 1, pick up and knit 36 (36/42) sts, evenly spaced around the armhole edge, place a BOR marker, and join in the round without twisting. Work in seed stitch until the Sleeve has reached a length of 13.8 in (35 cm). Change to Color 2, knit 1 round, then work 8 rounds in seed stitch.

SLEEVE CUFF

Change to US size 15 (10.0 mm) needles.

Round 1: * P1, work a single right-leaning decrease, keeping in seed stitch pattern (either k2tog or p2tog) *, rep from * to * to end of round, slip BOR marker.

Rounds 2–9: * P1, k1 *, rep from * to * to end of round, slip BOR marker.

Round 10: BO all sts in pattern.

FINISHING

Weave in all ends, dampen the sweater, and pull it into the desired shape.

ELISE

BOATNECK SWEATER WITH EXTRA-LONG CUFFS

SIZES
XS, S, M, L, XL, XXL

Numbers for size XS are listed before the parentheses, numbers for sizes S through XXL within parentheses. If only one number is listed, it applies to all sizes.

Size	Chest Circum-ference	Sleeve Length from Armhole	Garment Length from Armhole
XS	37.8 in (96 cm)	17.7 in (45 cm)	16.5 in (42 cm)
S	39.4 in (100 cm)	18.1 in (46 cm)	16.9 in (43 cm)
M	41 in (104 cm)	18.1 in (46 cm)	17.7 in (45 cm)
L	43.3 in (110 cm)	18.5 in (47 cm)	17.7 in (45 cm)
XL	48.8 in (124 cm)	18.9 in (48 cm)	18.5 in (47 cm)
XXL	52 in (132 cm)	19.3 in (49 cm)	18.5 in (47 cm)

MATERIALS AND TOOLS
— Lamana Como Tweed; 100% super-fine merino wool; 131 yd (120 m) per 0.9 oz (25 g): #57T Marble, 8 (9/10/10/12/13) skeins
— Circular knitting needle, US size 6 (4.0 mm), 32 in (80 cm) long
— If desired, a DPN set in US size 4 (3.5 mm) for the sleeves
— Tapestry needle
— 2 stitch markers

GAUGE
In stockinette stitch on US size 6 (4.0 mm) needles: 21 sts and 35 rows = 4 x 4 in (10 x 10 cm)

CONSTRUCTION NOTES
The sweater is worked from the top to the bottom. First, Front and Back are worked separately in turned rows. Under the arm, pieces are joined and continued in the round down to the hem ribbing. Purl stitch columns at the sides of the body create a false-seam look. The Sleeves are knitted on at the end, with sleeve stitches picked up around the armhole.

RIBBING
1x1 ribbing: * K1, p1 *, rep from * to * continuously.

STOCKINETTE STITCH
In rows: Knit on RS, purl on WS.
In the round: Knit all sts in all rounds.

SELVEDGE STITCHES
In RS and WS rows, slip first/last stitch as indicated purlwise with yarn in front of work (= selv st).

CONTINUED

Model is
wearing size L

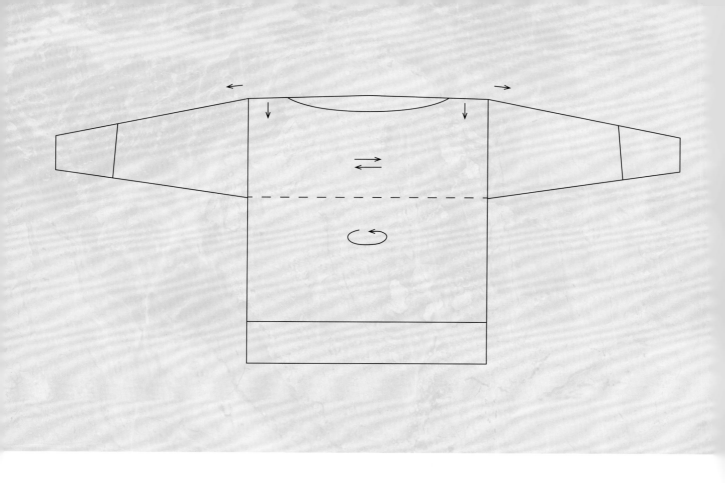

INSTRUCTIONS

With US size 6 (4.0 mm) needles, cast on 101 (105/109/115/129/139) sts for the Front, and work the Front as follows:

Row 1 (WS): * K1, p1 *, rep from * to * to last stitch, k1.

Row 2 (RS): K1, * k1, p1 *, rep from * to * to last 2 sts, k2.

Row 3 (WS): Work the same as Row 1.

Rows 4–9: Repeat Rows 2 and 3 another 3 times.

Row 10 (RS): Knit all stitches.

Row 11 (WS): K1, purl to last stitch, k1.

Repeat Rows 10 and 11 until the piece has reached a length of 7.1 (7.5/7.9/ 7.9/8.3/8.7) in [18 (19/20/20/21/22) cm], ending having just completed a WS row. Transfer all stitches to stitch holders or a piece of waste yarn, but do not break the working yarn; the Back will be worked next.

Pick up and knit the first 27 (29/30/ 32/39/44) sts from the cast-on edge, cast on 47 (47/49/51/51/51) sts using backwards cast-on, then pick up and knit the last 27 (29/30/32/39/44) sts from the cast-on edge. This yields a total of 101 (105/109/115/129/139) sts.

Now, work the Back the same as the Front, ending having just completed a WS row, then break the working yarn on this piece.

Take up the formerly held sts again. Using the working yarn previously left hanging, knit all sts, cast on 1 st using backwards cast-on, knit the sts of the Back, cast on 1 st using backwards cast-on, place a BOR marker, and join in the round without twisting. You should now have 204 (212/220/ 232/260/280) sts on the needles.

Row 1: * Knit to 1 st before next m, p1, slip m *; rep from * to* once more.

Repeat Row 1 until the sweater has either reached a length of 13.4 (13.8/14.6/14.6/15.4/15.4) in [34 (35/37/37/39/39) cm], measured from the underarm, or is 3.1 in (8 cm) shorter than desired Body length to accommodate ribbing to be added. During the last row, end 2 sts before the BOR marker.

RIBBING

First, the ribbing section is divided into Front and Back, then both halves are worked separately, one after another, but the same way.

In the following setup round, stitches are crossed to the right and decreased at the same time.

Setup round: Remove m; insert the right needle into the 3rd st on the left needle and pull the working yarn through for a knit stitch, leaving the old stitch on the left needle. Knit the preceding 1st and 2nd st together, and let the resulting stitch and the previously retained 3rd st slip off the left needle. Knit to 2 sts before m; insert the right needle into the 3rd st on the left needle, and pull the working yarn through for a knit stitch, leaving the old stitch on the left needle.Knit the preceding 1st and 2nd st together, and let the resulting stitch and the previously retained 3rd st slip off the left needle. Knit to last stitch of this row, selv st.

The sts for the Front ribbing can be placed aside for the time being; the Back ribbing will be worked first. Front and Back ribbing each have 101 (105/109/115/129/139) sts.

Row 1 (WS): * K1, p1 *, rep from * to * to last stitch, selv st.

Row 2 (RS): K1, * k1, p1 *, rep from * to * to last 2 sts, k1, selv st.

Repeat Rows 1 and 2 until the ribbing has reached a length of 3.1 in (8 cm), ending having just completed a WS row. In the following RS row, bind off all sts in pattern. Work the Front ribbing the same way.

SLEEVES

Both Sleeves are worked the same. Pick up and knit stitches around the armhole at a rate of 3 sts picked up from every 4 sts, making sure the total number of stitches picked up is an even number. Place a BOR marker, and join in the round.

Work the Sleeve in stockinette stitch, at the same time, in every 9th row, decrease as follows a total of 11 times: K2tog, work in pattern to 3 sts before m, skp, p1, slip m.

Work the Sleeve in stockinette stitch in the round until the sleeve has either reached a length of 9.7 (10.1/10.1/10.5/10.9/11.3) in [25 (26/26/27/28/29) cm] or is 8 in (20 cm) shorter than desired sleeve length to accommodate ribbing to be added.

SLEEVE CUFF

Work 1x1 ribbing, at the same time continuing to work sleeve tapering decreases in every 9th row as described above. When the ribbing has reached a length of 8 in (20 cm), bind off all sts in pattern.

FINISHING

Weave in all ends, dampen the sweater, and pull it into the desired shape.

IRMA

BASIC SWEATER WITH DEEP, ROUND NECKLINE

SIZES
XS, S, M, L, XL, XXL

Numbers for size XS are listed before the parentheses, numbers for sizes S through XXL within parentheses. If only one number is listed, it applies to all sizes.

Size	Chest Circum-ference	Sleeve Length from Armhole	Garment Length from Armhole
XS	37.4 in (95 cm)	18.9 in (48 cm)	13.8 in (35 cm)
S	39 in (99 cm)	18.9 in (48 cm)	13.8 in (35 cm)
M	40.6 in (103 cm)	19.3 in (49 cm)	14.2 in (36 cm)
L	45.3 in (115 cm)	19.3 in (49 cm)	14.2 in (36 cm)
XL	48.4 in (123 cm)	19.7 in (50 cm)	14.6 in (37 cm)
XXL	52.8 in (134 cm)	19.7 in (50 cm)	15 in (38 cm)

MATERIALS AND TOOLS
— Buttinette Woll Butt Primo Madeleine 150; 100% merino wool; 164 yd (150 m) per 1.75 oz (50 g): #381.51 Black, 7 (8/9/11/12/14) skeins
— Circular knitting needle, US size 4 (3.5 mm), 32 in (80 cm) long
— Circular knitting needle, US size 2.5 (3.0 mm), 32 in (80 cm) long
— If desired, one DPN set each in sizes US 4 (3.5 mm) and US 2.5 (3.0 mm) for the sleeves
— Tapestry needle
— 2 stitch markers

GAUGE
In stockinette stitch on US 4 (3.5 mm) needles: 24 sts and 30 rows = 4 x 4 in (10 x 10 cm)

CONSTRUCTION NOTES
The sweater is worked from the top to the bottom. First, Front and Back are worked separately in turned rows. Shoulder sloping is achieved with short row shaping. To shape the neckline, stitches are increased. Under the arm, pieces are joined in the round, and a few decreases are worked to bring the sleeves closer to the Body, which results in the Body having an approximately 2.8 in (6–7 cm) smaller circumference than the listed chest circumference. The Sleeves are knitted on at the end; Sleeve stitches are picked up and knit around the armhole. This understated and timeless sweater is truly a basic piece and a useful addition to any wardrobe since it can be paired with just about everything.

RIBBING
1x1 ribbing: * K1, p1 *, rep from * to * continuously.

STOCKINETTE STITCH
In rows: Knit on RS, purl on WS.
In the round: Knit all sts in all rounds.

TURNING STITCHES (T-ST)
Place the working yarn behind work, turn work, slip 1 stitch purlwise, move the working yarn over the right needle from front to back and pull up on the stitch. This creates a turning stitch (t-st) with two legs sitting on the needle. The "double stitch" will be worked and counted as one stitch further on. Knit stitches can be worked immediately; for purl stitches, the working yarn first needs to be moved to the front of the work between the needles.

SELVEDGE STITCHES
In RS and WS rows, knit the first and the last stitch of the row (= selv st).

CONTINUED

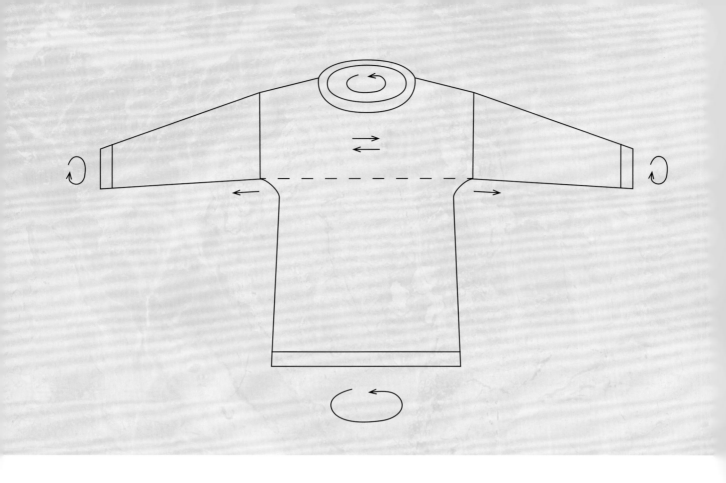

INSTRUCTIONS

With US size 4 (3.5 mm) needles, cast on 114 (119/124/138/147/160) sts, then work the Back as follows:

Row 1 (WS): Selv st, p37 (39/41/47/52/58), place m, p38 (39/40/42/43/44), place m, purl to last st, selv st.

Row 2 (RS): Knit to last m, slip m, k5, turn work.

Row 3 (WS): T-st, purl to last marker, p5, turn work.

Row 4 (RS): T-st, knit to 5 sts past the last t-st, turn work.

Row 5 (WS): T-st, purl to 5 sts past the last t-st, turn work.

Repeat Rows 4 and 5 another 4 (5/5/6/7/8) times.

Now, row counting starts anew from Row 1, beginning with a RS row.

Row 1 (RS): Knit all stitches.

Row 2 (WS): Selv st, purl to last stitch, selv st.

Repeat Rows 1 and 2 until the piece has reached a length of 7.1 (7.5/7.5/7.9/7.9/8.3) in [18 (19/19/20/20/21) cm], ending having just completed a WS row. Transfer all stitches

to stitch holders or a piece of waste yarn for holding, and break the working yarn; the Left Front will be worked next.

LEFT FRONT

Pick up and knit the last 38 (40/42/48/52/58) sts from the cast-on edge, then proceed as follows:

Row 1 (WS): Selv st, purl to last stitch, selv st.

Row 2 (RS): K5, turn work.

Row 3 (WS): T-st, purl to last stitch, selv st.

Row 4 (RS): Knit to 5 sts past the last t-st, turn work.

Row 5 (WS): Work the same as Row 3.

Repeat Rows 4 and 5 another 4 (5/5/6/7/8) times.

Now, row counting starts anew from Row 1, beginning with a RS row.

Row 1 (RS): Knit all stitches.

Row 2 (WS): Selv st, purl to last stitch, selv st.

Rows 3–10: Repeat Rows 1 and 2 four times.

Row 11 (RS): K2, M1L, knit to end of row. You should now have 39 (41/43/49/53/59) sts on the needles.

Row 12 (WS): Work the same as Row 2.

Rows 13 and 14: Work the same as Rows 1 and 2.

Rows 15–22: Repeat Rows 11–14 twice. You should now have 41 (43/45/51/55/61) sts on the needles.

Row 23 (RS): Work the same as Row 11. You should now have 42 (44/46/52/56/62) sts on the needles.

Row 24 (WS): Work the same as Row 2.

Rows 25–34: Repeat Rows 23 and 24 five times more. You should now have 47 (49/51/57/61/67) sts on the needles.

Row 35 (RS): K2, M1L, kfb, knit to end of row. You should now have 49 (51/53/59/63/69) sts on the needles.

Row 36 (WS): Work the same as Row 2.

Rows 37 and 38: Work the same as Rows 35 and 36. You should now

have 51 (53/55/61/65/71) sts on the needles.

Transfer all stitches to stitch holders or a piece of waste yarn for holding, and break the working yarn, the Right Front will be worked next.

RIGHT FRONT

Pick up and knit the first 38 (40/42/ 48/52/58) sts from the cast-on edge.

Row 1 (WS): Selv st, purl to last stitch, selv st.

Row 2 (RS): Knit all stitches.

Row 3 (WS): Selv st, p4, turn work.

Row 4 (RS): T-st, knit to last stitch of this row, selv st(s).

Row 5 (WS): Selv st, purl to 5 sts before the last t-st, turn work.

Repeat Rows 4 and 5 another 4 (5/5/ 6/7/8) times.

Now, row counting starts anew from Row 1, beginning with a RS row.

Row 1 (RS): T-st, knit all sts.

Row 2 (WS): Selv st, purl to last stitch, selv st.

Row 3 (RS): Knit all stitches.

Row 4 (WS): Work the same as Row 2.

Rows 5–10: Repeat Rows 3 and 4 three times.

Row 11 (RS): Knit to last 2 sts, M1R, k2. You should now have 39 (41/43/49/53/59) sts on the needles.

Row 12 (WS): Work the same as Row 2.

Rows 13 and 14: Work the same as Rows 3 and 4.

Rows 15–22: Repeat Rows 11–14 twice. You should now have 41 (43/45/51/55/61) sts on the needles.

Row 23 (RS): Work the same as Row 11. You should now have 42 (44/46/52/56/62) sts on the needles.

Row 24 (WS): Work the same as Row 2.

Rows 25–34: Repeat Rows 23 and 24 five times more. You should now have 47 (49/51/57/61/67) sts on the needles.

Row 35 (RS): Knit to last 3 sts of this row, kfb, M1R, k2. You should now have 49 (51/53/59/63/69) sts on the needles.

Row 36 (WS): Work the same as Row 2.

Rows 37 and 38: Work the same as Rows 35 and 36. You should now have 51 (53/55/61/65/71) sts on the needles.

In the following row, the two halves of the Front will be joined. For this, knit the 51 (53/55/61/65/71) sts of the Right Front, cast on 12 (13/14/16/17/18) new sts, then knit the 51 (53/55/61/65/71) formerly held sts of the Left Front. You should now have 114 (119/124/ 138/147/160) sts on the needles.

Row 1 (WS): Selv st, purl to last stitch, selv st.

Row 2 (RS): Knit all stitches.

Row 3 (WS): Work the same as Row 1.

Repeat Rows 2 and 3 until the piece has reached a length of 7.1 (7.5/7.5/7.9/7.9/8.3) in [18 (19/19/20/20/21) cm], ending having just completed a WS row; do not break the working yarn.

BODY

Now, Front and Back are joined, then work is continued in the round. For this, knit all sts of the Right Front, place m, knit the formerly held Back sts, place a BOR marker, and join in the round without twisting. You should now have 228 (238/248/276/294/320) sts on the needles.

Round 1: Knit all stitches, slipping markers as you encounter them.

Round 2: * K1, k2tog, knit to 3 sts before the next marker, skp, k1, slip m *, rep from * to* once more. You should now have a total of 224 (234/244/272/290/316) sts for the body on the needles.

Repeat Rounds 1 and 2 another 3 times. You should now have a total of 212 (222/232/260/278/304) sts for the body on the needles.

Now, continue working the sweater in stockinette stitch in the round until it has either reached a length of 13.4 (13.4/13.8/13.8/14.2/14.6) in [34 (34/35/35/36/37) cm], measured from the underarm, or is 0.4 in (1 cm) shorter than desired body length to accommodate ribbing to be added.

RIBBING

Change to US size 2.5 (3.0 mm) needles.

Rounds 1–4: * K1, p1 *, rep from * to * to end of round.

Round 5: BO all sts in pattern.

SLEEVES

Both Sleeves are worked the same. With US size 4 (3.5 mm) needles, pick up and knit stitches around the armhole at a rate of 3 sts picked up from every 4 sts, making sure the total number of stitches picked up is an even number, place m and join in the round.

The Sleeve is worked in the round from here on; the marker indicates the BOR. Work the Sleeve in stockinette stitch, at the same time, work Sleeve tapering decreases in every 10th round through the end of the Sleeve as follows: K1, k2tog, work in stockinette stitch to 3 sts before m, skp, k1, slip m.

Work the Sleeve in stockinette stitch until the Sleeve has either reached a length of 18.5 (18.5/18.9/18.9/19.3/19.3) in [47 (47/48/48/49/49) cm] or is 0.4 in (1 cm) shorter than desired sleeve length to accommodate ribbing to be added.

SLEEVE CUFF

Change to US size 2.5 (3.0 mm) needles.

Rounds 1–4: * K1, p1 *, rep from * to * to end of round.

Round 5: BO all sts in pattern.

RIBBED NECKBAND

Using US size 2.5 (3.0 mm) needles and beginning at the left shoulder, pick up and knit stitches around the neckline edge as follows: On slanted sections, pick up at a ratio of 3 sts from every 4 sts from the newly cast-on sts and, from the cast-on edge of the Back neckline, pick up every stitch. Make sure that the total number of stitches picked up is an even number. Join in the round.

Rounds 1–4: * K1, p1 *, rep from * to * to end of round.

Round 5: BO all sts in pattern.

FINISHING

Weave in all ends, dampen the sweater, and pull it into the desired shape.

OLIVIA

OVERSIZED CARDIGAN WITH DEEP V-NECK AND OPTIONAL BELT

SIZES

XS, S, M, L, XL, XXL

Numbers for size XS are listed before the parentheses, numbers for sizes S through XXL within parentheses. If only one number is listed, it applies to all sizes.

Size	Chest Circumference	Sleeve Length from Armhole	Garment Length from Armhole
XS	41.0 in (104 cm)	17.3 in (44 cm)	13.4 in (34 cm)
S	44.1 in (112 cm)	17.3 in (44 cm)	13.4 in (34 cm)
M	47.2 in (120 cm)	17.7 in (45 cm)	13.8 in (35 cm)
L	53.5 in (136 cm)	17.7 in (45 cm)	13.8 in (35 cm)
XL	56.7 in (144 cm)	18.1 in (46 cm)	14.2 in (36 cm)
XXL	59.8 in (152 cm)	18.1 in (46 cm)	14.6 in (37 cm)

MATERIALS AND TOOLS

— Lana Grossa Lovely Cashmere Lala Berlin; 60% cashmere, 25% polyamide, 15% virgin wool; 66 yd (60 m) per 0.9 oz (25 g): #09 Gray/Beige Heathered, 12 (12/14/16/20/22) skeins
— Circular knitting needle, US size 15 (10.0 mm), 32 in (80 cm) long
— Circular knitting needle, US size 13 (9.0 mm), 32 in (80 cm) long
— If desired, one DPN set each in sizes US 15 (10.0 mm) and US 13 (9.0 mm) for the sleeves
— Tapestry needle
— 2 stitch markers
— 4 snap fasteners, approx. 1 in (25 mm)
— 4 horn buttons, approx. 1.1 in (28 mm)

GAUGE

In stockinette stitch on US 15 (10.0 mm) needles: 10 sts and 16 rows = 4 x 4 in (10 x 10 cm)

CONSTRUCTION NOTES

The cardigan is worked from the top to the bottom in turned rows. First, stitches for the Back are cast on; the Back is worked top down in the shape of a rectangle. After this, one after the other, stitches for the shoulders and Fronts are picked up and knit. Shoulders are shaped with short rows, increases and decreases. Neckline increases are worked next. Under the arm, the stitches of both Fronts and of the Back are combined on one needle and continued together in turned rows. Sleeve stitches are picked up and knit around the armhole, then the sleeves knitted onto the Body, working from the top down. An all-around buttonband without buttonholes is knitted on at the end. The cardigan is closed with sewn-on snap fasteners and a separately knitted belt. All of the ribbing as well as the belt are worked with slipped stitches. Working steps in the instructions are sometimes different for different sizes; for this reason, all sizes to which a particular step does not apply are marked with "-".

TURNING STITCHES (T-ST)

Place the working yarn behind the work, turn work, slip 1 stitch purlwise, move the working yarn over the right needle from front to back and pull up on the stitch. This creates a turning stitch (t-st) with two legs sitting on the needle. This "double stitch" will be worked and counted as one stitch further on. Knit stitches can be worked immediately; for purl stitches, the working yarn first needs to be moved to the front of work between the needles.

SLIPPED STITCHES WITH YARN OVER (SL1-W/YO)

Work each slipped stitch with yarn over as follows: Slip 1 stitch purlwise, and make a yarn over. This creates a stitch resembling a double stitch. This stitch is worked and counted as 1 stitch.

SELVEDGE STITCHES

In RS and WS rows, knit the first and the last stitch of the row as indicated (= selv st).

CONTINUED

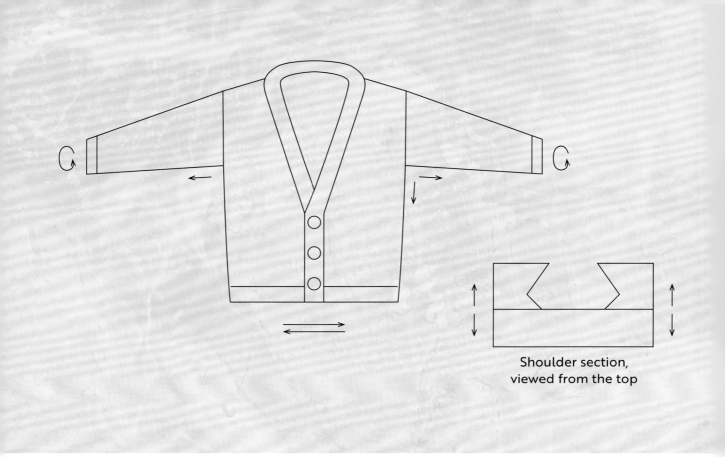

Shoulder section,
viewed from the top

INSTRUCTIONS

BACK

With US size 15 (10.0 mm) needles, cast on 52 (56/60/68/72/76) sts, and work the Back as follows:

Row 1 (WS): Selv st, purl to last stitch, selv st.

Row 2 (RS): Knit all stitches.

Repeat Rows 1 and 2 until the piece has reached a length of 7.5 (7.5/8.3/8.3/8.7/8.7) in [19 (19/21/21/22/22) cm], measured along the knotted selvedge of the armhole, ending having just completed a WS row.

Place all stitches on holders, and break the working yarn; the Right Front will be worked next.

RIGHT FRONT

Pick up and knit the last 16 (17/19/22/24/26) sts from the cast-on edge.

Sizes XS (S/-/-/-/-)

Row 1 (WS): Selv st, purl to last 2 sts of this row, turn work.

Row 2 (RS): T-st, knit all sts to last 3 sts of this row, k2tog, k1. You should now have 15 (16/-/-/-/-) sts on the needles.

Row 3 (WS): Selv st, purl to 2 sts before the last t-st, turn work.

Row 4 (RS): Work the same as Row 2. You should now have 14 (15/-/-/-/-) sts on the needles.

Rows 5 and 6: Work the same as Rows 3 and 4. You should have 13 (14/-/-/-/-) sts on the needles.

Row 7 (WS): Selv st, purl to last stitch, selv st.

Row 8 (RS): Knit all stitches.

Row 9 (WS): Selv st, p6 (5/-/-/-/-), turn work.

Row 10 (RS): T-st, k to last stitch of this row, M1R, k1. You should now have 14 (15/-/-/-/-) sts on the needles.

Row 11 (WS): Selv st, purl to 3 sts past the last t-st, turn work.

Row 12 (RS): T-st, knit to end of row.

Row 13 (WS): Work the same as Row 11.

Rows 14 and 15: Work the same as Rows 10 and 11. You should now have 15 (16/-/-/-/-) sts on the needles.

Row 16 (RS): T-st, knit to end of row.

Row 17 (WS): Selv st, purl to last stitch, selv st.

Row 18 (RS): Knit to the last stitch of this row, M1R, k1. You should now have 16 (17/-/-/-/-) sts on the needles.

Row 19 (WS): Work the same as Row 17.

Sizes - (-/M/L/XL/XXL)

Row 1 (WS): Selv st, purl to last 2 sts of this row, turn work.

Row 2 (RS): T-st, knit all sts to last 3 sts of this row, k2tog, k1. You should now have - (-/18/21/23/25) sts on the needles.

Row 3 (WS): Selv st, purl to 2 sts before the last t-st, turn work.

Row 4 (RS): Work the same as Row 2. You should now have - (-/17/20/22/24) sts on the needles.

Rows 5–8: Repeat Rows 3 and 4 twice. You should now have - (-/15/18/20/22) sts on the needles.

Row 9 (WS): Selv st, purl to last st, selv st.

Row 10 (RS): Knit all stitches.

Row 11 (WS): Selv st, p - (-/3/6/8/10), turn work.

Row 12 (RS): T-st, knit to last stitch, M1R, k1. You should now have - (-/16/19/21/23) sts on the needles.

Row 13 (WS): Selv st, purl to 3 sts past the last t-st, turn work.

Row 14 (WS): T-st, knit to end of row.

Row 15 (WS): Work the same as Row 13.

Rows 16 and 17: Work the same as Rows 12 and 13. You should now have - (-/17/20/22/24) sts on the needles.

Row 18. (RS): T-st, knit to end of row.

Row 19 (WS): Selv st, purl to last stitch, selv st.

Row 20 (RS): Knit to last stitch, M1R, k1. You should now have - (-/18/21/23/25) sts on the needles.

Row 21 (WS): Work the same as Row 19.

Row 22 (RS): Knit all stitches.

Row 23 (WS): Work the same as Row 19.

Rows 24 and 25: Work the same as Rows 20 and 21. You should now have - (-/19/22/24/26) sts on the needles.

At this point, all sizes have again reached the initial stitch count of 16 (17/19/22/24/26) sts. Now, increases will be continued in every other RS row until the piece has reached a length of 7.5 (7.5/8.3/8.3/8.7/8.7) in [19 (19/21/21/22/22) cm], measured along the knotted selvedge of the armhole, ending having just completed a Row 4 (WS), as follows:

Row 1 (RS): Knit all stitches.

Row 2 (WS): Selv st, purl to last stitch, selv st.

Row 3 (RS): Knit to last stitch, M1R, k1. You should now have 17 (18/20/23/25/27) sts on the needles.

Row 4 (WS): Work the same as Row 2.

LEFT FRONT

Pick up and knit the first 16 (17/19/22/24/26) sts from the cast-on edge.

Sizes XS (S/-/-/-/-)

Row 1 (WS): Selv st, purl to last stitch, selv st.

Row 2 (RS): Selv st, skp, knit to last 2 sts, turn work. You should now have 15 (16/-/-/-/-) sts on the needles.

Row 3 (WS): T-st, purl to last stitch, selv st.

Row 4 (RS): Selv st, skp, knit to 2 sts before the last t-st, turn work. You should now have 14 (15/-/-/-/-) sts on the needles.

Row 5 (WS): Work the same as Row 3.

Rows 6 and 7: Work the same as Rows 3 and 4. You should now have 13 (14/-/-/-/-) sts on the needles.

Row 8 (RS): Knit all stitches.

Row 9 (WS): Selv st, purl to last st, selv st.

Row 10 (RS): K1, M1L, k6 (5/-/-/-/-), turn work. You should now have 14 (15/-/-/-/-) sts on the needles.

Row 11 (WS): T-st, purl to last stitch, selv st.

Row 12 (RS): Knit to 3 sts past the last t-st, turn work.

Row 13 (WS): Work the same as Row 11.

Row 14 (WS): K1, M1L, knit to 3 sts past the last t-st, turn work. You should now have 15 (16/-/-/-/-) sts on the needles.

Row 15 (WS): Work the same as Row 11.

Rows 16 and 17: Work the same as Rows 12 and 13.

Row 18 (RS): K1, M1L, knit to end of row. You should now have 16 (17/-/-/ -/-) sts on the needles.

Row 19 (WS): Selv st, purl to last stitch, selv st.

Sizes - (-/M/L/XL/XXL)

Row 1 (WS): Selv st, purl to last stitch, selv st.

Row 2 (RS): Selv st, skp, knit to last 2 sts of this row, turn work. You should now have - (-/18/21/23/25) sts on the needles.

Row 3 (WS): T-st, purl to last stitch, selv st.

Row 4 (RS): Selv st, skp, knit to 2 sts before the last t-st, turn work. You should now have - (-/17/20/22/24) sts on the needles.

Row 5 (WS): Work the same as Row 3.

Rows 6–9: Repeat Rows 3 and 4 twice. You should now have - (-/15/18/20/22) sts on the needles.

Row 10 (RS): Knit all stitches.

Row 11 (WS): Selv st, purl to last st, selv st.

Row 12 (RS): K1, M1L, k - (-/3/6/8/10), turn work. You should now have - (-/16/19/21/23) sts on the needles.

Row 13 (WS): T-st, purl to last stitch, selv st.

Row 14 (WS): Knit to 3 sts past the last t-st, turn work.

Row 15 (WS): T-st, purl to last stitch, selv st.

Row 16 (RS): K1, M1L, knit to 3 sts past the last t-st, turn work. You should now have - (-/17/20/22/24) sts on the needles.

Row 17 (WS): T-st, purl to last stitch, selv st.

Rows 18 and 19: Work the same as Rows 14 and 15.

Row 20 (RS): K1, M1L, knit to end of row. You should now have - (-/18/21/23/25) sts on the needles.

Row 21 (WS): Selv st, purl to last stitch, selv st.

Row 22 (RS): Knit all stitches.

Row 23 (WS): Work the same as Row 21.

Rows 24 and 25: Work the same as Rows 20 and 21. You should now have - (-/19/22/24/26) sts on the needles.

At this point, all sizes have again reached the initial stitch count of 16 (17/19/22/24/26) sts. Now, increases will be continued in every other RS row until the piece has reached a length of 7.5 (7.5/8.3/8.3/8.7/8.7) in [19 (19/21/21/22/22) cm], measured along the knotted selvedge of the armhole, ending having just completed a Row 4 (WS), as follows:

Row 1 (RS): Knit all stitches.

Row 2 (WS): Selv st, purl to last stitch, selv st.

Row 3 (RS): K1, M1L, knit to end of row. 17 (18/20/23/25/27) sts should remain on the needles.

Row 4 (WS): Work the same as Row 2.

Place all stitches on holders, and break the working yarn.

BODY

Now, Front and Back are joined, then work is continued over all stitches. For this, work all sts of the Left Front, place m, knit the formerly held Back sts, place m, and knit the formerly held sts of the Right Front. You should now have a total of 86 (92/100/114/122/130) sts on the needles, of these, 52 (56/60/68/72/76) sts for the Back, and 17 (18/20/23/25/27) sts each for the Fronts.

During this, continue to work in pattern, and continue to work increases in every other RS row for a total of 13 (14/15/17/17/17) increases worked (counted from the first increase); the pattern is again written out here for better overview:

Row 1 (WS): Selv st, purl to last stitch, selv st.

Row 2 (RS): K1, M1L, knit to last stitch, M1R, k1. You should now have 88 (94/102/116/124/132) sts on the needles, 52 (56/60/68/72/76) sts for the Back and 18 (19/21/24/26/28) sts each for the Fronts.

After all increases have been completed, you should have a total of 104 (112/120/136/144/152) sts on the needles, 52 (56/60/68/72/76) sts for the Back and 26 (28/30/34/36/38) sts each for the Fronts.

Then, the Body is worked even in stockinette stitch with selv sts without further increases until it has either reached a length of 11.8 (11.8/12.2/12.2/12.6/12.6) in [30 (30/31/31/32/32) cm], measured from the armhole, or is 1.6 in (4 cm) shorter than other desired body length to accommodate ribbing to be added.

RIBBING

Change to US 13 (9.0 mm) needles.

Row 1 (RS): Selv st, * k1, p1 *, rep from * to * to last stitch, selv st.

Row 2 (WS): Selv st, * k1, sll-w/yo *, rep from * to * to last stitch, selv st.

Rows 3–8: Repeat Rows 1 and 2 three times.

Row 9 (RS): BO all sts in pattern.

FRONT BANDS

Using US size 13 (9.0 mm) needles, pick up and knit stitches from the knotted selvedge at a rate of 3 sts picked up from every 4 sts, pick up and knit stitches 1:1 along the Back, then pick up and knit stitches from the knotted selvedge at a rate of 3 sts picked up from every 4 sts; make sure that the total number of stitches picked up is even.

Row 1 (WS): Selv st, * k1, sll-w/yo *, rep from * to * to last stitch, slip 1 st purlwise with yarn in front of work.

Row 2 (RS): Selv st, * k1, p1 *, rep from * to * to last stitch of this row, slip 1 st purlwise with yarn in front of work.

Row 3 (WS): Work the same as Row 1.

Rows 4–7: Repeat Rows 2 and 3 twice.

Row 8 (RS): BO all sts in pattern.

SLEEVES

Both Sleeves are worked the same. Using US 15 (10.0 mm) needles, pick up and knit stitches around the armhole at a rate of 3 sts picked up from every 4 sts so that the total number of stitches picked up is even, place BOR marker, and join in the round. Work the Sleeve in stockinette stitch, at the same time, in every 8th round, decrease as follows throughout to the end of the Sleeve: K1, k2tog, work in pattern to 3 sts before m, skp, k1, slip m.

Work the Sleeve in stockinette stitch until the Sleeve has either reached a length of 15.7 (15.7/16.1/16.1/16.5/16.5) in [40 (40/41/41/42/42) cm] or is 1.6 in (4 cm) shorter than desired sleeve length to accommodate ribbing to be added.

SLEEVE CUFF

Change to US size 13 (9.0 mm) needles.

Round 1: * K1, p1 *, rep from * to * to end of round.

Round 2: * Sll-w/yo, p1 *, rep from * to * to end of round.

Rounds 3–8: Repeat Rounds 1 and 2 three times.

Round 9: BO all sts in pattern.

BELT (OPTIONAL)

Using US 15 (10.0 mm) needles, cast on 7 sts.

Row 1 (WS): P1, * k1, sll-w/yo *, rep from * to* once more, k1, slip 1 st purlwise with yarn in back of work.

Row 2 (RS): * K1, p1 *, rep from * to * 2 times more, slip 1 st purlwise with yarn in front of work.

Repeat Rows 1 and 2 until the belt has reached a length of 88.5 (90.5/92.5/94.5/98.5/102.4) in [225 (230/235/240/250/260) cm]. BO all stitches in pattern.

FINISHING

Weave in all ends, dampen the cardigan, and pull it into the desired shape. Sew the four snap fasteners to the outside of the Left Front band and the inside of the Right Front band, and the horn buttons to the outside of the Right Front band, in the same spots where the snap fasteners are located inside.

NOEMI

TOP-DOWN CARDIGAN IN A SLIGHTLY CROPPED LENGTH WITH INTEGRATED CABLE BAND

SIZES

XS, S, M, L, XL, XXL

Numbers for size XS are listed before the parentheses, numbers for sizes S through XXL within parentheses. If only one number is listed, it applies to all sizes.

Size	Chest Circum-ference	Sleeve Length from Armhole	Garment Length from Armhole
XS	34.6 in (88 cm)	11 in (28 cm)	12.6 in (32 cm)
S	36.6 in (93 cm)	11 in (28 cm)	12.6 in (32 cm)
M	39.4 in (100 cm)	11.4 in (29 cm)	13.8 in (35 cm)
L	43.3 in (110 cm)	11.4 in (29 cm)	13.8 in (35 cm)
XL	47.2 in (120 cm)	11.8 in (30 cm)	15.4 in (39 cm)
XXL	51.2 in (130 cm)	11.8 in (30 cm)	15.4 in (39 cm)

MATERIALS AND TOOLS

— Rosy Green Wool Cheeky Merino Joy; 100% organic merino extra fine wool; 350 yd (320 m) per 3.5 oz (100 g): #62 Isar Pebble, 3 (4/4/5/6/7) skeins
— Circular knitting needle, US size 6 (4.0 mm), at least 32 in (80 cm) long
— If desired, a DPN set in US size 6 (4.0 mm) for the sleeves
— 4 stitch markers
— Stitch holder or waste yarn
— Tapestry needle
— Cable needle

GAUGE

In garter stitch on US size 6 (4.0 mm) needles: 21 sts and 40 rows = 4 x 4 in (10 x 10 cm)

CONSTRUCTION NOTES

The cardigan is worked as a modified top-down raglan in one piece in garter stitch in turned rows. Work starts with the ribbed neckband in the back, from which stitches for the Sleeves and the Back are picked up and knit. The cabled front band is worked at the same time as the main part of the cardigan. First, all typical sleeve and back raglan increases are worked. After this, stitches for the Front are picked up along the sleeve increase lines and knit. The Front is shaped with short rows. Because of its special construction, the cardigan is shorter in the front than in the back. The narrow, tapered sleeves in a three-quarter length are worked without cuff so as to not distract from the main eye-catching detail of the garment—the unusual construction and all-around cabled band. Short rows are worked throughout the whole Body to compensate for the different gauges of the garter stitch of the Body and the cable pattern at the edge.

TURNING STITCHES (T-ST)

Place the working yarn in back of the work, turn work, slip 1 stitch purlwise, move the working yarn over the right needle from front to back and pull up on the stitch. This creates a turning stitch (t-st) with two legs sitting on the needle. This "double stitch" will be worked and counted as one stitch further on. Knit stitches can be worked immediately; for purl stitches, the working yarn first needs to be moved to the front of the work between the needles.

SELVEDGE STITCHES

Work all sts listed as "selv st" in the instructions as follows: In RS and WS rows, slip the first/last stitch as indicated (= selv sts) purlwise with yarn in front of work.

Attention: At the beginning of the instructions, this is not done on both ends of the row. Please follow the respective instructions for each specific row worked.

CONTINUED

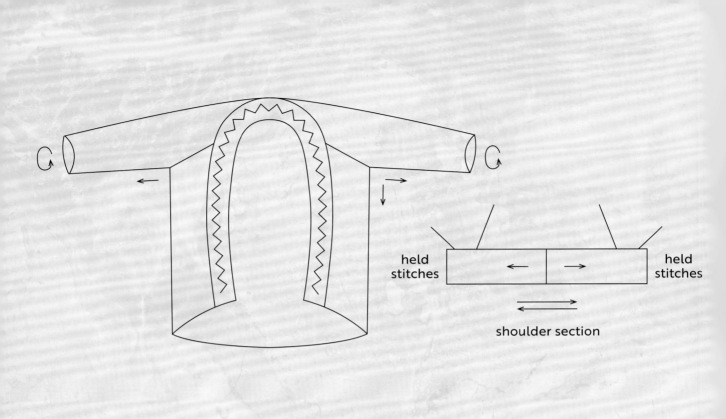

held stitches

held stitches

shoulder section

GARTER STITCH
In rows: Knit all sts in RS and WS rows.
In rounds: Alternate knit 1 round, purl 1 round.

CABLE PATTERN OVER 16 STITCHES
In every 10th RS row, work a cable crossing as follows: Hold 4 sts on a cable needle behind work, knit the next 4 sts, then k4 from cable needle, hold 4 sts on a cable needle in front of work, k4, then k4 from cable needle.

Any other 16-stitch-wide cable can be substituted for this cable.

INSTRUCTIONS

First, the ribbed neckband in the Back is worked, beginning in the center of the Back. For this, using US size 6 (4.0 mm) needles, cast on 20 sts.

Row 1 (WS): K2, p16, k2.

Row 2 (RS): Knit to the last stitch of this row, selv st.

Row 3 (WS): Work the same as Row 1.

Rows 4–7: Repeat Rows 2 and 3 twice.

Row 8 (RS): Knit 2, hold 4 sts on a cable needle behind work, knit the next 4 sts, then k4 from cable needle, hold 4 sts on a cable needle in front of work, k4, then k4 from cable needle, k1, selv st.

Row 9 (WS): Work the same as Row 1.

Rows 10–17: Repeat Rows 2 and 3 four times.

Row 18 (RS): Work the same as Row 8.

Row 19 (WS): Work the same as Row 1.

Repeat Rows 10–19 until a total of 55 (55/57/57/59/59) rows have been worked, ending having just completed a WS row. Break the working yarn and transfer all stitches to a stitch holder or a piece of waste yarn for holding.

Pick up and knit 20 sts from the cast-on edge; the ribbed neckband will now be continued in the opposite direction.

Row 1 (WS): K2, p16, k1, 1 selv st(s).

Row 2 (RS): Knit all stitches.

Row 3 (WS): Work the same as Row 1.

Rows 4–7: Repeat Rows 2 and 3 twice.

Row 8 (RS): Knit 2, hold 4 sts on a cable needle behind work, knit the next 4 sts, then k4 from cable needle, hold 4 sts on a cable needle in front of work, k4, then k4 from cable needle, k2.

Row 9 (WS): Work the same as Row 1.

Rows 10–17: Repeat Rows 2 and 3 four times.

Row 18 (RS): Work the same as Row 8.

Row 19 (WS): Work the same as Row 1.

Repeat Rows 10–19 until a total of 55 (55/57/57/59/59) rows have been worked, ending having just completed a WS row. Do not break the working yarn; transfer all stitches to a stitch holder or a piece of waste yarn for holding.

Now, stitches for the Sleeves and Back will be picked up from the knotted selvedge and knit. The two cables remain on holders and will be continued later. In the following WS row, stitch markers will be placed to divide into the sections for the Sleeves and Back. After this, raglan increases for Sleeves and Back begin.

Pick up and knit stitches from the knotted selvedge at a rate of 3 sts picked up from every 4 sts, for a total of 90 (90/94/94/98/98) sts.

Row 1 (WS, raglan division): K1, place m, k22 (22/23/23/24/24), place m, k44 (44/46/46/48/48), place m, k22 (22/23/23/24/24), place m, k1. Now, raglan increases begin.

Row 2 (RS, increase row): * K1, slip m, k1, M1L, knit to 1 st before m, M1R, k1, slip m, M1L, knit to marker, M1R, slip m, k1, M1L, knit to 1 st before m, M1R, k1, slip m, k1.

You should have 25 (25/26/26/27/27) sts each for the Sleeves and 46 (46/48/48/50/50) sts for the Back on the needles.

Row 3 (WS): Knit all stitches, slipping markers as you come to them.

Repeat Rows 2 and 3 another 16 (20/22/27/33/38) times. You should now have 57 (65/70/80/93/103) sts each for the Sleeves and 76 (84/92/102/116/126) sts for the Back on the needles.

From here on, increases will only be worked in every other RS row. For ease of counting, row counting begins anew with Row 1 here.

Row 1 (RS): Knit all stitches, slipping markers as you come to them.

Row 2 (WS): Work the same as Row 1.

Row 3 (RS, increase row): * K1, slip m, k1, M1L, knit to 1 st before m, M1R, k1, slip m, M1L, knit to m, M1R, slip m, k1, M1L, knit to 1 st before m, M1R, k1, slip m, k1.

You should have 59 (63/72/82/95/105) sts each for the Sleeves and 74 (82/94/104/118/128) sts for the Back on the needles.

Row 4 (WS): Knit all stitches, slipping markers as you come to them.

Repeat Rows 1–4 another 2 (2/2/2/1/0) time(s); you should have 63 (71/76/86/97/105) sts each for the Sleeves and 82 (90/98/108/120/128) sts for the Back on the needles.

From here on, increases will only be worked in every 3rd RS row. For ease of counting, row counting begins anew with Row 1 here.

Rows 1–4: Knit all stitches, slipping markers as you come to them.

Row 5 (RS, increase row): * K1, slip m, k1, M1L, knit to 1 st before m, M1R, k1, slip m, M1L, knit to m, M1R, slip m, k1, M1L, knit to 1 st before m, M1R, k1, slip m, k1.

You should now have 65 (73/78/88/99/107) sts each for the Sleeves and 84 (92/100/110/122/130) sts for the Back on the needles.

Row 6 (WS): Knit all stitches, slipping markers as you come to them.

Repeat Rows 1–6 another 3 (2/2/1/0/0) time(s), then additionally only Rows 1–4 a total of 0 (0/1/1/1/1) time(s). You should now have 71 (77/82/90/99/107) sts each for the Sleeves and 90 (96/104/112/122/130) sts for the Back on the needles. Break the working yarn. Now, all stitches are combined on one needle, and at the same time, the Sleeve stitches placed on holders.

SLEEVE SEPARATION ROUND

Take up the formerly held cable stitches again and continue, using the working yarn previously left hanging.

Row 1 (RS): K2, work 16 sts in cable pattern, k1, place m, pick up and knit stitches from the knotted selvedge at a rate of 2 sts picked up from every 3 sts = a total of 44 (48/53/56/58/61) sts, knit the first stitch of the Sleeve, * remove m, transfer the next 71 (77/82/90/99/107) sts (Sleeve) to next m to a stitch holder or a piece of waste yarn for holding, cast on 1 (1/1/2/2/3) new underarm st(s), place m, cast on 1 (1/1/2/2/3) new underarm st(s) *, knit the 90 (96/104/112/122/130) sts of the Back to m, rep from * to* once more, knit the last stitch of the Sleeve. Pick up and knit stitches from the knotted selvedge at a rate of 2 sts picked up from every 3 sts = a total of 44 (48/53/56/58/61) sts, place m, k1, work 16 sts in cable pattern, k1, selv st. You should now have a total of 220 (234/252/268/282/298) sts on the needles, 65 (69/74/78/80/84) sts for each Front and 90 (96/104/112/122/130) sts for the Back.

Row 2 (WS): K2, p16, knit to last m, k1, p16, k1, selv st.

LEFT FRONT

Now, the Left Front is shaped with short rows. Work according to instructions, after each cable crossing row always working the next WS row as follows: T-st, knit to m, turn work.

Row 1 (RS): K2, work 16 sts in cable pattern, k1, slip m, knit to 1 (5/5/4/1/5) st(s) before the next m, turn work.

Row 2 (WS): T-st, knit to m, k1, p16, k1, selv st.

Row 3 (RS): K2, work 16 sts in cable pattern, k1, slip m, knit to 4 sts before the last m, turn work.

Row 4 (WS): Work the same as Row 2.

Repeat Rows 3 and 4 another 8 (9/10/11/12/13) times. Work the next RS row as follows: K2, work 16 sts in cable pattern, k1, slip m, knit to last m, k1, work 16 sts in cable pattern, k1, selv st.

RIGHT FRONT

Now, the Right Front is shaped with short rows. Work according to instructions, after each cable crossing row always working the next RS row as follows: T-st, knit to marker, turn work.

Row 1 (WS): K2, p16, k1, slip m, knit to 1 (5/5/4/1/5) st(s) before next m, turn work.

Row 2 (RS): T-st, knit to m, k1, work 16 sts in cable pattern, k1, selv st.

Row 3 (WS): K2, p16, k1, slip m, knit to 4 sts before the last m, turn work.

Row 4 (RS): Work the same as Row 2.

Repeat Rows 3 and 4 another 8 (9/10/11/12/13) times. Work the next WS row as follows: K2, p16, k1, slip m, knit to last m, k1, p16, k1, selv st.

BODY

To compensate for the different gauges of the garter stitch of the Body and the cable pattern at the edge, after each cable crossing row, short rows are worked in the next row between the markers for the cable sections as follows:

Row 1 (WS): K2, p16, knit to last m, turn work.

Row 2 (RS): T-st, knit to m, turn work.

Row 3 (WS): T-st, knit to last m, k1, p16, k1, selv st.

Except for the short row section, work the Body in the established pattern, instructions are written out here again for clarification. Begin with a RS row.

Row 1 (RS): K2, work 16 sts in cable pattern, k1, slip m, knit to last m, k1, work 16 sts in cable pattern, k1, selv st.

Row 2 (WS): K2, p16, k1, slip m, knit to last m, k1, p16, k1, selv st.

Repeat this pattern until the cardigan has either reached a length of 12.6 (12.6/13.8/13.8/15.4/15.4) in [32 (32/35/35/39/39) cm], or other desired length. During a RS row, bind off all sts.

SLEEVES

Both Sleeves are worked the same. For the Sleeves, first take up the 71 (77/82/90/99/107) formerly held sts using US size 6 (4.0 mm) needles, pick up and knit 1 (1/1/2/2/3) st(s) of the cast-on underarm sts, place m, pick up and knit another 1 (1/1/2/2/3) st(s) of the cast-on underarm sts, and join in the round. The Sleeves are worked in the round from here on; the marker indicates the BOR. You should now have a total of 73 (79/84/94/103/113) sts on the needles.

Work the Sleeve in garter stitch, at the same time, in every 10th row, work knitwise decreases throughout to the end as follows: K1, k2tog, work in pattern to 3 sts before m, skp, k1, slip m.

Work the Sleeve in garter stitch until it has either reached a length of 11 (11/11.4/11.4/11.8/11.8) in [28 (28/29/29/30/30) cm] or desired sleeve length. Bind off during a knit round.

FINISHING

To finish, weave in all ends, dampen the cardigan, and pull it into the desired shape.

PAOLA

LOOSELY FITTING RIBBED SWEATER WITH PRONOUNCED SHOULDER SLOPING AND CURVED HEM

SIZES
XS, S, M, L, XL, XXL

Numbers for size XS are listed before the parentheses, numbers for sizes S through XXL within parentheses. If only one number is listed, it applies to all sizes.

Size	Chest Circum-ference	Sleeve Length from Armhole	Garment Length from Armhole
XS	36.6 in (93 cm)	16.1 in (41 cm)	9 in (23 cm)
S	38.2 in (97 cm)	16.5 in (42 cm)	9 in (23 cm)
M	41.7 in (106 cm)	16.9 in (43 cm)	9 in (23 cm)
L	45.7 in (116 cm)	16.9 in (43 cm)	9 in (23 cm)
XL	49.6 in (126 cm)	16.9 in (43 cm)	9 in (23 cm)
XXL	53.5 in (136 cm)	16.9 in (43 cm)	9 in (23 cm)

MATERIALS AND TOOLS
— Lamana Cosma; 60% pima cotton, 40% modal; 109 yd (100 m) per 1.75 oz (50 g): #05 Silver Gray, 9 (10/11/12/13/15) skeins
— Circular knitting needle, US size 8 (5.0 mm), 32 in (80 cm) long
— If desired, a DPN set in US size 8 (5.0 mm) for the sleeves
— Tapestry needle
— 2 stitch markers

GAUGE
In 1x1 ribbing pattern on US size 8 (5.0 mm) needles: 20 sts and 23 rows = 4 x 4 in (10 x 10 cm)

CONSTRUCTION NOTES
The sweater is worked from the top to the bottom. First, Front and Back are worked in one piece in the round. To shape the sloped shoulders, stitches are increased at the shoulders, then the neckline is shaped with short rows. Armholes are created by dividing Front and Back, which are then continued separately in turned rows. Under the arm, pieces are joined again, then continued in the round. At the bottom of the Body, short row shaping is used to create the curved hemline. Since the sweater is worked in 1x1 ribbing throughout, additional cuffs or hem ribbing are not needed. It can be worn either the regular way or off-shoulder. If desired, the 1x1 ribbing can be substituted with either stockinette stitch or seed stitch in the same gauge. This will give the garment a completely different character. If opting for stockinette stitch, it would be prudent to add ribbing to all open edges to prevent unwanted rolling.

RIBBING PATTERN
1x1 ribbing: * K1, p1 *, rep from * to * continuously.

TURNING STITCHES (T-ST)
Place the working yarn behind work, turn work, slip 1 stitch purlwise, move the working yarn over the right needle from front to back and pull up on the stitch. This creates a turning stitch (t-st) with two legs sitting on the needle. This "double stitch" will be worked and counted as one stitch further on. Knit stitches can be worked immediately; for purl stitches, the working yarn first needs to be moved to the front of work between the needles.

SELVEDGE STITCHES
In RS and WS rows, knit the first and the last stitch of the row (= selv st).

CONTINUED

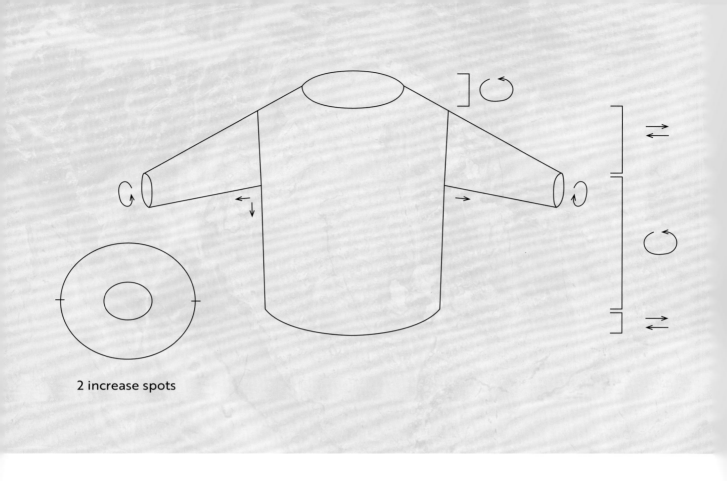

2 increase spots

INSTRUCTIONS

With US size 8 (5.0 mm) needles, cast on 96 (96/100/100/104/104) sts, place BOR marker, join in the round.

Round 1 (setup round): * K1, p1 *, rep from * to * until 48 (48/50/50/52/52) sts have been worked, place m, rep from * to * to end of round.

Now, the neckline is shaped with short rows.

Row 1 (RS): K1, M1L in pattern, work in pattern to m, M1R in pattern, slip m, k1, M1L in pattern, work 1 st in pattern, turn work. You should now have 99 (99/103/103/107/107) sts on the needles.

Row 2 (WS): T-st, * work in pattern to 1 st before m, M1R in pattern, p1, slip m, M1L in pattern *, rep from * to * once more, work 1 st in pattern, turn work. You should now have 103 (103/107/107/111/111) sts on the needles.

Row 3 (RS): T-st, * work in pattern to m, M1R in pattern, slip m, k1, M1L in pattern *, rep from * to * once more, work in pattern to 6 sts past the last t-st, turn work. You should now have 107 (107/111/111/115/115) sts on the needles.

Row 4 (WS): T-st, * work in pattern to 1 st before m, M1R in pattern, p1, slip m, M1L in pattern *, rep from * to * once more, work in pattern to 6 sts past the last t-st, turn work. You should have 111 (111/115/115/119/119) sts on the needles.

Row 5 (RS): T-st, * work in pattern to m, M1R in pattern, slip m, k1, M1L in pattern *, rep from * to * once more, work in pattern to 2 sts past the last t-st, turn work. You should have 115 (115/119/119/123/123) sts on the needles.

Row 6 (WS): T-st, * work in pattern to 1 st before m, M1R in pattern, p1, slip m, M1L in pattern *, rep from * to * once more, work in pattern to 2 sts past the last t-st, turn work. You should now have 119 (119/123/123/127/127) sts on the needles.

Rows 7–10: Repeat Rows 5 and 6 twice. You should now have 135 (135/139/139/143/143) sts on the needles.

Row 11 (RS): T-st, * work in pattern to m, M1R in pattern, slip m, k1, M1L in pattern *, rep from * to * once more, work in pattern to 3 sts past the last t-st, turn work. You should now have 139 (139/143/143/147/147) sts on the needles.

Row 12 (WS): T-st, * work in pattern to 1 st before m, M1R in pattern, p1, slip m, M1L in pattern *, rep from * to* once more, work in pattern to 3 sts past the last t-st, turn work. You should have 143 (143/147/147/151/151) sts on the needles.

Rounds 13–18: Repeat Rounds 11–12 three times. You should now have 167 (167/171/171/175/175) sts on the needles.

Now, the short row section has been completed, and you will work in the round again.

Round 19: T-st, * work in pattern to m, M1R in pattern, slip m, k1, M1L in pattern *, rep from * to * once more, work in pattern to m, M1R, slip m. You should now have 172 (172/176/176/180/180) sts on the needles.

Round 20: * K1, M1L in pattern, work in pattern to m, M1R in pattern, slip m *, rep from * to * once more. You should now have 176 (176/180/180/184/184) sts on the needles.

Work Round 20 another 2 (4/8/13/17/22) times, you should have 184 (192/212/232/252/272) sts on the needles, 92 (96/106/116/126/136) sts each for Front and Back.

From here on, Front and Back are continued separately in turned rows to shape the armholes.

BACK

The Back is worked over the following 92 (96/106/116/126/136) sts.

Row 1 (RS): Work in pattern to 1 st before m, selv st, turn work.

Row 2 (WS): Selv st, work in pattern to 1 st before m, selv st, turn work.

Row 3 (RS): Selv st, work in pattern to 1 st before m, selv st.

Row 4 (WS): Work the same as Row 2.

Repeat Rows 3 and 4 until the armhole measures 5.9 (6.3/6.7/6.7/7.1/7.5) in [15 (16/17/17/18/19) cm]. Place all stitches on holders and break the working yarn.

FRONT

Work the same as the Back; do not place the stitches on hold; do not break the working yarn.

BODY

Now that Front and Back are joined in the round, work continues in the round. For this, work in pattern over all sts of the Front, place m, knit the formerly held Back sts, place m, and join in the round. You should now have 184 (192/212/232/252/272) sts on the needles.

Work in pattern until the Body has either reached a length of 9 in (23 cm) or is 4 in (10 cm) shorter than desired body length to accommodate the curved hem to be added. This will now be shaped using short rows.

FRONT HEM

Row 1 (RS): Work in pattern to 1 st before m, turn work.

Row 2 (WS): T-st, work in pattern to 1 st before m, turn work,

Row 3 (RS): T-st, work in pattern to last t-st, turn work.

Row 4 (WS): Work the same as Row 3.

Rows 5–16: Repeat Rows 3 and 4 another 6 times.

Rows 17–20: T-st, work in pattern to 1 st before previous t-st, turn work.

Rows 21–24: T-st, work in pattern to 2 sts before previous t-st, turn work.

Rows 25–28: T-st, work in pattern to 4 sts before previous t-st, turn work.

Row 29 (RS): T-st, work in pattern to last m.

Rows 30–56: Work the same as Rows 2–28.

Row 57 (RS): T-st, work in pattern to m.

In the following round, bind off all sts in pattern.

SLEEVES

Both Sleeves are worked the same. Pick up and knit stitches around the armhole edge at a rate of 4 sts picked up from every 5 sts, making sure the total number of stitches picked up is an even number, place marker for BOR, and join in the round.

Work the Sleeve in the established pattern, at the same time, in every 10th (10th/10th/8th/8th/6th) round, decreasing for Sleeve tapering a total of 4 (5/5/6/7/8) times as follows: K1, depending on the pattern either k2tog or p2tog, work in pattern to 2 sts before marker, depending on the pattern either ssk or ssp, slip m.

Work the Sleeve in the established pattern until the Sleeve has reached a length of 16.1 (16.5/16.9/16.9/16.9/16.9) in [41 (42/43/43/43/43) cm].

FINISHING

Weave in all ends, dampen the sweater, and pull it into the desired shape.

DORITA

NARROW TURTLENECK SWEATER WITH INTEGRATED SLEEVE CAP SHAPING AND SLEEVES WITH A TIED CORD DETAIL

SIZES

XS, S, M, L, XL, XXL

Numbers for size XS are listed before the parentheses, numbers for sizes S through XXL within parentheses. If only one number is listed, it applies to all sizes.

Size	Chest Circum-ference	Sleeve Length from Armhole	Garment Length from Armhole
XS	33.8 in (86 cm)	18.9 in (48 cm)	17.7 in (45 cm)
S	35.4 in (90 cm)	18.9 in (48 cm)	18.1 in (46 cm)
M	39 in (99 cm)	19.3 in (49 cm)	18.1 in (46 cm)
L	42.9 in (109 cm)	19.3 in (49 cm)	18.5 in (47 cm)
XL	46.9 in (119 cm)	19.3 in (49 cm)	18.9 in (48 cm)
XXL	50.8 in (129 cm)	19.3 in (49 cm)	19.3 in (49 cm)

MATERIALS AND TOOLS

— Lana Grossa Alpaca Peru 200; 100% alpaca, 219 yd (200 m) per 1.75 oz (50 g): #218 Light Gray, 9 (10/11/12/14/15) skeins
— Circular knitting needle, US size 8 (5.0 mm), 32 in (80 cm) long
— If desired, a DPN set in US size 8 (5.0 mm) for the sleeves
— Tapestry needle
— 5 stitch markers

GAUGE

In stockinette stitch on US 8 (5.0 mm) needles with yarn held double: 17 sts and 27 rows = 4 x 4 in (10 x 10 cm)

CONSTRUCTION NOTES

The sweater is worked with two strands of yarn held together throughout. While similar in outward appearance to a classic construction with sewn-in sleeve and shaped sleeve cap, this garment does not require any seaming at all. The sweater is first worked from bottom to top in the round, and from the armholes on, work is continued in turned rows, while the armholes are shaped with decreases. Shoulder seams are joined using the 3-needle bind-off method. Then, first the sleeve caps are shaped with short rows, then the remainder of the sleeve is worked from top to bottom in the round. Turtleneck and folded-over sleeve cuff lend the sweater a special touch. Working steps in the instructions are sometimes different for different sizes.

RIBBING

2x2 ribbing: * K2, p2 *, rep from * to * continuously.

TURNING STITCHES (T-ST)

Place the working yarn behind work, turn work, slip 1 stitch purlwise, move the working yarn over the right needle from front to back and pull up on the stitch. This creates a turning stitch (t-st) with two legs sitting on the needle. This "double stitch" will be worked and counted as one stitch further on. Knit stitches can be worked immediately; for purl stitches, the working yarn first needs to be moved to the front of work between the needles.

SELVEDGE STITCHES

In RS and WS rows, knit the first and the last stitch of the row (= selv st).

STOCKINETTE STITCH

In rows: Knit on RS, purl on WS.
In the round: Knit all sts in all rounds.

CONTINUED

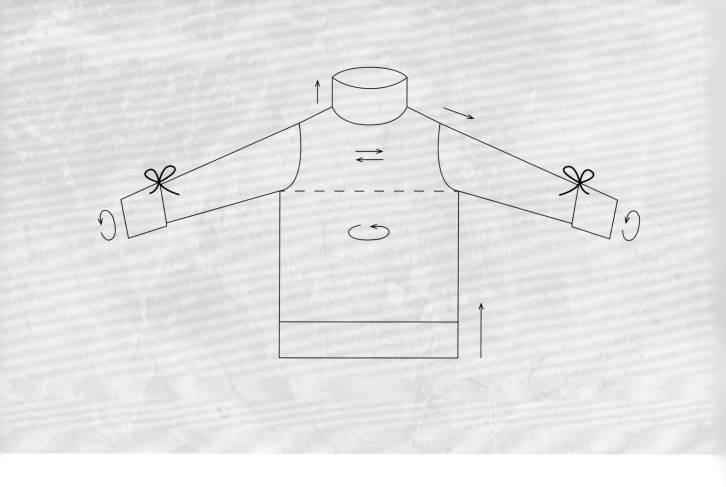

INSTRUCTIONS

With US size 8 (5.0 mm) needles and 2 strands of yarn held together, cast on 148 (156/168/188/204/220) sts, place a BOR marker, and join in the round without twisting. In Round 1, place an additional marker after having worked the first 74 (78/84/94/102/110) sts. First, work hem ribbing as follows:

Rounds 1–28: * K2, p2*, rep from * to * to end of round, slip BOR marker.

After this, work in stockinette stitch until the piece has reached a height of 17.7 (18.1/18.1/18.5/18.9/19.3) in [45 (46/46/47/48/49) cm], measured from the cast-on edge. In the last round, end 3 sts before the BOR marker. From here on, continue Back and Front separately, each one of them over 74 (78/84/94/102/110) sts, working in turned rows.

SLEEVE SEPARATION ROUND

BO 6 (6/6/8/10/10) sts, knit to 3 (3/3/4/4/5) sts before m, BO 6 (6/6/8/10/10) sts, knit to end.

Back and Front have now been separated, each one of them has 68 (72/78/86/92/100) sts.

BACK

Row 1 (WS): Selv st, purl to last stitch, selv st.

Row 2 (RS): Selv st, k1, sssk, knit to last 5 sts, k3tog, k1, selv st. You should now have 64 (68/74/82/88/96) sts on the needles.

Row 3 (WS): Work the same as Row 1.

Sizes XS (S/M/L/-/-)

Row 4 (RS): Selv st, k1, skp, knit to last 4 sts, k2tog, k1, selv st. You should now have 62 (66/72/80/-/-) sts on the needles.

Row 5 (WS): Work the same as Row 1.

Rows 6–13: Repeat Rows 4 and 5 four times. You should now have 54 (58/64/72/-/-) sts on the needles.

Row 14 (WS): Knit all stitches.

Row 15 (WS): Work the same as Row 1.

Rows 16 and 17: Work the same as Rows 4 and 5. You should now have 52 (56/62/70/-/-) sts on the needles.

Rows 18 and 19: Work the same as Rows 14 and 15.

Rows 20 and 21: Work the same as Rows 4 and 5. You should now have 50 (54/60/68/-/-) sts on the needles.

Rows 22 and 23: Work the same as Rows 14 and 15.

Sizes - (-/-/-/XL/XXL)

Rows 4 and 5: Work the same as Rows 2 and 3. You should now have - (-/-/-/84/92) sts on the needles.

Row 6 (RS): Selv st, k1, skp, knit to last 4 sts, k2tog, k1, selv st. You should now have - (-/-/-/82/90) sts on the needles.

Row 7 (WS): Work the same as Row 1.

Rows 8–15: Repeat Rows 6 and 7 four times. You should now have - (-/-/-/74/82) sts on the needles.

Row 16 (RS): Knit all stitches.

Row 17 (WS): Work the same as Row 1.

Rows 18 and 19: Work the same as Rows 6 and 7. You should now have - (-/-/-/72/80) sts on the needles.

Rows 20 and 21: Work the same as Rows 16 and 17.

Rows 22 and 23: Work the same as Rows 6 and 7. You should now have - (-/-/-/70/78) sts on the needles.

Rows 24 and 25: Work the same as Rows 16 and 17.

All Sizes

Work in stockinette stitch with selv sts until the Back measures 7.1 (7.1/7.9/8.3/8.7/9.5) in [18 (18/20/21/22/24) cm] from beginning of armhole, ending having just completed a WS row. You should now have 50 (54/60/68/70/78) sts on the needles.

SHOULDER SLOPING

Row 1 (RS): K17 (18/23/25/26/30), BO 16 (16/16/18/18/20) sts, knit to end of row, turn work.

You should now have 2 times 17 (18/23/25/26/30) sts on the needles. We will next work across one set of these sts for the left side.

Next, the **Back left shoulder** as well as the **Neckline** will be worked.

Row 2 (WS): T-st, purl to last stitch, selv st.

Row 3 (RS): K2, sssk, knit to 2 sts before the previous t-st, turn work. You should now have 15 (16/21/23/24/28) sts on the needles.

Row 4 (WS): Work the same as Row 2.

Rows 5 and 6: Work the same as Rows 3 and 4. You should now have 13 (14/19/21/22/26) sts on the needles.

Row 7 (RS): K2, skp, knit to 2 sts before the previous t-st, turn work. You should now have 12 (13/18/20/21/25) sts on the needles.

Row 8 (WS): Work the same as Row 2.

Sizes XS (S/-/-/-/-)

Place remaining stitches on holder and break the working yarn.

Sizes - (-/M/L/XL/XXL)

Row 9 (RS): Knit to 2 sts before the last t-st, turn.

Row 10 (WS): Work the same as Row 2.

Repeat Rows 9 and 10 another - (-/1/1/2/3) time(s), then, in the following RS row, knit all sts, place stitches on a holder, and break the working yarn.

RIGHT SHOULDER

Row 1 (WS): Purl to last 2 sts of this row, turn work.

Row 2 (RS): T-st, knit to last 5 sts, k3tog, k2. You should now have 15 (16/21/23/24/28) sts on the needles.

Row 3 (WS): Purl to 2 sts before the last t-st, turn work.

Rows 4 and 5: Work the same as Rows 2 and 3. You should now have 13 (14/19/21/22/26) sts on the needles.

Row 6 (RS): T-st, knit to last 4 sts, k2tog, k2. You should now have 12 (13/18/20/21/25) sts on the needles.

Row 7 (WS): Work the same as Row 3.

Sizes XS (S/-/-/-/-)

Place stitches on holder and break the working yarn.

Sizes - (-/M/L/XL/XXL)

Row 8 (RS): Knit to 2 sts before the last t-st, turn.

Row 9 (WS): Work the same as Row 3.

Repeat Rows 8 and 9 another - (-/1/1/2/3) time(s), then work the next RS row as follows: T-st, knit all sts, place stitches on a holder, and break the working yarn.

FRONT

Work the Front the same as the Back in stockinette stitch with selv sts as described until the Front has either reached a length of 6.3 (6.3/7.1/7.5/7.9/8.7) in [16 (16/18/19/20/22) cm] from armhole edge or is 8 rows shorter than the Back up to the separation. You should now have 50 (54/60/68/70/78) sts on the needles.

Row 1 (RS): K17 (18/23/25/26/30), BO 16 (16/16/18/18/20) sts, knit to end of row, turn work.

You should have 2 times 17 (18/23/25/26/30) sts on the needles. You will next work across one set of these stitches for the right shoulder.

Next, the **Front right shoulder** as well as the **Neckline** will be worked.

Row 2 (WS): Purl to last stitch of this row, selv st.

Row 3 (RS): K2, sssk, knit to end of row. You should now have 15 (16/21/23/24/28) sts on the needles.

Row 4 (WS): Work the same as Row 2.

Rows 5 and 6: Work the same as Rows 3 and 4. You should now have 13 (14/19/21/22/26) sts on the needles.

Row 7 (RS): K2, skp, knit to end of row. You should now have 12 (13/18/20/21/25) sts on the needles.

Row 8 (WS): Purl to last 2 sts of this row, turn work.

Row 9 (RS): T-st, knit to end of row.

Row 10 (WS): Purl to 2 sts before the last t-st, turn work.

Repeat Rows 9 and 10 another 4 (4/6/6/7/8) times. In the following RS row, knit all sts.

Take up the formerly held sts of the Back right shoulder, and join them with the live stitches of the Front

right shoulder using the 3-needle bind-off method. For this, place the shoulders right sides facing each other, and wrong sides facing out.

LEFT SHOULDER

Row 1 (WS): Purl to last stitch, selv st.

Row 2 (RS): Knit to last 5 sts of this row, k3tog, k2. You should now have 15 (16/21/23/24/28) sts on the needles.

Row 3 (WS): Purl to last stitch, selv st.

Rows 4 and 5: Work the same as Rows 2 and 3. You should now have 13 (14/19/21/22/26) sts on the needles.

Row 6 (RS): Knit to last 2 sts, k2tog, k2. You should now have 12 (13/18/20/21/25) sts on the needles.

Row 7 (WS): Purl to last 2 sts, turn work.

Row 8 (RS): T-st, knit to end of row.

Row 9 (WS): T-st, purl to 2 sts before the last t-st, turn work.

Repeat Rows 8 and 9 another 4 (4/6/6/7/8) times, then work the next RS row as follows: T-st, knit all sts.

Take up the formerly held sts of the Back left shoulder, and join with the sts of the Front left shoulder, using the 3-needle bind-off method. For this, place the shoulders right sides facing each other, and wrong sides facing out.

TURTLENECK

Using US size 8 (5.0 mm) needles, pick up and knit stitches around the neckline edge. Make sure that the total number of stitches picked up is a multiple of 4. Place a BOR marker, and join in the round.

Now, work 2x2 ribbing as follows: * K2, p2 *, rep from * to * to end of round, slip m. Work ribbing until the turtleneck has reached a length of 9.5 in (24 cm). In the following row, bind off all sts in pattern.

SLEEVE CAP

Both Sleeves are worked the same. Pick up and knit the last 3 (3/3/4/4/5) sts of the bound-off sts under the arm; pick up and knit stitches from the knotted selvedge all around the edge at a rate of 3 sts picked up from every 4 sts; pick up and knit 3 (3/3/4/4/5) sts under the arm. Make sure to have picked up an even number of stitches. Place BOR marker. Now, place one marker each in the spots where the last armhole shaping decreases had been worked (markers #1 and #4). Now, count the stitches above these two markers, then divide the total into 3 equal sections, and in these spots, place one marker each (markers #2 and #3). If the stitch count between markers #1 and #4 is not a multiple of 3: if there's 1 extra stitch, add it to the middle section between markers #2 and #3. If there are 2 sts too many, add 1 stitch each to the side sections (the first third between markers #1 and #2 and the last third between markers #3 and #4). You now have a total of 5 markers in the armhole, beginning with marker #1, located at the last armhole decrease, 2 more markers (#2 and #3), each after 1/3 of the stitches to marker #4, marker #4 likewise located at the last armhole decrease, and the BOR marker at the end of the round.

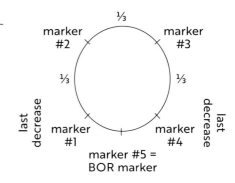

Now, the sleeve cap will be shaped with short rows.

Row 1 (RS): Knit to marker #3, turn work.

Row 2 (WS): T-st, purl to next marker, turn work.

Row 3 (RS): T-st, knit to 1 st past the last t-st, turn work.

Row 4 (WS): T-st, purl to 1 st past the last t-st, turn work.

Repeat Rows 1–4 until markers #1 and #4 have been reached.

After this, for ease of counting, counting starts anew with Row 1.

Row 1 (RS): T-st, knit to 2 sts past the last t-st, turn work.

Row 2 (WS): T-st, purl to 2 sts past the last t-st, turn work.

Repeat Rows 1 and 2 another 2 (2/2/2/3/3) times. Work the next RS row as follows: T-st, knit to BOR marker, removing all markers except for the BOR marker.

SLEEVE

Work the Sleeve in stockinette stitch in the round. At the same time, in every 12th (12th/10th/10th/8th/8th) round, decrease 2 sts each as follows a total of 7 (7/8/9/10/11) times: K1, k2tog, k to 2 sts before end of round, skp, slip BOR marker.

Continue the Sleeve in stockinette stitch until the Sleeve has either reached a length of 14.6 (14.6/15/15/15/15) in [37 (37/38/38/38/38) cm] or is 4.3 in (11 cm) shorter than desired Sleeve length to accommodate the ribbed cuff to be added.

SLEEVE CUFF

If the stitch count is not a multiple of 4, begin with Round 1. If the stitch count is a multiple of 4, begin with Round 2.

Round 1: K2tog, k1, * p2, k2 *, rep from * to * to last 3 sts of this round, p1, skp.

Round 2: * K2, p2 *, rep from * to * to end of round.

Repeat Round 2 until the ribbing has reached a length of 4 inches (10 cm).

Now, work a fold round as follows:

Round 1: * K2, yo, p2tog *, rep from * to * to end of round.

Round 2: Knit all stitches.

Round 3: * K2, p2 *, rep from * to * to end of round.

Repeat Round 3 until the ribbing from the turning round has reached a length of 4 in (10 cm). BO all sts in pattern.

TIES

Pick up and knit 6 stitches from the round before the ribbing, in the center of the top side of the Sleeve.

Work in turned rows as follows: K1, p1, k1, p1, k1, slip 1 st purlwise with yarn in front of work.

Work in this manner until the tie has reached a length of 10.2 in (26 cm). Bind off all sts in pattern. Fold the ribbed cuff to the outside along the fold round.

From the bound-off edge, pick up and knit 6 stitches, likewise in the center of the top side of the sleeve, and work another tie the same way.

Repeat on other Sleeve.

FINISHING

Weave in all ends, dampen the sweater, and pull it into the desired shape. Tie the two ties at each sleeve.

ELISA

LOOSELY FITTING TOP-DOWN JACKET WITH INTEGRATED SLEEVE CAP SHAPING, HOOD, AND NO-ROLL CUFFS

SIZES

XS, S, M, L, XL, XXL

Numbers for size XS are listed before the parentheses, numbers for sizes S through XXL within parentheses. If only one number is listed, it applies to all sizes.

Size	Chest Circumference	Sleeve Length from Armhole	Garment Length from Armhole
XS	37.8 in (96 cm)	16.9 in (43 cm)	18.9 in (48 cm)
S	39.8 in (101 cm)	16.9 in (43 cm)	18.9 in (48 cm)
M	43.3 in (110 cm)	17.3 in (44 cm)	19.7 in (50 cm)
L	46.1 in (117 cm)	17.3 in (44 cm)	19.7 in (50 cm)
XL	49.2 in (125 cm)	17.7 in (45 cm)	20.5 in (52 cm)
XXL	52.0 in (132 cm)	17.7 in (45 cm)	20.5 in (52 cm)

MATERIALS AND TOOLS

— Katia Cotton-Merino; 70% cotton, 30% extrafine merino wool; 115 yd (105 m) per 1.75 oz (50 g): #106 Light Gray, 13 (14, 15, 16, 18, 19) skeins
— Circular knitting needle, US size 8 (5.0 mm), 32 in (80 cm) long
— Circular knitting needle, US size 4 (3.5 mm), 32 in (80 cm) long
— If desired, one DPN set each in sizes US 8 (5.0 mm) and US 4 (3.5 mm) for sleeves and I-cord
— Tapestry needle
— 8 stitch markers

GAUGE

In stockinette stitch on US size 8 (5.0 mm) needles: 17 sts and 30 rows = 4 x 4 in (10 x 10 cm)

CONSTRUCTION NOTES

This cardigan has the classical appearance of a seamed cardigan worked in pieces with set-in sleeves. Its special feature is, however, the contiguous shoulder construction—the shape is achieved entirely by strategically placed increases, which makes it possible to work this garment from the top down. While the top of the sleeve is not quite the traditional round sleeve cap, it fits the shoulder just as well. In addition to this distinctive shoulder shaping, the cardigan features a stockinette stitch body with pockets, and special sleeve cuffs in a stockinette-stitch look, but with extra modifications preventing the typical rolling of the edges stockinette is known for. The hood, knitted on afterwards, has an incorporated drawstring tunnel and an I-cord drawstring.

SLIPPED STITCHES

Work each slipped stitch (sl1-pw-wyif) as follows: slip 1 stitch purlwise with yarn in front of work.

SLIPPED STITCHES WITH YARN OVER

Work each slipped stitch with yarn over (sl1-w/yo) as follows: slip 1 stitch purlwise and make a yarn over. This creates a stitch resembling a double stitch. This stitch is worked and counted as 1 stitch.

SELVEDGE STITCHES

Work all stitches noted as "selv st" as follows: In RS and WS rows, knit the first and the last stitch of the row (= selv st).

I-CORD

CO 3 sts, * k3, do not turn work, but slide the 3 sts to the other end of the needle. Move the working yarn behind work to the beginning of the needle, then again k3 *, rep from * to * until the desired length has been reached. Break the working yarn and pull it through the last 4 sts with the help of a tapestry needle.

CONTINUED

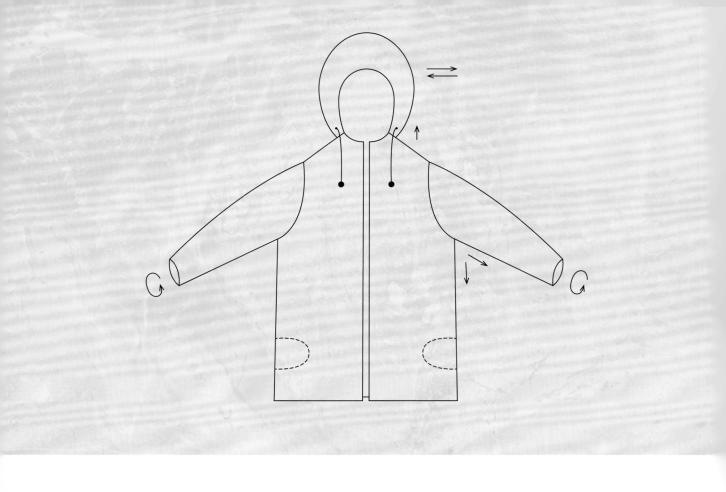

INSTRUCTIONS

With US 8 (5.0 mm) needles, cast on 30 (30/32/32/34/34) sts.

Row 1 (RS): Selv st, place m, k2, place m, k24 (24/26/26/28/28), place m, k2, place m, selv st. You should now have 1 st each for the Fronts, 2 sts each for the Shoulders, and 24 (24/26/26/28/28) sts for the Back on the needles.

Row 2 (WS): Selv st, * M1R-p, slip m, p2, slip m, M1L-p *, purl to next m, rep from * to * once more, selv st. You should now have 34 (34/36/36/38/38) sts on the needles: 2 sts each for the Fronts, 2 sts each for the Shoulders, and 26 (26/28/28/30/30) sts for the Back.

Row 3 (RS): * Knit to next m, M1R, slip m, k2, slip m, M1L *, rep from * to * once, knit to end of row. You should now have 38 (38/40/40/42/42) sts on the needles: 3 sts each for the Fronts, 2 sts each for the shoulders, and 28 (28/30/30/32/32) sts for the Back.

Row 4 (WS): Selv st, * purl to next m, M1R-p, slip m, p2, slip m, M1L-p *, rep from * to* once more, purl to last stitch, selv st. You should now have 42 (42/44/44/46/46) sts on the needles: 4 sts each for the Fronts, 2 sts each for the shoulders, and 30 (30/32/32/34/34) sts for the Back.

Rows 5–10: Repeat Rows 3 and 4 three times. You should now have 66 (66/68/68/70/70) sts on the needles, 10 sts each for the Fronts, 2 sts each for the shoulders, and 42 (42/44/44/46/46) sts for the Back.

Row 11 (RS): K1, M1L, * knit to next m, M1R, slip m, k2, slip m, M1L *, rep from * to * once, k to last stitch of this row, M1R, k1. You should now have 72 (72/74/74/76/76) sts on the needles: 12 sts each for the Fronts, 2 sts each for the shoulders, and 44 (44/46/46/48/48) sts for the Back.

Row 12 (WS): Work the same as Row 4. You should now have 76 (76/78/78/80/80) sts on the needles, 13 sts each for the Fronts, 2 sts each for the shoulders, and 46 (46/48/48/50/50) sts for the Back.

Rows 13 and 14: Work the same as Rows 3 and 4. You should now have 84 (84/86/86/88/88) sts on the needles: 15 sts each for the Fronts, 2 sts each for the shoulders, and 50 (50/52/52/54/54) sts for the Back.

Rows 15–20: Repeat Rows 11 and 12 three times. You should now have 114 (114/116/116/118/118) sts on the needles: 24 sts each for the Fronts, 2 sts each for the shoulders, and 62 (62/64/64/66/66) sts for the Back.

Row 21 (RS): Work the same as Row 3. You should now have 118 (118/120/120/122/122) sts on the needles: 25 sts each for the Fronts, 2 sts each for the shoulders, and 64 (64/66/66/68/68) sts for the Back.

Row 22 (WS): Selv st, M1L-p, * purl to next m, M1R-p, slip m, p2, slip m, M1L-p*, rep from * to* once more, purl to last stitch, M1R-p, p1, cast on 10 (10/12/12/14/14) new sts using backwards-loop cast-on. You should now have 134 (134/138/138/142/142) sts on the needles: 27 sts for the Right Front, 37 (37/39/39/41/41) sts for the Left Front, 2 sts each for the shoulders, and 66 (66/68/68/70/70) sts for the Back.

Row 23 (RS): * Knit to next m, M1R, slip m, k2, slip m, M1L *, rep from * to * once, knit to end of row, cast on 10 (10/12/12/14/14) new sts using backwards-loop cast-on. You should now have 148 (148/154/154/160/160) sts on the needles: 38 (38/40/40/42/42) sts each for the Fronts, 2 sts each for the shoulders, and 68 (68/70/70/72/72) sts for the Back.

Work the following Rows 24 and 25 a total of 0 (0/1/1/2/2) time(s).

Row 24 (WS): * Sl1-pw-wyif, k1 *, rep from * to * 2 times more, sl1-pw-wyif, place m, ** purl to next m, M1R-p, slip m, p2, slip m, M1L-p **, rep from ** to ** once more, purl to last 7 sts, place m, *** sl1-pw-wyif, k1 ***, repeat from *** to *** 2 times more, sl1-pw-wyif. You should now have - (-/158/158/164/164) sts on the needles, - (-/41/41/43/43) sts each for the Fronts, 2 sts each for the shoulders, and - (-/72/72/74/74) sts for the Back.

Row 25 (RS): * K1, sl1-pw-wyif *, rep from * to * 2 times more, k1, slip m, ** knit to m, M1R, slip m, k2, slip m, M1L **, repeat from ** to ** once, knit to m, slip m, *** k1, sl1-pw-wyif ***, repeat from *** to *** 2 times more, k1. You should now have - (-/162/162/168/168) sts on the needles: - (-/42/42/44/44) sts each for the Fronts, 2 sts each for the shoulders, and - (-/74/74/76/76) sts for the Back.

Shoulder sloping for all sizes has now been completed. In the next section, the sleeve cap will be shaped, for which row counting will start anew with Row 1 for ease of counting.

You should have 148 (148/162/162/176/176) sts on the needles: 38 (38/42/42/46/46) sts each for the Fronts, 2 sts each for the shoulders, and 68 (68/74/74/80/80) sts for the Back.

Row 1 (WS): * Sl1-pw-wyif, k1 *, rep from * to * 2 times more, sl1-pw-wyif, slip m, ** purl to 2 sts before next m, place m, M1R-p, purl to m, remove m, p2, remove m, p2, M1L-p, place m **, rep from ** to ** once more, purl to m before end, slip m, *** sl1-pw-wyif, k1 ***, repeat from *** to *** 2 times more, sl1-pw-wyif. You should now have 152 (152/166/166/180/180) sts on the needles: 38 (38/42/42/46/46) sts each for the Fronts, 4 sts each for the Sleeves, and 68 (68/74/74/80/80) sts for the Back.

Row 2 (RS): * K1, sl1-pw-wyif *, rep from * to * 2 times more, k1, slip m, ** knit to m, slip m, M1L, knit to next m, M1R, slip m **, repeat from ** to ** once, knit to m, slip m, *** k1, sl1-pw-wyif ***, repeat from *** to *** 2 times more, k1. You should now have 156 (156/170/170/184/184) sts on the needles: 38 (38/42/42/46/46) sts each for the Fronts, 6 sts each for the sleeves, and 68 (68/74/74/80/80) sts for the Back.

Row 3 (WS): * Sl1-pw-wyif, k1 *, rep from * to * 2 times more, sl1-pw-wyif, slip m, ** purl to next m, slip m, M1R-p, purl to m, M1L-p, slip m **, rep from ** to ** once more, purl to m before end, slip m, *** sl1-pw-wyif, k1 ***, repeat from *** to *** 2 times more, sl1-pw-wyif. You should now have 160 (160/174/174/188/188) sts on the needles: 38 (38/42/42/46/46) sts each for the Fronts, 8 sts each for the sleeves, and 68 (68/74/74/80/80) sts for the Back.

Repeat Rows 2 and 3 another 6 (7/8/8/9/9) times. You should now have 208 (216/238/238/260/260) sts on the needles: 38 (38/42/42/46/46) sts each for the Fronts, 32 (36/40/40/44/44) sts each for the sleeves, and 68 (68/74/74/80/80) sts for the Back.

From here on, sleeve increases will no longer be worked in every WS row. For ease of counting, row counting will start anew with Row 1, beginning with a RS row.

Row 1 (RS): * K1, sl1-pw-wyif *, rep from * to * 2 times more, k1, slip m, ** knit to m, slip m, M1L, knit to next m, M1R, slip m **, repeat from ** to ** once, knit to m, slip m, *** k1, sl1-pw-wyif ***, repeat from *** to *** 2 times more, k1. You should now have 212 (220/242/242/264/264) sts on the needles: 38 (38/42/42/46/46) sts each for the Fronts, 34 (38/42/42/

46/46) sts each for the Sleeves, and 68 (68/74/74/80/80) sts for the Back.

Row 2 (WS): * Sl1-pw-wyif, k1 *, rep from * to * 2 times more, sl1-pw-wyif, slip m, purl to last m, slip m, ** sl1-pw-wyif, k1 **, repeat from ** to ** 2 times more, sl1-pw-wyif.

Row 3: Work the same as Row 1. You should now have 216 (224/246/246/268/268) sts on the needles: 38 (38/42/42/46/46) sts each for the Fronts, 36 (40/44/44/48/48) sts each for the Sleeves, and 68 (68/74/74/80/80) sts for the Back.

Row 4 (WS): * Sl1-pw-wyif, k1 *, rep from * to * 2 times more, sl1-pw-wyif, slip m, ** purl to next m, slip m, M1R-p, purl to m, M1L-p, place m **, rep from ** to ** once more, purl to m before end, slip m, *** sl1-pw-wyif, k1 ***, repeat from *** to *** 2 times more, sl1-pw-wyif. You should now have 220 (228/250/250/272/272) sts on the needles: 38 (38/42/42/46/46) sts each for the Fronts, 38 (42/46/46/50/50) sts each for the Sleeves, and 68 (68/74/74/80/80) sts for the Back.

Repeat Rows 1 and 2 another 1 (2/3/3/4/5) time(s). You should now have 224 (236/262/262/288/292) sts on the needle:, 38 (38/42/42/46/46) sts each for the Fronts, 40 (46/52/52/58/60) sts each for the Sleeves, and 68 (68/74/74/80/80) sts for the Back.

Now, increases next to the Sleeves will be worked to shape the armhole. For ease of counting, row counting will start anew with Row 1, beginning with a RS row.

Row 1 (RS): * K1, sl1-pw-wyif *, rep from * to * 2 times more, k1, slip m, ** knit 1 st before m, M1R, k1, slip m, knit to next m, slip m, k1, M1L **, repeat from ** to ** once, knit to m, slip m,

*** k1, sl1-pw-wyif ***, repeat from *** to *** 2 times more, k1. You should now have 228 (240/266/266/292/296) sts on the needles, 39 (39/43/43/47/47) sts each for the Fronts, 40 (46/52/52/58/60) sts each for the Sleeves, and 70 (70/72/72/82/82) sts for the Back.

Row 2 (WS): * Sl1-pw-wyif, k1 *, rep from * to * 2 times more, sl1-pw-wyif, slip m, purl to last m, slip m, ** sl1-pw-wyif, k1 **, repeat from ** to ** 2 times more, sl1-pw-wyif.

Rows 3 and 4: Work the same as Rows 1 and 2. You should now have 232 (244/270/270/296/300) sts on the needles: 40 (40/44/44/48/48) sts each for the Fronts, 40 (46/52/52/58/60) sts each for the Sleeves, and 72 (72/78/78/84/84) sts for the Back.

Row 5 (RS): Work the same as Row 1. You should now have 236 (248/274/274/300/304) sts on the needles: 41 (41/45/45/49/49) sts each for the Fronts, 40 (46/52/52/58/60) sts each for the Sleeves, and 74 (74/80/80/86/86) sts for the Back.

Row 6 (WS): * Sl1-pw-wyif, k1 *, rep from * to * 2 times more, sl1-pw-wyif, slip m, ** purl to 1 st before next m, M1L-p, p1, slip m, purl to m, slip m, p1, M1R-p **, rep from ** to ** once more, purl to m before end, slip m, *** sl1-pw-wyif, k1 ***, repeat from *** to *** 2 times more, sl1-pw-wyif. You should now have 240 (252/278/278/304/308) sts on the needles: 42 (42/46/46/50/50) sts each for the Fronts, 40 (46/52/52/58/60) sts each for the Sleeves, and 76 (76/82/82/88/88) sts for the Back.

Repeat Rows 3 and 4 another 0 (1/1/2/2/3) time(s). You should now have 240 (256/282/286/312/320) sts on the needles: 42 (43/47/48/52/53) sts each for the Fronts, 40

(46/52/52/58/60) sts each for the Sleeves, and 76 (78/84/86/92/94) sts for the Back.

BODY

Now, Sleeve stitches will be placed on holders; you will work over the stitches of the Body only.

Row 1 (RS, raglan division): * K1, sl1-pw-wyif *, rep from * to * 2 times more, k1, slip m, knit to next m, ** remove m, transfer the next 40 (46/52/52/58/60) sts to a stitch holder or a piece of waste yarn for holding, cast on 3 (3/4/5/5/6) new underarm sts using backwards CO, place m, cast on 3 (3/4/5/5/6) new underarm sts using backwards CO **, knit to next m, rep from ** to ** once more, knit to last m, slip m, *** k1, sl1-pw-wyif ***, repeat from *** to *** 2 times more, k1. You should now have 172 (176/194/202/216/224) sts on the needles: 45 (46/51/53/57/59) sts each for the Fronts, and 82 (84/92/96/102/106) sts for the Back.

Row 2 (WS): * Sl1-pw-wyif, k1 *, rep from * to * 2 times more, sl1-pw-wyif, slip m, purl to last m, slip m, ** sl1-pw-wyif, k1 **, repeat from ** to ** 2 times more, sl1-pw-wyif.

Row 3 (RS): * K1, sl1-pw-wyif *, rep from * to * 2 times more, k1, slip m, knit to last m, slip m, ** k1, sl1-pw-wyif **, repeat from ** to ** 2 times more, k1.

Row 4 (WS): Work the same as Row 2.

Repeat Rows 3 and 4 until the Body has reached a length of 9.8 (9.8/10.6/10.6/11.4/11.4) in [25 (25/27/27/29/29) cm]. Now, the pockets will be worked. If you don't want pockets, this step can be skipped.

POCKETS

To keep the Pocket instructions usable for pockets with any stitch count, specific stitch counts are not mentioned in the following section, but the method is described in general terms. If your gauge does not match, more or fewer pocket stitches may need to be cast on, and the row count adjusted as well.

Row 1 (RS): * K1, sl1-pw-wyif *, rep from * to * 2 times more, k1, slip m, ** knit to 1 st before next m, p1, slip m, cast on 20 sts using backwards CO, place m, cast on 20 sts using backwards CO, place m, p1 **, rep from ** to ** once more, knit to last m, slip m, *** k1, sl1-pw-wyif ***, repeat from *** to *** 2 times more, k1.

Row 2 (WS): * Sl1-pw-wyif, k1 *, rep from * to * 2 times more, sl1-pw-wyif, slip m, ** purl to 1 st before the m, k1, slip m, purl to the m after the next m, slip m, k1 **, rep from ** to ** once more, purl to last m, slip m, *** sl1-pw-wyif, k1 ***, repeat from *** to *** 2 times more, sl1-pw-wyif.

Row 3 (RS): * K1, sl1-pw-wyif *, rep from * to * 2 times more, k1, slip m, ** knit to 1 st before next m, p1, slip m, knit to 1 st before next m, M1R, k1, slip m, k1, M1L, knit to next m, slip m, p1 **, rep from ** to ** once more, knit to last m, slip m, *** k1, sl1-pw-wyif ***, repeat from *** to *** 2 times more, k1.

Row 4 (WS): * Sl1-pw-wyif, k1 *, rep from * to * 2 times more, sl1-pw-wyif, slip m, ** purl to 1 st before the m, k1, slip m, purl to 1 st before next m, M1R-p, p1, slip m, p1, M1L-p, purl to next m, slip m, k1 **, rep from ** to ** once more, purl to last m, slip m, *** sl1-pw-wyif, k1 ***, repeat from *** to *** 2 times more, sl1-pw-wyif.

Rows 5–8: Repeat Rows 3 and 4 twice.

Row 9 (RS): Work the same as Row 3.

Row 10 (WS): Work the same as Row 2.

Row 11 (RS): * K1, sl1-pw-wyif *, rep from * to * 2 times more, k1, slip m, ** knit to 1 st before the next m, p1, slip m, knit to 1 st after the next m, slip m, p1 **, rep from ** to ** once more, knit to last m, slip m, *** k1, sl1-pw-wyif ***, repeat from *** to *** 2 times more, k1.

Row 12 (WS): Work the same as Row 2.

Rounds 13–28: Repeat Rows 11 and 12 eight times.

Row 29 (RS): * K1, sl1-pw-wyif *, rep from * to * 2 times more, k1, slip m, ** knit to 1 st before next m, p1, slip m, knit to 3 sts before next m, skp, k1, slip m, k1, k2tog, knit to next m, slip m, p1 **, rep from ** to ** once more, knit to last m, slip m, *** k1, sl1-pw-wyif ***, repeat from *** to *** 2 times more, k1.

Row 30 (WS): * Sl1-pw-wyif, k1 *, rep from * to * 2 times more, sl1-pw-wyif, slip m, ** purl to 1 st before the m, k1, slip m, purl to 3 sts before next m, ssp, p1, slip m, p1, p2tog, purl to next m, slip m, k1 **, rep from ** to ** once more, purl to last m, slip m, *** sl1-pw-wyif, k1 ***, repeat from *** to *** 2 times more, sl1-pw-wyif.

Rows 31–34: Repeat Rows 29 and 30 twice.

Row 35 (RS): Work the same as Row 3.

Row 36 (WS): * Sl1-pw-wyif, k1 *, rep from * to * 2 times more, sl1-pw-wyif, slip m, ** purl to next m, remove m, bind off the next 40 sts, removing the m, slip m **, rep from ** to ** once more, purl to last m, slip m, ***

sl1-pw-wyif, k1 ***, repeat from *** to *** 2 times more, sl1-pw-wyif.

After this, the cardigan will be continued in pattern. In the first RS row, the holes resulting from binding off are closed. Work in pattern until the cardigan has either reached a length of 18.5 (18.5/19.3/19.3/20.1/20.1) in [47 (47/49/49/51/51) cm], measured from the underarm, or is 0.4 in (1 cm) shorter than desired body length to accommodate hem to be added.

HEM

Change to US size 4 (3.5 mm) needles.

Row 1 (RS): * K1, sl1-pw-wyif *, rep from * to * 2 times more, k1, slip m, ** k1, sl1-w/yo **, rep from ** to ** to last m, slip m, *** k1, sl1-pw-wyif ***, repeat from *** to *** 2 times more, k1.

Row 2 (WS): * Sl1-pw-wyif, k1 *, rep from * to * 2 times more, sl1-pw-wyif, slip m, ** sl1-w/yo, k1 **, rep from ** to ** to last m, slip m, *** sl1-pw-wyif, k1 ***, repeat from *** to *** 2 times more, sl1-pw-wyif.

Rows 3–8: Repeat Rows 1 and 2 three times.

Row 9 (RS): BO all sts in pattern. During this, work the first and the last 7 sts of the row as follows: K1, * k2tog, pass the previous stitch over the last stitch on the right needle, * rep from * to * 3 times more.

SLEEVES

Both Sleeves are worked the same. For the Sleeve, first take up the 40 (46/52/52/58/60) formerly held sts using US size 6 (4.0 mm) needles,

pick up and knit 3 (3/4/5/5/6) sts from the newly cast-on underarm sts, place m, pick up and knit another 3 (3/4/5/5/6) sts from the newly cast-on underarm sts, and join in the round. The Sleeve is worked in the round from here on; the marker indicates the BOR. You should now have a total of 46 (52/60/62/68/72) sts on the needles.

Continue the Sleeve in stockinette stitch, at the same time, decrease in every 7th round as follows to the end of the Sleeve:

K1, k2tog, work in pattern to 3 sts before m, skp, k1, slip m.

Work the Sleeve in the established pattern until the Sleeve has either reached a length of 16.5 (16.5/16.9/16.9/17.3/17.3 in [42 (42/43/43/44/44) cm] or is 0.4 in (1 cm) shorter than desired sleeve length to accommodate the sleeve cuff to be added.

SLEEVE CUFF

Change to US size 4 (3.5 mm) needles.

Round 1: * K1, sl1-w/yo *, rep from * to * to m.

Round 2: * Sl1-w/yo, k1 *, rep from * to * to m.

Rounds 3–8: Repeat Rows 1 and 2 three times.

Round 9: BO all sts in pattern. During this, work the first and the last 7 sts of the round: K1, * k2tog, pass the previous stitch over the last stitch on the right needle *, rep from * to * 3 times more.

HOOD

Using US size 8 (5.0 mm) needles, cast on 5 sts, then pick up and knit stitches as follows: 5 sts from the Front band, pick up and knit stitches from the knotted selvedge at a rate of 3 sts picked up from every 4 sts, the 2 sts of the shoulder seam, all sts along the Back, placing a marker in the middle of these stitches, the 2 sts of the other shoulder seam, pick up and knit stitches from the knotted selvedge at a rate of 3 sts picked up from every 4 sts, pick up and knit 5 sts from the Front band, cast on 5 additional sts using backwards CO. Make sure that the total number of stitches picked up is an even number.

To keep the Hood instructions usable for any stitch count, specific stitch counts will not be listed, but the method is described in general terms. To use these instructions for other garments, pick up and knit stitches according to the instructions, but cast on more stitches at the beginning and the end. These stitches will later be folded over and sewn down to form the drawstring tunnel—in this case, there are 5 sts each; if your gauge has more stitches in 4 in (10 cm), you will need to cast on more stitches. An odd stitch count is recommended.

Row 1 (WS): Purl all stitches.

Row 2 (RS): K6, skp, yo, knit to last 8 sts, yo, k2tog, knit to end. (If more or fewer stitches have been additionally cast on, the stitch counts over which the openings will be worked will be different here.)

Row 3 (WS): Purl all stitches.

Row 4 (RS): Knit to 1 st before m, M1R, k1, slip m, k1, M1L, knit to end of row.

Row 5 (WS): Purl all stitches.

Rows 6–15: Repeat Rows 4 and 5 five times.

Row 16 (RS): Knit all stitches.

Row 17 (WS): Purl all stitches.

Repeat Rows 16 and 17 until the hood has reached a length of 13.4 in (34 cm). 12 sts total have been increased.

Now, stitches will be decreased again; for this, row counting starts anew with Row 1, beginning with a RS row.

Row 1 (RS): Knit to 4 sts before m, sssk, k1, slip m, k1, k3tog, knit to end of row.

Row 2 (WS): Purl all stitches.

Repeat Rows 1 and 2 another 10 times, 44 sts have been decreased in total. Now, distribute the stitches evenly on two needles, then graft them together.

Cast on 3 sts and work an I-cord 51.2 in (130 cm) long. Weave in the ends, then thread the I-cord through the two openings in the hood so that the two ends of the I-cord emerge in the front. Fold the additionally cast-on stitches to the inside all around and sew them down—5 sts in this pattern. This has created the I-cord tunnel; the I-cord is encased within. Sew the additionally cast-on stitches to the neckline seam—5 sts in this pattern. Make a knot in each of the two ends of the I-cord.

FINISHING

Graft the seams at the top and bottom of the pocket, tracing the first stitch from the body of the cardigan. This reinforces the edge and prevents unintentional holes in this spot. Weave in all ends, dampen the cardigan, and pull it into the desired shape.

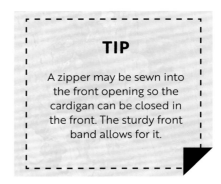

TIP

A zipper may be sewn into the front opening so the cardigan can be closed in the front. The sturdy front band allows for it.

ALLEGRA

SWEATER WITH CONTRASTING-COLOR LACE INSERTS ON THE SLEEVES

SIZES
XS, S, M, L, XL, XXL

Numbers for size XS are listed before the parentheses, numbers for sizes S through XXL within parentheses. If only one number is listed, it applies to all sizes.

Size	Chest Circum-ference	Sleeve Length from Armhole	Garment Length from Armhole
XS	33.8 in (86 cm)	19.7 in (50 cm)	12.6 in (32 cm)
S	35.4 in (90 cm)	20.1 in (51 cm)	13 in (33 cm)
M	39 in (99 cm)	20.1 in (51 cm)	14.2 in (36 cm)
L	42.9 in (109 cm)	20.1 in (51 cm)	14.6 in (37 cm)
XL	46.9 in (119 cm)	20.1 in (51 cm)	15.7 in (40 cm)
XXL	50.8 in (129 cm)	20.5 in (52 cm)	16.1 in (41 cm)

MATERIALS AND TOOLS
— Schachenmayr Merino Extrafine 120; 100% virgin wool;131.2 yd (120 m) per 1.75 oz (50 g): #101 White, 2 (2/3/3/3/3) skeins; and #190 Light Gray Heathered, 7 (8/9/10/12/13) skeins
— Circular knitting needle, US size 6 (4.0 mm), at least 32 in (80 cm) long
— Circular knitting needle, US size 4 (3.5 mm), 16 in (40 cm) long, or a DPN set
— Stitch holder or waste yarn for holding stitches
— 2 stitch markers
— Row counter (optional)
— Tapestry needle

GAUGE
In stockinette stitch on US 6 (4.0 mm) needles: 22 sts and 32 rows = 4 x 4 in (10 x 10 cm)

CONSTRUCTION NOTES
This sweater does not correspond to any of the classic construction methods. First, the lace insert strips are worked in a contrasting color. For the Front, stitches for the first sleeve are picked up and knit along the long edge of the lace insert strip, additional stitches are cast on for the neckline, and stitches for the second sleeve are like-wise picked up and knit along the long edge of the other lace insert strip. Neckline and sleeves are shaped with the help of short rows. During this section, the sweater is worked in back-and-forth rows. The Back is worked the same way. When the sleeves have been completed, sleeve stitches are bound off, and the body joined in the round. The sleeves are grafted. Sleeve cuffs and ribbed neckband are knitted on at the end and worked in the round.

COLOR KEY
MC = Light Gray Heathered
CC = White

TURNING STITCHES (T-ST)
Place the working yarn behind work, turn work, slip 1 stitch purlwise, move the working yarn over the right needle from front to back and pull up on the stitch. This creates a turning stitch (t-st) with two legs sitting on the needle. This "double stitch" will be worked and counted as one stitch further on. Knit stitches can be worked immediately; for purl stitches, the working yarn first needs to be moved to the front of the work between the needles.

SELVEDGE STITCHES
In RS and WS rows, knit the first and the last stitch of the row (= selv st).

RIBBING PATTERN
1x1 ribbing: * K1, p1 *, rep from * to * continuously.

CONTINUED

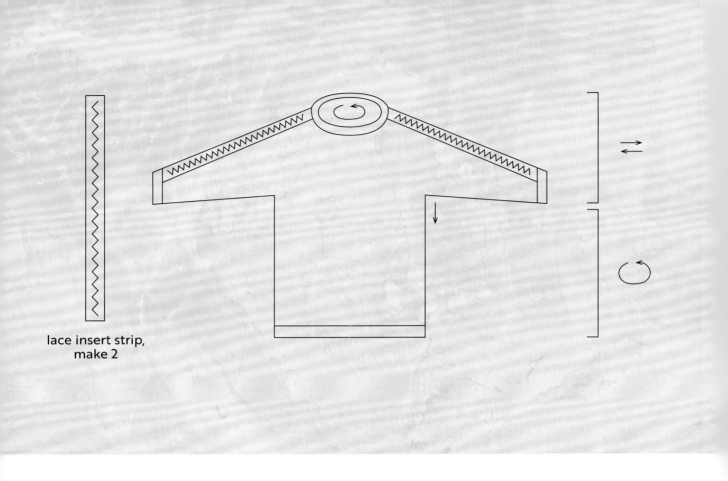

lace insert strip,
make 2

LACE INSERT STRIP, WORKED OVER 15 STITCHES

Please refer to chart and written in-structinos. Between selv sts (which are not shown in the chart), work from chart. Only RS rows are shown in the chart. Read chart rows from right to left. In WS rows, purl all stitches. Work Rows 1–23 once, then repeat Rows 2–23 heightwise. Begin and end with a WS row.

INSTRUCTIONS

First, work two identical lace insert strips for the sleeves. For this, using US size 6 (4.0 mm) needles and CC, CO 17 sts. Work the stitch pattern over 15 stitches widthwise, following the chart, and adding 1 selv st each at the beginning and the end of the row; these selv sts are not shown in the chart.

The stitch pattern for the lace insert strip, including the selv sts, is written out here for convenience:

Row 1 (WS) and all following WS rows: Selv st, p15, selv st.

Row 2 (RS): Selv st, k2, k2tog, yo, k1, k2tog, yo, k1, yo, skp, k1, yo, skp, k2, selv st.

Row 4 (RS): Selv st, k1, k2tog, yo, k1, k2tog, yo, k3, yo, skp, k1, yo, skp, k1, selv st.

Row 6 (RS): Selv st, k3, k2tog, yo, k2tog, yo, k1, yo, skp, yo, skp, k3, selv st.

Row 8 (RS): Selv st, k2, k2tog, yo, k2tog, yo, k3, yo, skp. yo, skp, k2, selv st.

Row 10 (RS): Selv st, k2, skp, k3, yo, k1, yo, k3, k2tog, k2, selv st.

Row 12 (WS): Selv st, k2, skp, k2, yo, k3, yo, k2, k2tog, k2, selv st.

Row 14 (WS): Selv st, k2, yo, skp, k1, yo, skp, k1, k2tog, yo, k1, k2tog, yo, k2, selv st.

Row 16 (RS): Selv st, k3, yo, skp, k1, yo, CDD, yo, k1, k2tog, yo, k3, selv st.

Row 18 (RS): Selv st, k2, yo, skp, yo, skp, k3, k2tog, yo, k2tog, yo, k2, selv st.

Row 20 (RS): Selv st, k3, yo, skp, yo, skp, k1, k2tog, yo, k2tog, yo, k3, selv st.

Row 22 (RS): Selv st, k2, yo, k3, k2tog, k1, skp, k3, yo, k2, selv st.

Work a total of 181 (189/195/201/207/217) rows, working Rows 1–23 once, then repeating Rows 2–23 heightwise. In the following RS row, bind off all sts knitwise. Break the working yarn, and weave in the end. Now, wash and block the two lace insert strips before proceeding.

FRONT

Using US size 6 (4.0 mm) needles and MC, pick up a total of 137 (142/146/151/156/163) sts from the knotted selvedge along the first lace insert strip at a rate of 3 sts picked up from every 4 sts, beginning at the bound-off edge, place m, cast on 40 (40/42/42/44/44) sts using backwards CO, place m, pick up and knit a total of 137 (142/146/151/156/163) sts from the knotted selvedge at a rate of 3 sts picked up from every 4 sts along the second lace insert strip, beginning at the cast-on edge. You should now have 314 (324/334/344/356/370) sts on the needles.

Row 1 (WS): Selv st, purl to 5 sts past the second m, turn work.

Row 2 (RS): T-st, knit to 5 sts past the second m, turn work.

Row 3 (WS): T-st, purl to 5 sts past the last t-st, turn work.

Row 4 (RS): T-st, knit to 5 sts past the last t-st, turn work.

Repeat Rows 3 and 4 another 7 (8/9/10/11/12) times. Now, more sts will be worked after the t-st; for ease of counting, row counting starts anew from Row 1 here.

Row 1 (WS): T-st, purl to 7 sts past the last t-st, turn work.

Row 2 (RS): T-st, knit to 7 sts past the last t-st, turn work.

Repeat Rows 1 and 2 another 4 (4/5/5/6/6) times. Now, more sts will be worked after the t-st; for ease of counting, row counting starts anew from Row 1 here.

Row 1 (WS): T-st, purl to 9 sts past the last t-st, turn work.

Row 2 (RS): T-st, knit to 9 sts past the last t-st, turn work.

Repeat Rows 1 and 2 another 3 (3/3/3/2/2) times. Now, the short row section has been completed, and you will be working in turned rows until the required sleeve circumference has been reached; for ease of counting, Row counting starts anew from Row 1 here.

Row 1 (WS): T-st, purl to last st, selv st.

Row 2 (RS): Knit all stitches.

Row 3 (WS): Selv st, purl to last st, selv st.

Repeat Rows 2 and 3 until the Sleeve has reached a length of 2.8 (2.8/3.1/3.1/3.5/3.5) in [7 (7/8/8/9/9) cm], measured from the picked up and knitted sts. Work the following RS row as follows: BO all sts knitwise to 27 (30/34/39/44/49) sts before marker #1, knit to 27 (30/34/39/44/49) sts after marker #2, removing the marker as you come to it, BO to end of row, place all stitches on a holder, and break the working yarn. 94 (100/110/120/132/142) sts remain.

BACK

Work the same as the Front; do not place the stitches on a holder, do not break the working yarn.

SLEEVES

Graft the open seams at the bottom of the sleeves.

SLEEVE CUFF

Using US size 4 (3.5 mm) needles and MC, pick up and knit stitches from the knotted selvedge at a rate of 3 sts picked up from every 4 sts, place BOR marker, and join in the round.

Rounds 1–6: * K1, p1 *, rep from * to * to end of row.

Round 7: BO all sts in pattern.

BODY

Now, Front and Back will be joined in the round. For this, take up the formerly held sts of the Front again, place m, and, using the working yarn previously left hanging at the Back, knit all sts, place m, and knit the sts of the Back to the m. The body has now been joined in the round, and the side seams have been marked in case a different body shape will be worked. You should now have a total of 188 (200/220/240/264/284) sts on the needles. In the pictured sample, the Body is now simply worked in stockinette stitch until the sweater has either reached a length of 11.8 (12.2/13.4/13.8/15/15.3) in [30 (31/34/35/38/39) cm] or is 0.8 in (2 cm) shorter than desired length to accommodate ribbing to be added.

RIBBING

Change to US size 4 (3.5 mm) needles.

Rounds 1–6: * K1, p1 *, rep from * to * to end of round.

Round 7: BO all sts in pattern.

RIBBED NECKBAND

Using US size 4 (3.5 mm) needles and MC, pick up and knit all sts along the cast-on edge, beginning at the left lace insert strip, place BOR marker, and join in the round.

Rounds 1–6: * K1, p1 *, rep from * to * to end of round.

Round 7: BO all sts in pattern.

FINISHING

To finish, weave in all ends, dampen the sweater, and pull it into the desired shape.

LACE CHART

Pattern repeat: 15 sts wide

Please note: Only RS rows are shown in the chart. Selvedge stitches are not shown in the chart.

Knitting symbol explanation

- ▣ = knit 1 stitch
- ○ = make 1 yarn over
- ◢ = knit 2 stitches together right-leaning: k2tog
- ◣ = knit 2 stitches together left-leaning (skp): slip 1 stitch, knit the next stitch, then pass the slipped stitch over the knitted one.
- ▲ = central double decrease (CDD): slip 2 stitches together knitwise, knit the next stitch, then pass the 2 slipped stitches over the knitted one.

ACKNOWLEDGMENTS

It goes without saying that at the end of this journey, I would like to express my thanks to all those dear people without whom this book would not have come into being. First of all, thank you to my family. To my husband, who has supported me greatly from the very beginning and took care of our children while I wrote. Additionally, to my wonderful children, who are so incredibly proud of their mom, and are excited for me. I love you very much! I'm also very pleased that my girls are already gladly wearing the countless pullovers and cardigans, even though these are actually still too big right now. This shows us that much love has been put into every knitted garment and how this love can be reflected to the knitter.

I would also like to thank all the women in my family after whom the designs in this book have been named. Of course, I'm also thanking the male part of the family, especially my son and my husband, whose names I have also used in a modified way.

A big thank you goes to the wonderful team at the publisher, EMF-Verlag, who believed in me and my vision, and with whom I had a lot of fun working together. I would like to especially thank Isabella Krüger and Regina Sidabras; both responded to my ideas with a great deal of patience and have helped to create a wonderful book.

Last, but not least, I would also like to thank the many sponsors who have provided yarn support for this book. In alphabetical order, a big thank you to: Buttinette, GGH Garn, Katia Yarns, Lamana, Lana Grossa, Lang Yarns, Prym, Rico Design, Rosy Green Wool, Sandnes, Schachenmayr, Union Knopf, and We Are Knitters.

ABOUT THE AUTHOR

Frauke Ludwig discovered knitting when her three children were young. She emphasizes timeless, classic designs with extra details that make them special. On Instagram, she regularly shows her finished knitting as @frauluknits and presents her own designs. On the blog of the same name, she also talks about all kinds of creative projects.

@FRAULUKNITS